EDUCATION'S SMOKING GUN

EDUCATION'S SMOKING GUN

How Teachers Colleges Have Destroyed Education in America

Reginald G. Damerell

FREUNDLICH BOOKS

NEW YORK

Copyright © Reginald G. Damerell

Library of Congress Cataloging in Publication Data

Damerell, Reginald G.
  Education's smoking gun.

  Bibliography: p.
  Includes index.
  1. Teachers colleges—United States. 2. Education—
United States—Aims and objectives. 3. Literacy—United
States. I. Title.
LB1811.D35 1985   370'.7'10973   85-10113
ISBN 0-88191-025-2

Published by Freundlich Books
80 Madison Avenue
New York, New York 10016

Distributed to the trade by
The Scribner Book Companies, Inc.

Manufactured in the United States of America

10 9 8 7 6 5 4 3 2 1

For Edna

. . . we and our colleagues have not spent our energies looking for villains to blame for the general conditions we deplore [in education]. In truth, there is plenty of culpability to go around, and no single "smoking gun" to search for. . . .

Chester E. Finn, Jr., Professor of Education
and Public Policy, Vanderbilt University
Diane Ravitch, Adjunct Professor of History,
Teachers College, Columbia University
Robert T. Fancher, Research Associate,
Vanderbilt University

Contents

1

Three Special Students

"Camera number one, slow zoom in," sounds the director's voice from the control room. Mary responds by gently pushing in on the knob at the back of the camera and watching the results on the monitor above it. As the image of the talent gradually looms larger it grows fuzzier. "Cut," calls the director over the headsets of the studio crew. "Floor manager, see if you can help Mary set up the zoom shot." Though this class is the next to the last class before the end of the term, Mary (not her real name) still does not know how to operate the camera properly. She still fails to keep the picture in focus throughout a zoom.

Mary is inept and an embarrassment to other students. Most have avoided having her as a crew member in their term productions. She is not the only black person in the class.

Ashley, the floor manager, is a black, from Jamaica, West Indies. He is in the course because somebody at the World Bank helped Jamaica's teacher-training school acquire a TV studio and other media equipment. Ashley, on the staff of the school, had been sent to the United States for a year to earn a master's degree in media. He is one of the eighteen students enrolled in the Educational TV Workshop and is a crew member in most of their term productions.

Ashley's specialty is mathematics and his own term production is one of two in the class with any educational content whatsoever. As the professor in charge, I had suggested that his production reflect his specialty. The time allowed was short, only three to five minutes, but was sufficient to teach a mathematical principle that lent itself to visual treatment. Ashley had been reluctant at first.

"Every time I tell people—here in the States and at home—that my field is mathematics, they look at me strangely and go away," he said. "I don't want to bore the rest of the class."

"Civilization is built on mathematics," I replied. "It's important. If the other students don't realize it, that's their loss. You're not here to entertain them."

Ashley had learned everything expected of him while Mary had learned nothing. Ashley explained to Mary as he set up the zoom shot for her: "First, you pull out this knob [at the back of the camera] all the way. Then, you focus the picture with this knob [on the side]. When it is focused, you don't touch it again. You go back to the first knob, push it all the way in and fine focus with it. Now, [demonstrating] the image remains in focus throughout the zoom."

Most students remember this sequence after a couple of demonstrations. Mary never retains it. In the control room she never learns how to operate the video and audio controls. During the practice productions, when everyone has a turn at every position, Mary has to be shown what to do each time. She is unable to write a script. For her term production she has one student interview another, relying on their ad libs. In directing, she is hopelessly inarticulate.

Unexpectedly, Mary's Graduate Record Examination (GRE) scores came across my desk early the following semester. "Of course!" I exclaimed to myself on seeing them. "Mary hasn't the tools of mind to organize and remember." In computation she had 210—in effect, nearly zero—and her verbal score of 240 was hardly better. She was innumerate and, at best, semi-literate.

Her exceptionally low GRE scores confirmed for me a part of the pattern I observed semester after semester among students in the TV Workshop, a "hands on" course teaching the operation of equipment. Students who have much trouble learning the equipment operations, like Mary, are also the ones who fail to write workable scripts for their term productions and cannot say what they mean while directing. On seeing

Mary's GRE scores, I anticipated that Ashley's might confirm the pattern's other half. Students who have no trouble learning the equipment operations, like Ashley, are adequate also in writing scripts and directing. On going to the records office and looking up Ashley's GRE scores, I found that they were at the other end of the scale from Mary's. Out of a possible 800, Ashley scored 780 in computation and 580 in verbal.

There is a different pattern for students of high and low ability. Learners have the tools of mind of literacy and numeracy; nonlearners do not. These tools of mind are critical for learning nonverbal and nonarithmetical tasks, even the fairly simple hands-on operations of TV studio equipment. This insight produced in me a "eureka!" feeling that owed much to recognizing what I had always known implicitly but never examined or questioned before joining the faculty of the School of Education of the University of Massachusetts at Amherst. For the first time in my life, including twenty years in the business world, I found myself surrounded with notions that were hostile to literacy and numeracy.

Mary was in the school's special program for mature people who had not completed (and in some cases never started) four years of college. Being admitted to the program was tantamount to being conceded a bachelor's degree. Once admitted, the person could immediately begin taking graduate courses toward a master's degree in education. Established chiefly for minorities, the special program was open to all. The dean's wife was in it. So was Bill Cosby, on whose doctoral dissertation committee I served.

Mary's adviser was Norma Jean Anderson, the assistant dean, who was in charge of the special program, and also black. She had admitted Mary despite the results of her GRE tests which the university requires all candidates for graduate study to take. University academic departments take the scores into account in admitting students but the School of Education does not. It considers all standardized tests to be racially discriminatory, culturally biased, and no indication of ability.

I happened to see Mary's GRE scores only because she applied for the doctoral program. She wanted an Ed.D. degree in media and I was the Media Program Director. Her scores were on her application, as the university required. With the concurrence of three media colleagues and a graduate student, I rejected her application, giving her low scores as the reason. A few days later the application came back to me from the division chairperson with a note saying that school policy forbade taking GRE scores into account in considering applicants for doctoral programs.

Professors in the school feared being labeled racist or, in its less strident version, "unsympathetic to minority students." The fear went beyond anxiously conforming to prevailing rhetoric. The school personnel committees usually included a minority faculty member, and often a black or Hispanic graduate student. The threat to pressure personnel committees to vote against any professor up for reappointment, tenure, or promotion who was deemed unsympathetic, was real.

The chairperson who returned Mary's application to me was an assistant professor in the reading program and had a Ph.D. in linguistics from an Ivy League university. Despite the admitted shortcomings of standardized tests, common sense showed that Mary's GRE scores were so nearly zero as to indicate gross academic deficiencies. But if the chairperson permitted common sense to prevail it might be held against her when she came up for a tenure review.

Pressure from minority students included pressure for financial assistance, often given in the form of teaching assistantships. Mary had one in the University Communication Skills Center. This surprised me, but not only because she lacked the rudimentary knowledge of the subjects she was supposed to teach. Some years before, while still new to the school, I had known another graduate student, almost as inept as Mary, who had had a teaching assistantship there.

When his assistantship papers came to my desk I had been surprised and puzzled because Spencer (not his real name) could not write coherently. I had telephoned the University Communication Skills Center and asked if it wanted a recommendation from me. "No," was the answer. "Dr. DeShields has interviewed Spencer and wants him to teach a course." All that was wanted from me was my signature as his faculty adviser. Still puzzled, I had gone to the division chairperson who knew Spencer, informed him of the situation, and asked what was going on.

"You have to be aware of campus politics," he began with a

smile. "You also have to know that Shirley DeShields [the center's director] is black and married to Jim DeShields, black, who is on the chancellor's staff. [The then chancellor was black.] Shirley knows that her job is to give assistantships to black students to keep them off the chancellor's back, so they can't say that he's not doing enough for minority students."

"But it's the blind leading the blind," I replied. "Students going to the center for help can't get it from the likes of Spencer."

"I would advise you, Reg, *not* to exercise your integrity in this," said the chairperson, a full professor, tenured, and one of the school's chief supporters of affirmative action.

I had signed the assistantship papers aware that everybody involved knew that Spencer was unable to help undergraduates, including those who were black, with reading, writing, and arithmetic deficiencies. Since then, I had heard that the center had improved the quality of its teaching assistantships. That's why Mary's assistantship there surprised me. She was less able to help students than Spencer.

Mary gets an M.Ed. degree

The media program rejected Mary's application for the doctoral program on grounds of poor course work. Though she deserved to fail in my TV Workshop course, I gave her a P for pass. No professor ever failed a minority student. It was also true that no one of whatever ethnicity ever failed an education course, although many did poor work. Some of these students were teachers currently employed in local school systems. A few were professors in community colleges. Nevertheless, none were as low in ability as Mary and other blacks and Hispanics who had GRE scores in the 200s. In some cases where course work remained unfinished, a few professors gave a grade of incomplete which in time automatically became an F. Mary received incompletes in two courses, one of mine and one of a media colleague. She never made up the work in either course.

The following academic year, the same colleague attended a dinner of School of Education graduates. To his surprise, he found Mary at the dinner. He discovered in talking to her that she had graduated with a master's degree. He subsequently looked up her records to see how it had been done. He found no record of his course or mine, which had been graded incomplete, but many credits for "independent study" and other noncourses.

Bill Cosby gets an Ed.D. degree

Bill Cosby's admission to the school in 1970 was national news. All the media that year and beyond carried stories of his "going back to school." A reporter acquaintance of mine, knowing I had just joined the school, telephoned me from New York City to find out if I could arrange an interview with Cosby. But I had no contact with him. I did not see Cosby on campus for a couple of years and then only by chance. I happened to be in the office of a university vice-chancellor when Cosby stuck his head in the door, chatted for a minute or two, and went on his way again.

I had no further firsthand knowledge of him until March 1975 when, out of the blue, I was asked to serve on his doctoral dissertation committee. I learned then that until some months before he had had a doctoral committee chaired by Atron Gentry. Gentry had been an assistant dean of the school the year before and was a leading figure in the school's Urban Education Center, which had large federal education grants. Following disclosure of the misappropriation of funds by a fellow faculty member in the center, Gentry had resigned his administrative post as had the school's dean, Dwight Allen. Allen also resigned from the school but Gentry retained his professorship and took a leave of absence. Bill Cosby let nearly a year go by and then telephoned the interim dean to find out where he stood with respect to his Ed.D. degree. He still had a dissertation to write. A new chairperson was appointed, the surviving assistant dean, Norma Jean Anderson. Cosby's dissertation was to be in media, my area of specialty, and she asked me to serve on his committee.

I had doubts about serving. Everybody knew that in no usual sense was Cosby a graduate student. Although he had a home in the area and a couple of his children attended Amherst public schools, he could hardly have fulfilled the residence requirement of two consecutive semesters on campus. His television programs, appearances, TV commercials, films, resort and casino engagements, and recordmaking had gone on uninterrupted. If Cosby had been enrolled in any semester-long courses everybody on campus would have known. But there were three-credit courses offered in the school which lasted no longer than a weekend. "Independent study" and "practicum" credits were also available. Such credits were on Cosby's records. When I mentioned to a colleague that I had been asked to be on his committee, he responded: "Don't touch it."

He did not have to elaborate. The year before, at the time the misappropriation of federal funds had been brought to light, a Northampton newspaper had run a series of articles charging that the School of Education was "a diploma mill." It reported that people were getting doctorates while working fulltime at their regular jobs. They included officials in U.S. and state education departments in Washington and Boston, superintendents of schools and others. The university had reacted by appointing a blue-ribbon committee of outside experts to investigate the school.

But little of significance had changed as far as I could see. Moreover, two facts indicated that Cosby's new doctoral committee would be as respectable as any other. The current administration supported it. The interim dean, an opponent of the former dean, had arranged for the committee. Also, the university's imprimatur was stamped on it. The committee's third faculty member was none other than the associate dean of the graduate school, supposedly the keeper of university standards. To no one involved could I give a reason for not serving that she or he would find acceptable, and I agreed to serve.

When the chairperson informed me of the location of the committee's first meeting, my doubts revived. It was to be at Cosby's home, for dinner, and with spouses. On the appointed evening my wife and I were the last to arrive. A servant let us in and Bill Cosby came down from the upstairs to greet us and take our coats.

The first order of business was a tour of Cosby's home, a 135-year-old, sixteen-room farmhouse that stood on two hundred or so hilltop acres and had been remodeled by the restorer of colonial houses in historic Old Deerfield. Up in the hills west of it, on a country road with no other houses nearby, Cosby's home was difficult to find without directions. At the entrance to his driveway, attached to the gated, split-rail fence that extended at right angles to it on both sides, were signs that read "If you are not invited do not pass through these gates." Cosby said that his former KEEP OUT sign had not stopped the curious from driving in. His present sign had.

My wife and I caught up with the tour in the master bedroom. Here, Cosby demonstrated an electronic noisemaker. One of its sounds was that of an electric fan. He explained that his wife Camille had grown up in Washington, D.C., where the heat of summer made sleeping impossible without an electric fan going. In the utter silence of those hills where at night it was always cool, she needed the electric fan sound to sleep. Identical noise making devices were also in the bedrooms of their children, aged three to eleven.

Like most old New England farmhouses, additions had been made to the original structure. One upstairs wing, off the master bedroom, had been remodeled by Cosby so that it was lined with nothing but clothes closets on one side and built-in drawers under the eaves on the other side. Cosby led his committee members and spouses down the corridor between them, opening closets and pulling out drawers. One closet was filled with just Camille's fur coats. Drawer after drawer displayed Cosby's shirts. The scene was right out of the pages of *The Great Gatsby*.

Ten of us sat down to dinner at the oval dining table that could seat twice as many. At one end sat Cosby facing beautiful Camille at the other, big with their fifth child. Between host and pregnant hostess sat committee members and spouses, including two graduate students. The associate dean of the graduate school was unaccompanied, but Bill Cosby's mother made the tenth at the table. The sumptuous dinner, prepared by Cosby's cook, was served by two servants.

During dinner Cosby did most of the talking. He was "on," regaling his committee members and spouses with stories about himself, his wife, and particularly about their other house in Los Angeles. He was just as entertaining in person as he was on records and television. His drive and competitiveness also showed. At one point, my wife turned to his silent mother and asked:

"Mrs. Cosby, do you have any other children besides Bill?"

"I have another son," she replied. "But he doesn't talk as much as Bill."

"He also lives in a smaller house," said Bill.

Dissertation work was not mentioned until after dinner when everyone retired to the large living room with an enormous coffee table in the center. Then, most of the talk was between Cosby and his chairperson, Norma Jean Anderson, with Cosby leaning forward over the coffee table making notes. The committee meeting and signing of doctoral forms lasted about thirty minutes.

A month later, committee members received Cosby's dissertation proposal from Norma Jean Anderson. In response, I gave her a four-page memo dealing with one aspect of it which she presumably passed on, in toto or in part, to Cosby. Two months later, committee members received his first three or four chapters about which the committee met, without Cosby. His research was still to come and there was little discussion of what was there. The chairperson's chief purpose, it seemed, was to set the date for his oral examination. I did not see the completed dissertation until his defense of it two months later. In his acknowledgments, where doctoral candidates make their obeisances to committee members, Cosby identifies me as the member who guided him in "the writing of the technical and creative components" of his "television research." My total guiding consisted of what I had written in my memo to his chairperson.

Cosby's oral examination or defense of dissertation was held in the dean's conference room the first Thursday in August at 8 A.M. Although professors and students were away and the campus was deserted, Norma Jean Anderson scheduled it at that early hour "to discourage a large attendance," she said. University regulations require that the title of a dissertation, the names of the candidate and committee chairperson, plus the time and place of the oral examination be published beforehand. The intent of announcing it in the university's bulletin was to permit any professor to attend and possibly challenge the proceedings and/or dissertation. It was publicized quality control that was seldom practiced.

Despite the early hour, Cosby's defense was attended by about thirty people, mostly admiring young black people whom I did not recognize. Cosby, running the projector himself, showed one of his *Fat Albert and the Cosby Kids* animated films that appeared Saturday mornings on CBS Television and which were marketed by McGraw-Hill Films. They were the subject of his dissertation research. Part of his presentation was an overview of it, after which he answered a few questions. The examination lasted two hours. Then he took his committee members, a school administrator or two, and a few friends to the Faculty Club for breakfast.

At graduation exercises the following May, held on the field of the university football stadium, press photographers captured William H. Cosby, Jr., in doctoral cap and gown, receiving his Ed.D. degree from the hands of the richly robed chancellor of the university. One of the many press photos taken appeared in *People* magazine. The caption for the full-page photograph read: "That doctorate after Bill Cosby's name is no honorary freebie." Another photo of the same scene appeared prominently as news in the Boston *Globe*. COSBY WINS HIS DOCTOR'S DEGREE said the headline, followed by the subhead: TO TEACH AT AMHERST. For the next two years he received appointments as an adjunct assistant professor in the media program of which I was the director, although I never saw Bill Cosby on campus again.

The dean's wife gets an M.Ed. degree

Mario D. Fantini became the dean of the school the summer of Bill Cosby's "defense" of dissertation. Fantini had previously been dean of the School of Education in the State University of New York at New Paltz. Before that, he had been Program Officer of Public Education at the Ford Foundation, where he was instrumental in setting up the Ocean Hill–Brownsville experimental school district that was the focus of the 1968 New York City teachers' strike. While Fantini was at the Ford Foundation, the U. Mass. School of Education received a large grant from it. At the same time Gerald Weinstein, with whom Fantini coauthored two books in the humanistic education vein, moved from the faculty of Columbia's Teachers College to become a tenured professor in the school. Subsequently, Gerald

Weinstein had been instrumental in Fantini's becoming the school's new dean that summer when some of the faculty who were labeled conservative and might have opposed his election, were away from the campus.

Fantini had also held appointments in the education departments of Temple and Syracuse universities. He was usually located where his wife had the opportunity to work for a bachelor's degree. The opportunity was at hand at the university in Amherst, too. Instead, Temmy Fantini entered the special program for mature people lacking bachelor's degrees and began taking courses toward an M.Ed. A few of the faculty muttered among themselves that it was unwise of the dean to put himself in a position of conflict of interest.

Temmy Fantini took my TV Workshop at the same time as Mary and Ashley, for which I gave her a grade of AB. She came to my office after receiving the grade in the mail, however, and complained that she should have had an A. The grade made not a particle of difference. The school was officially opposed to grades. It had long been on a Pass/Fail grading system. Professors were not permitted to give letter grades except in the case of master's degree candidates. It was the university that insisted that 18 of the 33 master's degree credits be letter-graded, but it was up to students to decide in which courses. Even if Temmy Fantini were not the dean's wife, in the School of Education she would get an M.Ed. degree regardless of grades. Since they made no difference, she was requesting an improved grade for reasons of her own. Politely but firmly I explained my methods of grading. Although she still insisted that she deserved an A, she left my office with the same grade she came in with.

Days later, the division chairperson suggested to me that I meet with the dean about a personnel matter, a media professor's leave of absence. A minute or two into the meeting the dean changed the subject, although to what was difficult for me to tell. Fantini usually spoke in circumlocutions. He seemed to be expressing dissatisfactions with the media program. I responded but he kept ignoring my responses. I gradually came to think that he was letting me know that he was dissatisfied with me personally, and for reasons he could not say aloud.

Before leaving his office I decided to review his wife's work.

I ran the videotapes of term productions on a monitor and then wrote a "Dear Temmy" letter. I told her that I had been unduly influenced in her favor because she was the wife of the dean who could determine the outcome of my tenure decision. I told her that I had overestimated the quality of her work, giving specific instances, and ended by saying that I was lowering her grade to a B.

I Xeroxed copies for the division chairperson, the associate dean for academic affairs, Temmy's adviser, Norma Jean Anderson, my personnel file, and two colleagues. The last were upset. They plainly believed that I had destroyed my chances for tenure and would have to leave the university.

No reaction came from any administrator in the school except the dean and it was nonverbal. When next we chanced to pass in the corridors he leaned away from me as if afraid I might strike him. My feelings were not so personal. They had more to do with the school's deficiencies which, to my relief, I finally permitted myself to see wholly.

2

No Body of Knowledge

Mary's and Temmy Fantini's M.Ed. degrees and Bill Cosby's Ed.D. do not attest to genuine academic achievement. They are empty credentials. Empty credentials are all that any school or department of education in any university in the United States gives to its graduates. The education field is devoid of intellectual content, has no body of knowledge of its own and acts as if bodies of knowledge do not exist in other university departments.

This sorry state of affairs is familiar to professors everywhere in departments of biology, engineering, English, history, mathematics, and others. A famous professor of economics says: "Anyone with any extensive personal experience with students— or professors—of education does not need any studies to tell him. . . . Schools and departments of education . . . [are] 'the intellectual slums' of the universities, and on most campuses they are held in contempt."[1] When he wrote this he was at the University of California in Los Angeles. Clear across the continent in New York City, the contempt is expressed on the Columbia campus by referring to 120th Street that separates Teachers College from the rest of the university as "the widest street in the world."

Professors nevertheless express their contempt among themselves, not, as a rule, in public. Nor do they, as one might expect, work to get rid of the pariah in their midst. The single exception is Yale, which eliminated its education department in 1955. Were professors in other universities to attempt the same removal they would stand little chance of success without outside support. State laws that have the effect of keeping schools and departments of education firmly cemented in place can be changed only by legislators with the support of their constituents. The general public must therefore take notice of what is wrong with departments of education.

Suppose that Mary, instead of applying to the School of Education, applied for graduate study in the chemistry department. Suppose, too, that the department took Mary's application seriously and made it possible for her to work for a master's degree. First, the department would have to arrange for Mary to learn mathematics from simple arithmetic through calculus, at least. She would also have to learn computer programming. Simultaneously, because all concepts, chemical and otherwise, are formulated in language, she would have to greatly improve her language abilities. The surest and most enjoyable way is to take English literature courses. Her competence would have to reach the point of being able to absorb new concepts. Mary would need to acquire the very idea of concept. Undergraduate courses in chemistry and other sciences would also be required of her. Gaining the prerequisites for graduate study would take Mary four or five years at a minimum.

Chemistry is highly structured and rule-governed and new structures and rules are frequently added. Chemistry is a body of knowledge. Moreover, it is based on other bodies of knowledge.

The School of Education, on the other hand, possessing no body of knowledge, admitted Mary to graduate study without prerequisites. But, of course, no base is necessary where nothing is to be added. Ignoring her GRE scores of close to zero meant that the school rejected the knowledge of the academic departments which placed a high value on literacy and numeracy.

Of what benefit was Mary's M.Ed. degree to her? I knew Mary continuously from the first to the last of her two consecutive semesters. Before the start of the first, in fact, we had conversations about an independent study she wanted me to sponsor. She had arranged a partial internship for herself with a Boston radio station and wanted three credits for it. In return, I required a written report of her activities and what she learned at the radio station. That was before I knew her GRE scores and of her ineptitude in the TV studio. Mary impressed me at first as an energetic, resourceful woman in her late thirties, eager to learn and better her position in life. She had been in several federally funded programs, the last with a black radio program on a Washington, D.C., station for which she claimed that she wrote scripts and conducted interviews. It was during our initial conversations that she told me of her teaching assistantship at the University Communication Skills Center that provided her with a waiver of tuition and money to live on.

Three or four weeks into the semester, her internship at the radio station abruptly ended. I imagine that she was just as inept at the radio station as she was in the TV studio, where all impression of energy and resourcefulness disappeared. She stood idle instead of practicing or asking questions. She did not pay attention to how other students operated equipment that she had not mastered. Even while being reinstructed in it, Mary's expression was devoid of curiosity, perplexity, or even frustration. Her face was blank. She may have had emotional problems or been mentally slow. I assumed that her difficulties were due to inadequate schooling.

Urban blacks were said in the school to be "streetwise." Mary was programwise. She had lived off several, and was adept at talking people into a better opinion of her than she was able to live up to. She also tried, in my case, to threaten. While I was going over some writing of hers and telling her how it needed to be improved, out of the blue she mentioned the word *racism*. She was hinting that she could accuse me of it.

Mary was searching for a niche and believed that an M.Ed. would help her find one. At first, she said she wanted to go into commercial media. Following her hapless experiences with the Boston radio station and my TV Workshop course, she spoke of going into geriatrics. She wanted an education degree solely because it was the only kind she could get, but she graduated no more prepared for any niche than when she came to the school. Her M.Ed. degree would no doubt help in getting jobs. Her problem would be in keeping one of the least complexity. If her jobs paid little or she became unemployed, her master's degree could be used to show that blacks earned less money than whites with the same degrees.

To Bill Cosby, the advertising spokesman, the publicity about his "going back to school" was worth millions. It gave him a distinctive image. He became known for his concern for children and the poor educations they were getting. Some of the early publicity had Cosby becoming a classroom teacher, leaving show business except for guest appearances on weekends and making movies during summers to support his teaching. Among celebrities, he became one of the few with ideals. The Los Angeles *Times* in an editorial thanked him for his idealism.

Cosby's image increased his value to advertisers of such products as Ford cars and Jell-O puddings. For products with educational applications such as computers made by Texas Instruments, Cosby was the celebrity of choice. In addition to the consumer market, there was the huge education market. Cosby's name and face promoted expensive videotape reading programs. Promotion pieces put out by McGraw-Hill Films placed "Dr." before his name and referred to him as an "educator." Cosby's image built by the "back to school" publicity starting in 1970, getting an M.Ed. degree in 1972, receiving an Ed.D. degree at graduation exercises in 1977, and successive appointments as adjunct professor in the School of Education, would add to his income for the rest of his career. In an age of sophisticated image building, it was an imagemaker's dream come true. Cosby and his attendants capitalized on it and worked to keep the image going. I was told as the media program director who had to write the recommendation for Cosby's appointment to adjunct assistant professor that someone identifying himself as his agent had telephoned the school to find out when the appointment would be forthcoming. In advertising for the concert film *Bill Cosby "Himself,"* released by Twentieth Century-Fox in 1983, "Dr." appeared in front of Cosby's name as the executive producer.

Self-serving can of course coexist with ideals. It was true that Cosby had an interest in teaching that predated his becoming a comedic actor. Some aspects of his background are very similar to those of others who are drawn to teaching. For one thing, he got low grades in school. The numbers of education majors everywhere who did poorly in elementary and high school are legion. Cosby was a high school dropout but completed a correspondence course for a high school equivalency while in the U.S. Navy. He later received an athletic scholarship to

Temple University. There, he was a physical education major before quitting to work as a comedian. He worked hard at it, studying from their records the techniques of other comedians like Lenny Bruce and Bob Newhart. He developed his early monologues out of his childhood experiences growing up poor in a Philadelphia ghetto. He used himself, his wholeness, which is the meaning of integrity, to succeed. His success indicated, as nothing else can, his exceptional drive, talent, and intelligence.

I believe that he took his schooling and his Ed.D. degree seriously, not cynically just to build an image. But, what is not generally known is that Cosby was recruited by the school. In his dissertation acknowledgments he wrote: "To Dr. Norma Jean Anderson, I am especially indebted for her faith in my doing graduate work, to the extent that she traveled to New York to personally recruit me into the graduate program." No celebrity was more hungry for publicity than the then dean of the school, Dwight Allen. Bringing Cosby in was a publicity coup for the school that contributed to its growing reputation.

Cosby was assured beforehand that enrolling would not interfere with his show business engagements, would not require him to take semester-length courses. He was already a teacher, he was told, for his involvement with *Sesame Street* and *The Electric Company,* which was equivalent to practice teaching. Independent study and practicum credits were not created for Cosby but predated him, as did weekend courses. For his dissertation, the school encouraged him to do research on his animated *Fat Albert* films created for CBS Television. Cosby could have put together all that is in his dissertation without ever enrolling in the school. Cosby knew, of course, that he was treated as a special case but accepted it as his due as a celebrity. Coming from his background and given the limitations of his formal education, it was easy for him to accept at face value what the school told him. From conversations with his friend Al Freeman, the actor on the TV soap opera *One Life to Live,* I believe that he took his degrees seriously. Al Freeman told me that Cosby urged him to take a degree at the school, and Freeman did, indeed, enroll and sign up for independent study credits.

Cosby could hardly be expected to recognize that his credentials stood for little. Only the professors in the academic departments of the university knew that, and they kept silent. On his own, Cosby could hardly have compared his Ed.D. with a Ph.D. in, for example, English literature. For that he would have had to become familiar with the works of Chaucer, Shakespeare, Donne, Milton, Dryden, Swift, Pope, Fielding, Johnson, Boswell, Burke, Gray, Burns, Blake, Wordsworth, Coleridge, Scott, Keats, Shelley, Bryon, Austen, Dickens, Thackeray, the Brontës, George Eliot, Trollope, Hardy, Stevenson, Kipling, Arnold, Tennyson, Browning, Wilde, Shaw, Yeats, T. S. Eliot, Conrad, Joyce, Woolf, and Forster, just for a beginning. Cosby would also have had to become proficient in reading a foreign language. I have no doubt that Cosby had the ability to earn a Ph.D. in English if he wanted to. Starting from where he was, however, it would have taken him at least six years of study and only if he gave up show business and studied fulltime. English literature is a *body of knowledge* and, like all bodies of knowledge, takes time and effort to acquire.

Absence of a body of pedagogical knowledge is inherent in the circumstances of my own appointment to associate professor. I first heard of the school in the spring of 1970 from a neighbor while I was commuting to and from midtown Manhattan. I was in advertising and Nat Rutstein was with NBC Television News. Each time we met, Rutstein brought me up to date on the latest developments in his planned change of careers. He intended to leave NBC and join the faculty of the school and become its media program director. While he was being interviewed at the school one of the associate deans asked him, because he lived in Teaneck, New Jersey, if he knew the author of the book about Teaneck, *Triumph in a White Suburb*.

My book had been published by William Morrow two years before and was a history of prejudice from the time that Jews began moving into the Protestant and Catholic suburb, to middle-class black families moving in, and the subsequent school-board election battles over the issue of integrating Teaneck's elementary schools. It had been widely and favorably reviewed, including a full-page review in *The New York Times Book Review*.[2]

All spring and into the summer Rutstein had described what he was going to accomplish at the school and, because my background fitted in with his plans, had asked if I would be interested in joining him. I had not taken the offer seriously until he told me of the unexpected and flattering recognition of my book. With it I had hoped to write myself out of advertising. Now it was happening. The prospect of living and working in the beautiful New England town of Amherst and no longer commuting to dirty, noisy New York City was also exceedingly pleasant. I agreed to join Rutstein even with an enormous reduction in income.

We started at the beginning of the academic year that fall, and found the school a bustling place, seemingly confirming what I had been told by all—that it was the only education school in the country that was "trying to *do* something." Dwight Allen, formerly of the Stanford School of Education, had been dean for just two and a half years. He had doubled the faculty and made the school famous and controversial. In the receiving line of a university reception, I overheard the president say: "Maybe we should pay Dwight Allen time and a half for the time he spends on campus." He said it facetiously, alluding to Allen's frequent trips to speak all over the United States and even Africa and the Middle East. At the university convocation, the chancellor, in his address, reported that an undergraduate had just died in the dorms from an attempted self-abortion. He added: "At least *that* cannot be blamed on the School of Education." When I remarked about the chancellor's poor taste, Dwight Allen said: "That's the man himself. You wouldn't think that he would be a supporter of the school. But when he visits other universities around the nation, we're the department in his university that he hears good things about. That's why he supports us." Rutstein and others had told me that Dwight Allen had been given a free hand in the school and it appeared to be true.

Part of the bustle of the school was a series of receptions and meetings connected with the forthcoming White House Conference on Children in Washington. Dwight Allen was chairman of one of the committees and its members flew in from all over the United States to plan for it. I undertook the preparation of a forty-eight-page booklet to be distributed at the conference and what amounted to a twenty-second educational commercial, both on the subject of myths in education. Having spent nearly twenty years in the creative departments of major advertising agencies writing every form of advertising, the assignment was an easy one.

Rutstein and I had purchased new homes in the Amherst area but our houses in Teaneck were still for sale. We commuted back to Teaneck for weekends. Because we did, I was able to use the services of my favorite art director at the Ted Bates agency, where I had spent eleven years. He designed the layout of the booklet, did the finished art, and made the drawings for the storyboard, the blueprint from which the film of the educational commercial would be made.

When the members of the White House Conference committee returned to the campus for a final meeting I had the mechanicals for the booklet completed—artwork and type all in place, camera-ready for the printer. Dwight Allen proudly passed them among the committee members. Not accustomed to seeing first-rate professional work, they were enormously impressed. When the discussion moved on to the closed-circuit television that was expected to be available at the conference in Washington, one of the committee members said: "What we really need is an educational commercial." Instantly, Allen held up my storyboard saying: "We have one ready." He then explained it frame-by-frame because they had never seen one before, and passed it among them.

The euphoria of Dwight Allen and his staff following the meeting was much the same as I had seen many times in advertising agencies after a successful presentation of new advertising to clients. Similarly, much of the credit for the success was attributed to the creator of the ads and commercials. Dwight Allen told me that had he known about me, he would have tried all the previous year to recruit me.

Even before the meeting, however, I had been told "Reg, you *have* to be faculty." I had come to the school with the rank of staff associate, a professional but nonteaching position. My intended role in Nat Rutstein's plans was to help create and market educational materials—films, video tapes, records, and printed materials. The income generated by selling them was to be plowed back into the media program to produce more materials, and pay salaries of a staff to be developed, and my own. But when Rutstein tried to set up the necessary framework, university officials said that state law prohibited the sale of any materials produced with state funds. Rutstein's salary and the equipment of the media program were paid for out of state funds. The whole basis for my coming to the school had therefore disappeared.

I never would have come to teach. My personality was not suited to it. I had accepted speaking engagements in connection with the publication of my book and found that talking before groups was painful. Had my wife and I been childless, I believe that I would have left the school rather than have to teach. But with three young daughters to raise and having burned my bridges behind me—I had left a good job in advertising, put my Teaneck home up for sale and purchased another in the Amherst area—I accepted a promotion to the rank of lecturer, the same as Rutstein's, with mixed emotions.

I was put on a major schoolwide committee for the development of "alternative" undergraduate teacher education programs. During months of meetings, twenty-two programs were approved. My committee contribution was publicizing them to freshmen and sophomores among the twenty thousand undergraduates on campus. Many of the programs were so similar that I had difficulty finding an exploitable difference. I took the center four pages of the campus newspaper and designed them to look like a separate section. When the issue appeared students came flocking to sign up and each of the twenty-two programs got a full enrollment. Once again, I was commended in glowing terms in letters of thanks from the committee chairman and the dean.

In the spring, too, the dean presented me with options for my future in the school. The first was becoming a doctoral candidate while continuing as a lecturer. On earning an Ed.D. degree he would appoint me an associate professor. He said that for my dissertation I could use the book I was planning and for which I had begun collecting information. It was to be on the first chancellor of the New York City public school system under the newly instituted decentralization. He was the chief hero of my Teaneck book where he had been the superintendent of schools. I had access to him and his staff at 110 Livingston Street in Brooklyn. The second option was that Allen could try to get me an immediate appointment to associate professor on the grounds that I had been hired at the wrong rank. Once appointed, working for an Ed.D. was no longer possible. Allen warned that universities and education departments placed great importance on the possession of a doctorate. He also warned that when I came up for a tenure decision he probably would no longer be dean. Security lay in the first option. I chose the second.

By university standards, my appointment to associate professor was due to my having published a book that was well reviewed in academic journals as well as the public press. It showed ability to do research, organize and present it coherently. It was the equivalent of a dissertation, and made up for not possessing a doctorate. My bachelor's degree, moreover, was from Columbia College.

Meeting university standards made it possible for Allen to get me the appointment. His reason for seeking it, however, was my advertising skills. They had contributed to his and the school's reputation, and would be available in the future. I was told "you *have* to be faculty" without any mention of *what* I would teach. I received no instructions or hints of what kind of courses were needed. Though everyone knew that I had no teaching experience, no one suggested anything that would help me to become a teacher—no books to read or courses to observe. What I would teach and how I would teach it were left up to me. The school offered no pedagogical knowledge or help because it had none to offer.

I recognized this situation, in part, at the time but I had expectations of my own. I knew that my advertising skills could be put to use for instructional purposes and had reason to believe that the dean thought so, too. Educational media, as a specialty within education departments, was misconceived as just equipment operation. I had said to the dean: "It's as if the great new medium of a newspaper had just been developed. But the only people in it are typesetters, printing press operators, and ink specialists." Allen had added: "And we have left out the reporters, columnists and editors."

No professor of educational media had my skills and I naively believed I could introduce them via courses and by developing instructional materials. I failed to recognize the futility of making the attempt when the specialty, as well as the larger field of which it was a part, had nothing to build on.

3

Then and Now

Not so long ago, within memory of the eldest of our senior citizens, there were no education majors, no M.Ed. and Ed.D. degrees, and no professors of education. Schools and departments of education did not exist. Not until just before World War I did they become established in most universities. Educationists, the term critics use to distinguish them from educators in academic departments, are fairly recent arrivals.

Educationists have nevertheless been ensconced on university campuses long enough to carry out the purposes of the educationist curriculum. As framed by John Dewey: "to gather together and focus the best of all that emerges in the great variety of present practice, to test it scientifically, to work it out into shape for concrete use, and to issue it to the public educational system with the imprimatur ... of scientific verification."[1] This proposed rigorous and systematic study for the purpose of developing a body of pedagogical knowledge remained only a proposal. The new educationists never attempted to implement it, nor did any successive generation of educationists down to the present. Perhaps implementation was never possible, as some academicians believed then and some believe today.

The philosopher John Dewey, along with the presidents of Harvard, Johns Hopkins, and Columbia, and distinguished scholars such as Nicholas Murray Butler, urged establishing the to-be-developed discipline in universities shortly before the turn of the century. Schoolteachers at the time were trained in what were called normal schools. A university role was proposed to educate "the leaders of our educational system—teachers in normal and training schools, professors of pedagogy, superintendents, [and] principals in our large cities."[2]

The academicians saw a need for leadership in large cities strictly in *educational* terms, separate and apart from the *sociological*. The distinction is necessary because educationists have fused the two. The concerned academicians believed that new educational leaders were necessary to run city school systems that were growing to enormous size. A great increase in the school population was taking place due to rapid urbanization, new laws making school attendance mandatory, a high birthrate, and masses of immigrants pouring in from Europe. Many more teachers were needed and the academicians wanted to develop leadership qualities in those who taught the teachers-to-be in the normal schools by providing them with a to-be-developed pedagogical discipline.

Because educationists have concentrated on the sociological in the name of education, let us first look at the sociological circumstances prior to their inception. Although the migration of blacks from the south to the north had begun early in the century, they accounted for only 2 percent of New York City's population of roughly five million. In 1910, Harlem was still predominantly white. By contrast, 12 percent of the city's population were newly arrived Italians, chiefly from southern Italy. Fully 25 percent of the city's residents were Jews. Those from Germany were already established and accepted when the masses of Yiddish-speaking Jews began arriving from Russia and Poland in the 1880s. A half million of them came before the turn of the century. Subsequently, another million and a half arrived in the United States before World War I. Most ended up in Manhattan's lower east side, probably the most crowded slum in the world at the time, where they suffered all the privations of slum living.

As Thomas Sowell relates in his lucidly written *Ethnic America*, Jewish and Italian immigrants arrived destitute, speaking no English, and had high rates of illiteracy. For the Italians from southern Italy and Sicily, the illiterate portion was 54 percent and for Eastern European Jews it was 50 percent. Both groups lived in their own slum enclaves, worked at the most menial jobs, and were discriminated against. In reaction to the new Jewish immigrants, help wanted ads began to specify "Christian." German Jews looked down on the new arrivals from Eastern Europe, blamed them for a resurgence of anti-Semitism, and coined the epithet "kike" to disparage them. Immigrants from the north and south of Italy were separated by a similar caste attitude. The Catholic Church was dominated by Irish priests. Some made Italians sit at the back of the church and called them "dagos" from the pulpit.

Both the Italians and the Jews were typically small in stature and far from healthy when they arrived. From their pogrom-fearing days, Jews had a hunted look. They walked with bent heads in a "ghetto slouch," the unresisting target of street bullies.[3] The sociological disadvantages of most immigrants in New York City at the time were far worse than for most blacks and Puerto Ricans in the post–World War II period. Some are glimpsed in the following from an Op-Ed piece that appeared in *The New York Times* in 1983:

> When I entered elementary school in 1913, I spoke only Yiddish. I was, in today's educational parlance, monolingual. And not surprisingly. My parents spoke no English. My recently arrived "greenhorn" relatives spoke no English. Neither did most of my friends.
>
> My parents came to the United States to escape Russian pogroms, Russian discrimination and Russian poverty.

In qualifying "discrimination" and "poverty" with "Russian," the writer allowed for American forms of discrimination and poverty. But they were of a different order and suffered in a state of freedom.

> America offered them instant freedom, hope, opportunity, peace and surcease from persecution. It could not, however, give them an instant language. But with what time and energy they had left after . . . working in the sweatshops, they went to the settlement houses and the "citizenship and Americanization" classes to learn the language, customs and traditions of their adopted country.

Much of the energy with which Jews eagerly grasped freedom and opportunity derived from a reverence for learning. More honor came to the woman in marrying a learned man than a rich one. Yet reverence for learning among Russian-Jewish immigrants was more tradition than practice. One-third of the men and two-thirds of the women were illiterate. Russia had suppressed the practice of their traditions: America gave them free rein. But although social conditions for them were by many measures far worse than for today's minorities, the *quality of the education* available to them was far superior.

> I have very vivid memories of my teachers. They were all women. They all wore long dresses with high lace collars. The tips of their black, shiny, "pointy" shoes peeped coyly from beneath their skirts. Some wore pince-nez. They were all extraordinarily clean-looking.
>
> They all seemed to be called Miss McDonald. And they didn't seem to like us or love us.

The teachers were principally Irish, two or three generations removed from the period of immigration of the great potato famine in Ireland. Jewish children had virtually no Jewish teachers as "role models," to mention a current educationist notion.

> But they *taught* us—firmly, thoroughly, relentlessly. They did not ask, nor did they seem to care, who we were, where we came from, what we wanted or what language we spoke at home.
>
> They knew what they were in school for: to civilize us, Americanize us, give us a common tongue and a common set of traditions. And they pursued these goals with an almost fanatical singlemindedness.
>
> They weren't about to let anything as irrelevant as our "roots" or our "ethnicity" or our many different mother tongues get in their way.
>
> And so, undistracted by bilingualisms, they quickly taught us to read, write and speak English.
>
> Before the end of my first year, I was teaching my parents what I had learned—with special emphsais on *speaking* English correctly so I wouldn't be ashamed of them when my gentile friends were around.
>
> Our class "readers," somewhat stodgy, stuffy, "noble" and, at times mind-stretching, were filled with "memory gems"—

lines, phrases, thoughts that resonated through our lives and gave a special tone and shape to our thinking, speaking and writing.

Happily, there were none of our contemporary "reading specialists" or "readability experts" pawing over our texts to turn them into the kinds of pap being served up to our kids in today's readers.

In referring to the current "pap" as the product of "reading specialists" and "readability experts," the writer speaks with some authority. He is Abraham H. Lass, a retired New York City high school principal who spent forty-one years in the city's public school system. He knows intimately the enormous difference in the quality of the education he received and the "pap" dished out to today's children.

Of course, not all our teachers made . . . a difference in our lives. Not all of them were kind, good, effective, dedicated.

Our vulnerability, our helplessness, our crudities brought out the worst in some of them. They looked upon us as the "great unwashed." Others didn't have the guts or the taste for the job.

Nor did all the kids get out of school what I did. Too many were casualties. They never made it out into America, the beautiful.

But I loved all those Miss McDonalds. I owe them everything. They made me possible.

The credit that Lass gives to his teachers is substantiated by statistics for Jews as a group, most of whom were of Eastern European extraction. They immediately became upwardly mobile despite their social handicaps, handicaps reflected in low IQ scores. American soldiers in World War I of Russian origin, mostly Jewish, averaged among the lowest of any ethnic group tested. But by the middle of the twentieth century, despite continuing discrimination against them, they had more education, higher IQ scores, and higher incomes than other Americans.

Toward the end of Lass piece, he refers to "today's troubled" and "rudderless" schools and looks back to ". . . when the classroom was a sanctuary, when teachers were secure in their profession, when they could teach with confidence, certainty and conviction."[4]

What enabled his teachers to "teach with confidence, certainty and conviction"? None had a university degree. Not all, possibly few, were high school graduates. The first class of students did not graduate from a public high school in New York City until 1902. Lass' teachers were products of normal schools where the training, often starting from the base of an elementary school education, lasted anywhere from six weeks to two years. Only in later years would normal schools require a high school diploma. Those of Lass' teachers who were hired after 1898 had to pass a competency examination. Some may have been trained in normal school by teachers who were products of the new Teachers College at Columbia, one of the first of the educationist institutions. If so, the initial professors of education were educated as academicians. It was the subsequent generations of educationists who had less and less academic training. The first education professors did not start our educational degeneration. That would begin imperceptibly in the next generation and thereafter accelerate with each successive generation.

Lass' teachers knew reading, 'riting, and 'rithmetic thoroughly. The 3Rs were part of their normal school training in subject matter. Moreover, the entire environment supported their knowledge and augmented it. Virtually all information at the time was conveyed by language, spoken and written. Photography existed but the technology to reproduce photographs cheaply in newspapers and magazines was still a long way off. Lass' teachers had not grown up with motion pictures, which were still new and infrequent when Lass was a boy. Telephones were not yet in general use and communicating with people at a distance meant writing them letters.

The strongest support for literacy was the practice of reading short stories and novels as the chief means of entertainment, including reading or being read to aloud. The practice was widespread. All general magazines carried short stories. Newspapers and magazines serialized novels. Charles Dickens' novels, considered great literature today, had a mass audience, were best-sellers at the time Lass' teachers were growing up. Books of fiction far outsold nonfiction. It was not until the 1930s that sales of nonfiction books exceeded those of fiction, and some general magazines stopped carrying short stories.

Print, as it exists and is used in the world, is the most highly developed form of language. Its capacity to convey ideas and experiences in a great variety of forms is infinite. The range of existing print permits a range in fluency of comprehension and composition. Lowest in the range are people able to write their names and read street signs and little more. Filling out an application blank for employment or a bank loan is beyond their competence. Such people can sometimes be seen these days struggling to get money from the cash machines of banks, unable to follow the machines' printed instructions. Most who understand the instructions may not be sufficiently competent to make sense of a textbook—even that rarity, the well-written textbook. To comprehend unfamiliar material, they may need the help of a course and an instructor. For the fortunate few, many bodies of knowledge are within easy reach through reading about them. New concepts and information are grasped from the printed page, aided only by a dictionary and sometimes an encyclopedia.

The hardest half of literacy, of course, is writing. The ability to compose a straightforward letter, memo, or page of paragraphs is becoming rare, and separates those who are adequately literate from those who are not. At the highest end of the literacy scale are the composers of our literary masterpieces.

The practice of reading even second-rate fiction, which may be what Lass' teachers chiefly read, helps develop a fair degree of literacy. Even trashy novels have a structure and logical flow of language not present in everyday speech. Written language is not everyday talk set down on paper. It is normally profoundly different from spoken language, although the two share a common grammar and vocabulary. Written language demands a precision and completeness that is not necessary when talking to others in many social situations. People in the same room or on the telephone can always ask for clarification when others fail to make themselves clear. Frequently, the setting in which every day speech takes place is purely situational. Meaning is inherent in the situation rather than the words spoken. If in a crowded bus or subway we say, "You're standing on my foot," the meaning is "Get off my foot." We could say that, or say, "You weigh a ton," or "What do you think you're doing?" or a dozen other sentences. All would mean "Get off my foot." Sometimes in situations meanings can be conveyed just by pointing.[5]

Printed sentences on the page, on the other hand, refer to persons, places, times, and ideas not present to the senses. Written language is an escape from the here and now. It communicates over space and time, one of its many virtues. The habit of reading, especially when combined with practice in writing, helps develop a similar precision and completeness in speaking. A person's spoken language takes on the attributes of written language.[6]

Indeed, the oral communication of complex information and knowledge requires that the speaker use the exactness and fullness of written language. Ideally, medical doctors and scientists in hospitals and laboratories speak the written form of language. Lawyers pleading cases in court speak the written form. So do diplomats and businessmen conducting complicated negotiations. So should teachers in instructing their classes.

Abraham Lass' "Miss McDonalds" were sufficiently literate to speak with the precision and completeness of written language. They could say what they meant when instructing. I can report this unequivocally because my experience with teachers in school is entirely consistent with Lass'. I entered elementary school in New York City in 1926, just thirteen years after Lass entered school. My teachers were still "Miss McDonalds," chiefly Irish, although no longer wearing ankle length skirts and pince-nez. Like Lass' teachers, mine were highly effective. They taught with "confidence, certainty and conviction," speaking with written language's attributes.

The school experiences of Dr. Kenneth B. Clark, the psychologist, apparently were also much the same as Lass' and mine, even to having chiefly Irish teachers. As Clark recollects:

> I went to school in Harlem and I remember my teachers in Junior High School 139. I knew Miss McGuire insisted that I respect the structure of a sentence and she explained to me what a sentence was. Those teachers had standards that we knew we had to meet. Why is it that that could be done in the late 1920s and the early 1930s and not in the 1970s and 1980s? Why?
>
> All of them—Mr. Deegan, Miss McGuire, Miss Smith, and Mr. Mitchell—never asked whether I came from a broken home. They weren't social workers; they were teachers. As far as I recall, for five or six hours, five days a week, the universe

was what was happening in that classroom. Mr. Ruprack kept me after school if I didn't get those equations and there was respect for us that was indicated by the standards to which we were held and by the sense of achievement that we felt. If we had thought that Mr. Ruprack thought that we couldn't have done algebra then we would have felt badly. Public education is a cornerstone of the stability of this democracy. If that isn't maintained there is no solution to the urban crisis. The public school system in this country can't be sacrificed on the altar of race.[7]

Kenneth Clark, Abraham Lass and I were seldom, if ever, confused by our teachers. They never left us in doubt about what they were saying. We were never confused by them as children have been in recent decades by their teachers.

In the college and university town of Amherst, Massachusetts, many of my daughters' teachers often failed to say what they meant. In the seventh grade, my youngest daughter's social studies teacher assigned a research paper and told the class to use "original sources." Holly chose to write about Charles Lindbergh's solo flight across the Atlantic in 1927. In the town's library she found the two books he had written about it, and based her paper on them. But her teacher refused to accept it because it was not based on newspaper accounts.

Holly pointed out to the teacher that she had specified "original sources." Lindbergh's own account was *the* original source. No one was with him on his flight across the Atlantic. Her teacher nevertheless rebuffed Holly's protest, saying that she had meant newspaper accounts. Not only had the teacher failed to make herself clear, she exposed a faulty notion of journalism. Newspapers are collections of news from other sources usually—the police in the case of crimes, press releases put out by businesses and government bureaus, and so forth. Only in rare cases where a reporter happens to witness an event is the report original.

Another time from another teacher, Holly brought home a mimeographed assignment. The words took up more than half a page but Holly could decipher no meaning in them, could not tell what was expected. In an effort to help, I read the assignment through several times. It had no subject. What it was about was not stated. Although I questioned my daughter about her classwork for the previous several weeks, trying to find a context from which to infer the subject of the assignment, neither of us could relate it to anything. The words were gibberish.

Of my daughters' teachers, some were adequate, some good, and a few excellent. But so many were inadequate that examples of their ineptitude would fill pages. A frequent complaint, especially in math, was that a teacher could not elaborate on, or clarify, new material. When students asked questions, the teachers responded in the exact same words that prompted the questions. The teachers appeared to have memorized the material from a teacher's manual or textbook without real understanding. They were unable to restate the material in other ways.

The town of Amherst is more "gown" than "town." Home of Amherst and Hampshire colleges and the University of Massachusetts' largest campus, the town's only industry is education. Professors in the academic departments of the three institutions far outnumber the professors in the university's School of Education. Given the contempt of most academicians for educationists, as well as concern for their children's schooling, one might expect the academicians to limit the influence of educationists. They do not. The school system in Amherst is dominated by educationists as are all school systems elsewhere.

Time magazine in its cover story entitled "Help! Teacher Can't Teach," gave examples from all over the nation. In Chicago, a television news reporter was told by a teacher: "I teaches English." In a Milwaukee suburb, teachers—not one but many—submitted a curriculum proposal to the board of education that was riddled with grammatical errors and misspellings. Examples of the latter were: "dabate," "documant," and "woud." In Oregon, a kindergarten teacher who had As and Bs in her education courses at Portland State University was found to be functionally illiterate. In Mobile, Alabama, a fifth grade teacher with an M.Ed. degree sent home the following note: "Scott is dropping in his studies he acts as if he don't Care. Scott want pass in his assignment at all, he a had a poem to learn and he fell to do it." This note eventually reached the hands of a board of education member who was so shocked that he called it to the attention of the superintendent of schools. But the superintendent was not shocked.[8]

Few of the teachers currently employed in American schools are nearly as literate as the teachers who taught Abraham Lass. Many are not up to giving clear instruction and being models of language usage for their students. Their deficiencies in math are even greater.

Teacher training in the normal schools of eighty and ninety years ago was better than the teacher training in today's university schools and departments of education. Teachers-to-be then had a clear idea of what was expected of them. They knew the 3Rs were important and that they were expected to know them thoroughly and teach them rigorously. In ghetto schools—those that were all Jewish, all Italian, or mixtures of these and others from non-English speaking homes—teachers had the additional task of teaching them English from scratch. The adequate literacy of Lass' teachers was only partly due to their teacher training. Their skill was largely developed by the habit of reading fiction for pleasure, as was true of the rest of the population, excluding, of course, the millions of recently arrived immigrants who spoke little or no English.

Today's educationists can try to excuse themselves for producing teachers who are inadequately literate. They can point to the change in the culture from chiefly reading to chiefly watching. It is not the fault of educationists that today's entertainment consists largely of watching television, films, and looking at magazines and newspapers filled with photographs. The excuse would be valid except for three historical facts.

First, the rapid and continuously accelerating technological developments in the larger culture, including computers, made it continuously apparent that knowledge of math was becoming increasingly important. It was obvious that larger numbers of students were going to have to be prepared to learn advanced forms of mathematics—calculus and beyond. Yet, the teaching of math in public schools today is at the lowest ebb in the history of public schooling. In math instruction, educationists have gone against the technological tide, gone against the obvious needs of the larger society.

Second, there exist in the United States a few high schools where student achievement is greater today than at any former time. The number of such schools is small, amounting to less than one percent of the total. The student achievement in them is also due to special circumstances. Their existence nevertheless demonstrates that today's students can become highly literate and numerate despite all the distractions of the larger culture.

The third historical fact that invalidates blaming the culture is that educationists have actively promoted the decline in the 3Rs. They have aggressively attacked them. They have trained teachers-to-be as attackers and dispersed them to schools throughout the United States. Some of the attacks have been overt and frontal. Most have been covert and indirect, some in the guise of furthering literacy and numeracy. Few of the attacks have been deliberately malicious. It would be a mistake to ascribe to education professors any intellectual understanding of the consequences of their actions. They do not recognize that the literature of Greece, Rome, and modern Europe made today's culture possible. They do not realize that despite the technologies of current communications and computers, further cultural, social, and technological progress is dependent on literacy; that without it we descend into anarchy.

Educationists' attacks on the 3Rs have been made out of ignorance compounded by self-interest. Having no body of knowledge of their own and having never made a positive contribution to public schooling, educationists have had to keep putting out new notions to justify their existence. The attacks on the 3Rs and the development of literacy and numeracy have to be seen in that light as they are documented in detail in all that is to follow.

4

Attacking Literacy with Pseudoliteracies

"What is visual literacy?" I asked this question of a media colleague after hearing him use the term to a group of students. Being still fresh from the advertising agency world, where talent in communicating with visuals is concentrated, to my ears the term sounded strange. Photographs, drawings, moving pictures, animation, and television images are the domain of art directors, film and television directors in ad agencies, but never did I hear any of them, nor anyone else, use the phrase "visual literacy."

In response to "What is visual literacy?" I got silence and a funny look. My colleague's reaction might be due, I thought, to feeling at a disadvantage. I had recently arrived from the world of commercial television, the most visual of the visual media. Dean Allen and his staff had told people about me as one of the new faculty in the school and many professors and students knew about my background. Students, especially, wanted to know if it was true that I had created such-and-such famous TV commercials, parodied by all the comedians.

I had written commercials, along with every form of print advertising, since the inception of television. In the beginning they were scripts for commercials that were broadcast live within live programs. When programs and commercials came to be filmed, I worked with art directors to develop commercials on storyboards and with Hollywood-trained producers during the production of them.

My media colleague was in the specialty that was promoting the use of television in schools. One of the rationales given was that since television teaches people to buy products, it can also teach school curricula. I was the only one in the school, however, with experience in the area that was the basis for the claim.

When next I asked "What is visual literacy?" I asked it of Ray Wyman, a full professor and senior member of the media program. He knew so much about technology, I was told, that he was practically an engineer. Wyman, too, gave me a funny look but muttered something about looking into "the literature." But it was not until several years later that I followed Wyman's suggestion.

During my first years in the school I spent my research efforts at 110 Livingston Street in Brooklyn observing the first chancellor under decentralization, Harvey B. Scribner, and collecting information about his administration. As superintendent of schools in Teaneck, New Jersey, Scribner had been the most visible leader in the fight to integrate its elementary schools, and was one of the heroes of that fight in my Teaneck book. I still admired him for that. My new colleagues in the U. Mass School of Education said that Scribner was doing the right things as New York City's schools chancellor, and I was still trying to accommodate myself to the school and believed that its soaring national and international reputation was deserved. I continued to see Scribner in a favorable light during his chancellorship and wrote a book-length manuscript showing him as the victim of the school system's established powers. Fortunately, I did not find a publisher for it. I say "fortunately" because my view of Scribner changed drastically after he joined the U. Mass School of Education as a professor and I observed him as a colleague. Moreover, rapid deterioration in New York City schools became obvious in the years immediately following his chancellorship, and I became progressively more aware of the deficiencies of the education field.

During my first four years I kept hearing and seeing the phrase "visual literacy" more frequently. It made no sense and, having many questions about the specialty I was in, I finally read its "literature." The specialty is variously known as audio-visual instruction, educational technology, and educational communications. The people in it are media professors in colleges and media specialists in public schools.

An invention of Eastman Kodak

Linking "visual" to "literacy" was full of intent. The two words together suggest an equivalence to reading and writing. They suggest that pictures can convey the same information.

I found that the literature of the specialty credits the invention of visual literacy to John L. Debes, a marketing executive of Eastman Kodak.[1] Debes introduced the term at the national convention of the Association of Educational Communications and Technology (AECT) in Houston in 1968. Kodak, of course, makes cameras, film for still photographs and slides, motion picture cameras and film to use in them, movie and slide projectors, photographic papers, and other photographic and darkroom supplies. Thanks to the efforts of media professors in university departments of education, their graduates in state education departments, as well as in elementary, junior high, and high schools, photography had been included in classroom curricula. Unlike schools before the 1950s when photography had been a camera-club activity after school, schools now purchased all kinds of equipment and supplies manufactured by Kodak. The education market for such wares had grown enormously. As a Kodak executive, John L. Debes had a profit motive.

Not always, but usually, the profit motive operates in the public interest. Profit is the incentive that keeps the supplies of what people need and want flowing to them. Suppliers to schools provide what schools will buy, whether educationally sound or not. Like all marketers, Kodak's marketing executive needed ideas to promote his products. But instead of inventing the term visual literacy, I believe that Debes found it, came across it as I did in an article in *Audiovisual Instruction* that predates his presentation of it at the 1968 AECT national convention. He probably recognized that it would serve the purposes of media specialists, and in doing so, contribute to Kodak's profits. Both wanted a larger share of school budgets.

The discretionary portion of any school budget is tiny compared to the whole. Almost all of a school budget goes for fixed costs—teachers' salaries, debt retirement, plant maintenance, electricity, heating, etc. Only in the spending of what is left over is there any choice. Most of the remaining money goes for various kinds of supplies, including books for the library. But from the 1950s on, as new schools were built all over the United States, schools changed drastically. For one thing, libraries became "resource centers." They no longer contained "just books." Many schools were built with TV studios, closed-circuit television, and quantities of other media equipment—TV monitors, movie projectors, filmstrips and viewers, audio recorders and cassettes, slide- and overhead-projectors, etc. Schools became staffed with media specialists to operate and take care of the media equipment. Discretionary funds now could be used for purchasing media supplies as well as books. In many instances where discretionary funds, and even capital funds, were insufficient to do both, books suffered.

Books suffered in Amherst. The year before I joined the School of Education, a beautiful new junior high school opened for classes. Wonderfully equipped, it had an indoor twenty-five-yard, six-racing-lane swimming pool and a TV studio, but few books in its library. My wife's first involvement in Amherst schools was to serve on a committee of parents that petitioned the school committee (the name for the board of education in Massachusetts) to make a special appropriation to purchase books. In the college/university town of Amherst, books in the new junior high had been neglected in favor of media paraphernalia.

How widespread was the competition for money between books and what media specialists often called nonprint, may be judged by the following lament published in a library journal in 1974:

> Educational technologists, with the industry they support, have nearly completed their invasion of library territory undertaken 15 to 20 years ago. The success of the operation can be seen in the epidemic conversion of school and college libraries into media or learning-resource centers; it is also apparent in state and national library standards, and in the curriculum of library schools. . . . the printed page has been demoted in favor of other "commodities."[2]

Dating from the 1968 AECT national convention, Kodak and media professors aggressively promoted the notion of visual literacy. An article on it written by Debes appeared later that year in *Audiovisual Instruction*,[3] another by him was published by Eastman Kodak,[4] and they formed the International Visual Literacy Association. It held its first conference the following year in Rochester, New York, the home city of Eastman Kodak. The conference issued this definition:

> Visual literacy refers to a group of vision competencies a human being can develop by seeing and at the same time having and integrating other sensory experiences. The development of these competencies is fundamental to normal human learning. When developed, they enable a visually literate person to discriminate and interpret the visual reactions, objects and symbols natural and man-made, that he encounters in his environment. Through the creative use of these competencies he is able to comprehend and enjoy the masterworks of visual communications.[5]

The murkiness of these words embarrassed even media professors. Advocates nevertheless defended visual literacy by saying that it was a mistake to overdefine it, and claimed that it was "a new field—perhaps not quite definable for some years."[6]

Visual literacy never would be defined, though in 1975 Eastman Kodak made a grant of $338,925 to the University of Iowa for a five-year Visual Scholars Program. The so-called scholars in it attempted to make visual literacy mean something, which was impossible. There is and can be no language of vision.

True languages are abstract, rule-governed, and the information they carry can be made available across *all* the major senses. A native language is spoken to be understood through the sense of hearing; in script and printed forms, made available to the sense of sight; in raised points and dots of Braille for the blind, its meaning is received through the sense of touch; pressures into the hands, finger spelling, is the way Helen Keller learned language, and "spoke" to her teacher, Anne Sullivan.

Being abstract and rule-governed, languages lend themselves to an infinite number of notational systems—the dots and dashes of the Morse Code; the short and long flashes of light of the heliograph; the arrangements and gestures of fingers and arms in signed spelling for the deaf; the shorthand of stenographers; the punch holes in cards for computers, phonetic symbols, etc. Because notation makes music a language, the deaf Beethoven communicated his compositions to other musicians via his written scores. Languages are *escapes* from the sensory; they are only *incidentally* sensory.

Some information in the physical world is, of course, entirely sensory; and is detectible by just *one* sense. Smells and tastes can be perceived only by the senses of smell and taste respectively. Nothing can make smells and tastes perceivable to the other senses. The same holds true for the purely visual—the looks of things. Purely visual information is what a blind man can never see, nor perceive with his other senses—the physical appearances of buildings, parks, street scenes, rivers, clouds, mountains, or human faces. Nothing can make these appearances available in any other form, although they can be replicated in copies and recordings. Attempts have been made to develop "a notational system for pictures, a device . . . that would enable people to 'write' pictures to each other much as engineers can write circuits, musicians can write sounds, and poets can write language."[7]

But all such efforts were foredoomed. No language of vision is possible because of the nature of physical reality. Cameras and graphic artists can record and copy its appearances. But how things look in drawings, photographs, motion pictures, videotapes, and television remains much the same as they look in physical reality. Although the looks of things can be modified to a certain extent, appearances can only be perceived as appearances.

Since visual literacy pertained to no language, Eastman Kodak and media professors could take it no further than the suggestiveness of the two words placed next to each other. The one tiny furtherance, from their point of view, was the headline in the full-page ad that Kodak ran in *The New York Times Magazine*. The headline was LITERACY, PLAIN OR VISUAL. The ad contained no pictures, depending entirely on words to convey its message. The body copy urged the teaching of visual literacy in the schools, with the last paragraph stating: "If you have read this far, you deserve compliments on your persistence. You are, we suspect, one of a small minority of readers of this magazine. Most people abandon an unillustrated bare stream of words like this. We don't blame them. There are too many other rewarding attractions for the eye and, through it, the mind."[8]

The ad insulted intelligence. It assumed that the reader would not recognize the ad's internal contradiction—urging the teaching of visual literacy and saying that words are boring while using no pictures, only words.

The ad's claim of the eye being the avenue to the mind is contrary to the history of the discovery of most of the world's knowledge. Ever since the invention of written language and mathematics, the human mind has used these two tools to discover information *below the surfaces* of physical reality, *beyond the purely sensory* of just the looks of things. All the seeing, touching, and tasting of water will not reveal that water is composed of two gases, one of which burns and the other supports combustion. To discover the chemistry of water, the tools of mind of literacy and numeracy were necessary. They remain necessary for the comprehension of all important knowledge—the psychological, social, economic, historical, and literary, as well as the scientific.

The promotion of visual literacy led future teachers and teachers in schools in the direction diametrically opposite to what is true. Visual literacy contributed—without the general public ever becoming aware of the term—to miseducation and our educational degeneration.

The complete acceptance of the non-language

Depravity in the eyes of the uncorrupted exerts a certain fascination. It is due, perhaps, to a lingering desire to disbelieve the enormity of it and its consequences.

It was with some fascination that I went to the national conference on visual literacy in 1976 at the Regency Hyatt Hotel in Nashville. It was the eighth annual conference of the Visual Literacy Association. Expecting to find John Debes of Kodak there, indeed I saw his name immediately following mine in the alphabetical listing of those making presentations.

By this time I had lost my former uneasiness in speaking to groups. No longer self-conscious while addressing audiences, I could think clearly on my feet, seldom at a loss in responding to the reactions of students and others. I felt no anxiety about making a presentation on the television medium that went against the notions of those who would be attending. I felt somewhat smug, too, knowing that *Phi Delta Kappan,* a general educationist journal, had accepted for publication my paper that showed that visual literacy is a nominalistic fallacy, a name for something that does not exist. I had titled my paper "Beware of the 'literacy' for which there is no language." *Kappan*'s editor had telephoned me to get the names of visual literacy advocates, saying that he wanted to elicit a rebuttal article and run it side by side with mine. Confident that my paper could not be rebutted successfully, I had given Debes's name with a couple of others to the editor. During the three-day conference, I wondered if anybody there had been sent a copy of my paper and would connect me with it.

I found the conference clothed in respectability. Among its supporters were the Tennessee Arts Commission/National Endowment for the Arts, the Middle Tennessee State University, and the University of Tennessee/Nashville. A principal presenter was from the federal Office of Education, and the banquet/keynote speaker was Tennessee's commissioner of education.

Seventy-one different presentations, some given more than once, were offered at the conference by professors of education and by elementary and high school teachers. A sampling of the presentation titles includes:

> Visual literacy and photography: the tie that binds.
> Photography philosophy and visual literacy.
> Materials production by and for children: visual literacy at work.
> Visual learning in practice: an exemplary program from San Diego.
> Visual literacy through media.
> The effectiveness of visual learning and communication skills development in teacher training programs.
> Integrating the visual literacy concept into any curriculum.
> Aspects of visual grammar and syntax: multilevel probes.
> Organizing teaching for learning visually.
> Visual literacy: teaching non-verbal communication through television.
> Teaching visual literacy at the college level: Success !!!!!!!!!!!!
> Piaget: Ramifications for visual literacy.
> Media assignments in the regular english classroom. [Yes, "english" with a small *e*.]

The title of Debes's presentation was "The Democracy of the Intellect," and befitting his status as a principal speaker, it was given in one of the ballrooms. He introduced what was labeled "the new Debes model." He talked about the right and left hemispheres of the brain, with what he called "visual languaging" occurring in the right. Debes was trying to freshen up visual literacy by linking it to an emerging fad touched off by *The Psychology of Consciousness* by Robert Ornstein. A British brain researcher commented:

> Ornstein has claimed that the two halves of the cerebrum serve two different types of consciousness. The left hemisphere generally containing the speech centres, is associated with the logical, rational thought processes typical of the scientific culture of western society. The right hemisphere is associated with intuitive processes, holistic understanding and the life style of the "mystic" east. Scientists, presumably, are left-hemisphere dominant, poets right. The future of humanity lies in reintegrating left and right hemispheres. Fashionable though such ideas may be, there seems little necessity to take them seriously.[9]

Debes's "new model" made no more sense than the old. But he did not have to make sense. My impression was that he, or rather Eastman Kodak through him, owned the conference. Kodak's influence was everywhere. The cash bar/hors d'oeuvres at the end of the day, before dinner, was "Courtesy, The Eastman Kodak Company." Debes held open house in his personal hotel suite after dinner where the liquor flowed freely and I had a chance to observe him and his followers, the media professors who worked with him. Without Kodak, there probably would have been no Visual Literacy Association, nor annual conferences. I suspect that Debes and perhaps some of his hangers-on believed in visual literacy no more than I did. But it was good business, and it gave the media professors a specialty within a specialty, conferences and publications to add to their curriculum vitas, and probably some extra consultancy money.

Kodak must have found the promotion of visual literacy to be cost effective to continue promoting it eight years after Debes had introduced it. Sales must have increased. Kodak's promotions included heavy mailings to teachers, media specialists in schools systems and professors in education departments. I received them several times a year, year after year. There was the $338,925 grant made the year before to the University of Iowa for a five-year Visual Scholars Program. Kodak also advertised to teachers and school administrators in magazines such as *Scholastic*. The ad in *The New York Times Magazine* with the headline LITERACY, PLAIN OR VISUAL, previously quoted, had run the prior Sunday. When I mentioned to Debes that I had seen it, he told me that the first thing on Monday morning, before he left his office for the conference, he had had phone calls from teachers wanting to know more about visual literacy.

The term had gained a wide currency. It was showing up in textbooks used in media courses, in advertising by suppliers of media equipment and materials, including film rentals. Two years before, a book with the title of *A Primer of Visual Literacy* had been published. The term appeared in education journals having nothing to do with media. *Change* magazine quoted Dwight Allen as saying in an interview: "Visual literacy is extremely important in all societies. My hunch is that the less literate the society, the more intuitively present visual literacy is."[10] The *English Journal*, published by the National Council of Teachers of English, had a regular department called Multi-Media. Its editor urged English teachers to "further develop the visual literacy that children have acquired watching TV," suggesting that students be allowed to express themselves "in the visual language that is the natural language of their times."[11] A writer in *Language Arts* stated: "The possibilities for development of visual literacy skills are enormous."[12] The National Education Association (NEA) had recently published its own booklet with the title *Visual Literacy* for its 1.7-million members.

The general acceptance of the nominalistic fallacy was so great that few teachers escaped its influence. It is difficult to separate how they were affected by it from such parallel notions as students being supposedly visually oriented due to television, and the everyday presence of visual media in many schools. Many teachers tried to be more visual in their teaching methods, often with disastrous results.

Take, for example, the seventh grade math teacher of one of my daughters in the Amherst junior high. She introduced the concept that if a number is halved an infinite number of times, the number will approach zero but never reach zero. This being an abstract principle, she should have treated it as an abstraction.

She could have made it perfectly clear by writing on the blackboard a series of numbers such as 1, ½, ¼, ⅛, ¹/₁₆, ¹/₃₂, ¹/₆₄, /₁₂₈, ¹/₂₅₆, ¹/₅₁₂, ¹/₁₀₂₄. Students would have readily understood that the number, although rapidly diminishing, could never become zero.

Instead, the teacher tried to make the concept visual, using the distance from her desk to the classroom door. She paced off half of it, then half the remaining distance, and so on. She told the class that she would never reach the door, but by the fourth or fifth time that she halved the distance, she was *at the door*. Her feet were against it. She had demonstrated the opposite of what she said she was demonstrating. The students, astonished and confused, were in the position of pointing out the obvious, with the attendant danger of retaliation from the teacher.

Stressing visuals, the concrete over the abstract, the sensory over the incidentally sensory, contributed to inferior teaching in schools everywhere.

As reading, writing, and math skills declined at all levels of schooling, educationists proliferated pseudoliteracies. Besides visual literacy, there was film literacy, television literacy, multimedia literacy, social literacy—part of the title of a federally funded program—and even ethnic literacy. A professor in the School of Education used, as part of a course title, personal literacy. No advertising copywriter I ever knew could have invented these terms—for the serious purpose of furthering education—without feeling ashamed.

5

Undermining Literacy with Television

Prior to steeping myself in the literature of educational technology, I assumed that television had helped bring the specialty into being. Those in it, however, attributed its birth to the success of the U.S. Navy and Army in developing and using visual aids during World War II.

The urgent training task of the armed forces was to turn millions of civilians into sailors and soldiers prepared for combat. That included teaching them to recognize the differences between the naval and military hardware of the U.S. and allied forces and that of our enemies. Aircraft recognition charts and posters were a major type of visual aid. They presented, for example, the side-by-side silhouettes of American and Japanese fighter planes, making the differences between them discernible. Knowing the differences was critical for recognition. Similar recognition charts were produced for U.S. and enemy aircraft carriers, battleships, tanks, etc. Other instructional aids included cutaway drawings of engines, and charts for all of the various kinds of rope knots used in the navy. Visual aids contributed so greatly to instructing servicemen that Fleet Admiral Chester N. Nimitz called their development "one of the educational achievements of the Second World War."[1]

The educationist technology specialty barely existed at the time and contributed no personnel to this achievement. But following the war when the specialty began to grow rapidly in schools and departments of education, it subsumed the success of the armed forces and said it was going to continue the success at every level of education from elementary school through college. The members of the specialty failed to distinguish between two very different kinds of information—the *purely visual* and the *incidentally visual*. The armed forces' visual aids showed the looks of things. The looks of planes, ships, and tanks are *purely visual*. The skills and knowledge taught in schools and colleges, on the other hand, are chiefly abstract. Reading, writing, and arithmetic, and the disciplines based on them, are only *incidentally visual*.

But the members of the specialty assumed that whatever words can do pictures can do better. They even stopped using "aids," which, until then, had always been coupled with "visual" and "audiovisual." They said they were going to spearhead a revolution with new teaching materials that they would create for the new technologies becoming available, including television. They spoke of themselves as "on the cutting edge of the future" that would soon end much "traditional" education. Within a decade, however, having produced no instructional materials themselves, they changed their rhetoric. They now said that teachers should create such materials and they would teach teachers how. When, in another decade, teachers had produced none to speak of, the rhetoric changed again. This time, they said students should be "involved" in creating their own instructional materials and "express" themselves with media technology. The specialty shifted responsibility from itself to teachers to students.

In the meantime, the specialty acquired tremendous quantities of the new technologies developed by manufacturers for the education market. Between 1959 and 1976, federal and state governments spent $2.13 billion for media equipment and materials under the National Education Defense Act.[2] This figure does not include all funds spent for such purposes by local school districts, by state education departments, nor by the federal government under other legislative acts.

Much of the money went for equipping new schools. School administrators and state departments of education, being unfamiliar with media hardware, needed experts to tell them what equipment to install, where it should go in new schools, and how to plan to use it. They consulted professors of media in university schools and departments of education. Manufacturers of the equipment also paid these professors to advise them, evaluate their hardware, and recommend it to schools and colleges. Self-interest in terms of extra income encouraged the professors to become hardware experts rather than take up the more difficult task of developing educational software.

University criteria also encouraged concentration on hardware. One of the criteria for tenure and promotion was publication, which meant writing articles for educational journals and books on school media. Universities offered no rewards for developing skills in any medium but print. Although media professors opposed traditional education, they sought its traditional rewards. They attained tenure and promotion by writing *about* the media they espoused, without attempting to become skilled in them.

Lack of skills did not stop media professors from writing as if they had them. They wrote textbooks telling how to create visuals and soundtracks for nonprint materials—for overhead projectors, slides, slide/audio tape productions, television, videotapes, film, and filmstrips. They gave step-by-step instructions and rules for each medium, arranged in long numbered lists. Schools, meanwhile, purchased readymade nonprint materials from commercial suppliers. Amherst elementary school librarians, or "resource center" personnel, were proud of integrating nonprint materials with books on the same shelves.

Media professors, meanwhile, concentrated on teaching equipment operations. They did not require their students to try to produce educational messages with the equipment. At the end of my first semester in the School of Education, receiving a general invitation to view the term productions of the students in the Educational TV Workshop, I went to the studio at the appointed time. Rows of movable chairs had been set up in front of a TV monitor. As I sat down the instructor with the euphonious name of Juan Caban handed me a list of student productions. "Don't judge the productions by their contents," he said, "just by their production values." Except for such elementary things as keeping cameras in focus and maintaining adequate sound levels, I could judge production values only by how well they added or detracted from the intended messages.

Juan Caban might just as well have asked me to judge a written paragraph but ignore its meaning. When he played the videotape of the student productions, which were indeed empty of content, the reason for his admonition was clear.

If a course in journalism were to be given in this manner, students would first be introduced to using typewriters, although fairly briefly. Next would come instruction on how to set type, whether on linotype or on a newer computer system. Then there would be lectures and labs on newsprint, printing inks, and printing-press operations. What students did for a term production would not be judged on news collection and writing.

So-called educational media was totally misconceived and I did not intend to contribute to its misconceptions even in my first semester. Since I had to teach, I wanted to introduce the means of creating software that would be substantive and useful to classroom teachers.

In my second semester, with considerable misgivings, I offered my first course. It was in the techniques of creating educational films and television on storyboards. The storyboard is a blank printed form available commercially in pads of fifty sheets, each with sixteen frames for pictures. Below each frame was space for writing in the soundtrack to be heard at the same time that the visuals were to be seen. One of my misgivings was that I could not draw well. In my advertising agencies, art directors always drew the visuals for me and much more. Art-school trained, they invariably improved on or substituted better visuals for mine. The same held true in creating magazine and newspaper ads and posters.

Graphic artists had similarly contributed their talents to creating visual aids in the U.S. Navy and Army during World War II. The officer in charge of the army's training aids, James D. Finn, wrote in a doctoral dissertation completed in 1949 at Ohio State University: ". . . *personnel from many different fields— advertising, commercial art, photography, electronics, etc.—fields not usually associated with school operations, are needed in quantity to support an instruction aids program.*" [Finn's italics][3]

Finn became a professor at the University of Southern California and the leader of the educational technology specialty. During the 1950s and '60s he was president of its national association, consultant to the U.S. Office of Education, and president of the Educational Media Council on which sat representatives of equipment manufacturers. Professor Finn ignored his own dissertation. On becoming a hardware specialist, he never mentioned again the need for graphic artists. Despite all the talk about teaching visually and visual literacy, media programs in schools and departments of education had electronics technicians on their support staffs but no graphic artists.

I partially quieted my misgivings about not being able to draw well by reminding myself that I had always created directly on storyboards, simultaneously writing the words and making my own rough visuals to form a single message. From now on I would have no choice but to draw as best I could, and try to get students to do the same.

My first classroom space was a dormitory "date room." It was lined with couches and easy chairs, and when I arrived students were sprawled in them, some with heads back in attitudes of sleep. I was appalled but the university was short of regular classrooms until completion of buildings under construction. Higher education was still a growth industry in the spring of 1971, as well as a time of "never trust anyone over thirty."

Introducing the course, I sensed that none in the class had ever heard of a storyboard. A student interrupted me to ask when we would get to film production. I answered that there would be none. Another student stood up and said that this was supposed to be a film production course. He asserted rather than asked, although the course was described in the course catalogue as "pre-production." I pointed out that all national TV commercials were on film and most had been made by following storyboards as blueprints, that I had created commercials without ever laying my hands on a piece of production equipment. Disbelief suffused the student's face and he walked out to drop the course.

The rest of the class did not accept authority readily, either. I had to sell them on the necessity for storyboards. Advertising agencies, I told them, spent weeks and sometimes months developing their very simple, simplistic messages. For the complex information that educational films should attempt to convey, careful development was much more necessary. Storyboards were the only means of doing that.

After some fumbling on how to conduct the class, I settled on giving a new assignment each week, to be done outside of class, with each student presenting his or her storyboard in class and getting criticism or feedback on it. I also collected assignments and returned them each week with my written comments. For the first month or so, students did all assignments in a TV commercial format. They assumed that that was what I wanted. I kept telling them each week not to limit themselves to it and to let the contents dictate the format. But they seemed not to hear or believe me. Finally, I told them that although I was from Madison Avenue, I was more than just an advertising man. I held up a copy of my book and said: "You see, I am also the author of a book that has nothing to do with advertising. I'm going to use it now to exorcise my Madison Avenue image." Thereupon, I waved it at them three times in the manner of a priest sprinkling holy water, and with each forward thrust of my book I said: "Out Madison Avenue image." Although I kept a straight face I expected the students to take it humorously. None smiled. In no eyes did a glint of humor appear. Their faces were inscrutable. After class I felt quite depressed.

When students presented their next assignment the following week none of their storyboards were in a TV commercial format, and they were much improved. My exorcism had apparently worked. I subsequently was able to give them examples of the use of storyboards by other than advertising agencies. *Sesame Street* was in its second year on the air. Its presumed success had made it the standard for how television could be used to teach. It became the new rationale, too, for media professors and media specialists to promote the use of television in schools. Portions of storyboards from *Sesame Street* teaching segments were published in the press and in publications of the Children's Television Workshop and the U.S. Office of Education. I had copies made for my class. I also learned that the storyboard had been invented in the early 1930s by a member of Walt Disney's creative staff and subsequently used to plan all Disney productions, live action films as well as animated cartoons.[4] Alfred Hitchcock, too, visualized all of his feature films first in storyboard form.[5] By the end of the term my students seemed to accept that I knew what I was talking about. Two had done excellent work and, to my surprise, I felt grateful. I wanted to grade them A but was prevented by school policy. I could give them only the same P that I gave the others.

I continued offering the course in subsequent semesters while recognizing some inherent shortcomings. Students had no further place to apply what they learned. They continued to express dissatisfaction at having no opportunity to produce films. The school offered no production course and the TV Workshop course concentrated merely on equipment operation. Beyond courses, the educationist field afforded little opportunity to create instructional software. This was the chief shortcoming in my eyes. I could not hope to pass on my skills and knowledge to students without software projects. The entire start-to-finish process was necessary—creating on storyboards, using them as blueprints during production, and testing the end result to determine effectiveness.

Remarks of a graduate student in the fall semester of 1972 put me on the trail of a possible software project. She was in the deaf-education program and after she mentioned the poor quality of captioned films, I invited her to show one to the class. It was an animated cartoon so ancient and poor that even Saturday morning cartoon programs on TV would not have used it. The graduate student said that such captioned films did not help deaf children learn to read.

Learning to read is an almost insurmountable task for those who are prelingually deaf—deaf at birth or before they learn spoken language. Children with normal hearing learn to read by making the connection between their spoken language and the marks on the page of written language. But for most children who are prelingually deaf, learning the language and learning to read tend to be one and the same. The prelingually deaf have little difficulty learning nouns such as door, window, floor, wall, book, desk, shirt, and all other objects that can be labeled, or action verbs, such as walk, run, jump, throw, that can be acted out. But understanding sentences is overwhelmingly difficult because of all the words in them that are not nouns and action verbs.

The graduate student told us that deaf education had made no progress in decades. Then I heard the head of the Clarke School for the Deaf in Northampton say the same thing. Considering that Anne Sullivan was able to impart language to deaf, mute, and blind Helen Keller in the 1880s, the lack of progress was startling.

Sensing that the deaf were in need of teaching materials, I investigated further. The school's deaf-education program consisted of training students with normal hearing to become media specialists in schools for the deaf. Professor Ray Wyman was head of the program, which was supported by a multimillion dollar grant from the Bureau of Education for the Handicapped of the U.S. Office of Education. The program had materials available that were supposed to teach word meanings visually. Among them was an elaborate teaching-machines program called Project Life, on which the bureau had spent millions. In looking over the different sets of materials I could tell at a glance that none could do more than confuse deaf children. To put my judgment to the test and demonstrate how very poor they were, I showed my class a number of typical examples from a set of materials designed for the overhead projector.

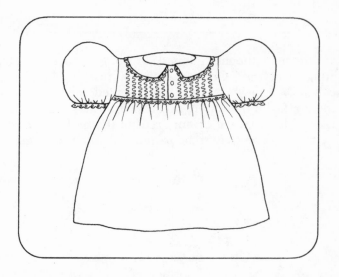

I showed this drawing by means of an overhead projector transparency, explaining that it was supposed to teach deaf children the meaning of a word. The word was on the transparency, just outside the frame at the upper right. I had covered it up with a small cardboard flap, making it opaque. I asked my students what they thought the intended word was. All said "dress." When I lifted the flap and revealed the intended word they gasped and exclaimed in surprise. The word was "clean." Next, I showed the following drawing, also with the intended word covered up with a flap.

For this one, students guessed "reading," "book," "holding," "sitting," and "girl." Once again they were amazed when I lifted the flap and they saw that the intended word was "big." A student asked if there were no other drawings to go with them. I assured her that out of hundreds in the set from which they were taken, none were to be paired with either drawing.

These next two transparencies were intended to be shown together. The differences between the two drawings were many, and I watched the eyes of the students shift back and forth between the two, comparing them. None in the class were able to tell that the intended words were "dull" and "sharp."[6] As instructional materials, the drawings were failures.

Unknown to me at the time, the first pictorial instructional materials for deaf-mutes had been devised by Thomas H. Gallaudet more than a hundred years before. His materials had either degenerated in the hands of subsequent teachers of the deaf or had always been ineffective. But Gallaudet believed that his materials could teach hearing children to read. In 1835 he published a reading primer based on them called *Mother's Primer*.[7] It was the forerunner of the reading primers using the "look-say" method, promoted by professors of education beginning in the 1920s, which was still the method in use to teach reading in 85 percent of the nation's schools at the beginning of the 1980s.

The ineffective pictures I demonstrated to my classes had been devised by Robert Newby, director of the Instructional Materials Center at the Pennsylvania School for the Deaf. Sets of them had been reproduced by the Bureau of Education of the Handicapped of the U.S. Office of Education and distributed to all schools of the deaf throughout the nation. Robert Newby was invited by the same federal bureau to present a paper about them at a conference it sponsored at the University of Nebraska. Newby did not claim that any deaf child had been helped to learn to read a word from them. The one and only claim he made was that he got favorable "classroom feedback" from teachers.[8]

Yet, this Nebraska conference at which he spoke was billed as celebrating A Decade of Progress. That was its theme. By progress the conference did not mean any increase in learning among deaf children. None had occurred and none was claimed. The only progress referred to was the installation by the media specialty in schools for the deaf of TV studios and all the paraphernalia that went with them, including equipment to record programs off the air and add captions. Professor Ray Wyman from my school presented a paper on the overhead projector. In just ten years, he boasted, it had become ubiquitous. The conference was a self-congratulatory meeting of hardware specialists with little concern for their failure to help prelingually deaf children to learn to read, their greatest difficulty and the one over which few ever triumphed.

From the time of the success of the armed forces in creating training aids in World War II and the subsumption of that success by the educationist media specialty, the ability to communicate visually had degenerated to zero. If the Navy's officer in charge of visual aids, William Exton, Jr., had been in charge of developing teaching materials for the deaf, I believe they would have succeeded. The principle he applied in creating aircraft recognition charts was the same as needed to convey meanings visually to deaf children. Just as there had been two side-by-side silhouettes of fighter planes, one with an American label and the other with a Japanese label, there should be two side-by-side dresses—one soiled and labeled "dirty" and the other unsoiled and labeled "clean." Furthermore, since words are generalizations, unlike the looks of fighter planes, a series of drawings of "dirty" and "clean" shirts, towels, hands, faces, plates, cups, and spoons was needed to form a pattern and permit deaf children to learn the meanings of the adjectives irrespective of the nouns they modified.

I pointed out to my class that side-by-side comparisons are seen every day of the year on television. Commercials show one brand of paper towel soaking up more liquid than another brand; one brand of hair spray holding hair in place better than another brand; one hand with "chocolate mess" while the other hand has "no chocolate mess." Contrary to the notion of teachers and educationists, virtually no one learns how to communicate visually from watching television. Children brought up with television probably know less about things visual than their counterparts of pretelevision days. They know less because they are less literate. What is *seen* largely depends on what is known *behind the eyes*; and most of what we know comes from language. Language conveys organized information; cameras convey the raw data of physical appearances. Raw data is difficult to learn from. Television viewers learn what advertising agencies take pains to organize into messages via side-by-side visual comparisons. Viewers understand the messages but fail to see the principle of how they are arranged. Principles, being abstract, are learned from language. In typical side-by-side advertising comparisons, the principle is that both brands are demonstrated in ways and settings that are identical in every respect except the one difference consumers are intended to notice.

The principle is the same as used in the armed forces aircraft recognition charts and the same that should be applied in creating materials for the deaf. I saw to it that students applied it in their assignments, which I broadened to include teaching meanings of words. I gave them simple adjectives like "tall" and "short" to define visually. When a student showed drawings in class that did not succeed, I sent him or her out into the halls of the school to ask the first person encountered to look at the drawings. If the person could not tell what the covered up words were, the student knew that the drawings did not work, that the principle had not been applied.

Two or three students in each class would come to realize that communicating with visuals was not easy but hard, and took the course seriously. Others, particularly those aiming to become media specialists, were made uneasy by my emphasizing principles and language. They sometimes indicated that they were not interested in deaf education. I responded that the course *had to have content* and that materials for the only population that takes in information almost exclusively through the eyes, made excellent content for a course in visual communication.

Some of my students who wanted jobs in the media specialty knew well its hardware emphasis and had a "so what" attitude. Though they could not fail to recognize the truths revealed in the course, the truths went against their self-interest.

To establish generally the credibility of what I taught, as well as for my own satisfaction, I needed a major software project. As ineffectual as the current materials for the deaf were, no channel existed to replace them. I knew better than to tell the Bureau of Education for the Handicapped how ineffectual they were. But I learned from a sign language instructor, whose own mother and father were deaf, that no teaching materials existed for the function words of language—the prepositions and conjunctions that pepper every page of print. Their meanings were considered so impossible to convey visually that no materials had been attempted for them.

I also learned that the Bureau of Education for the Handicapped funded proposals that the bureau deemed worthy. I could submit a proposal to visually define prepositions and conjunctions. First, I had to satisfy myself that I could, indeed, convey the meanings of such words as "to," "by," "of," "in," "out," "and," "if," and "but." I worked on several meanings of "to" on a storyboard that lengthened to 130 frames. Next, not wanting to waste my time by going to all the trouble of researching the literature on the deaf if there was no chance of my proposal being funded, I made an appointment with an official of the bureau. I took my 130-frame storyboard down to Washington, showed and explained it to him, and told him what I had in mind.

My proposal would entail developing storyboards for a number of prepositions and conjunctions while working with a panel of experts in deaf education. I would create the storyboards, review the storyboards with them and seek their criticisms, comments, and additional information, then revise the storyboards accordingly. I would keep working with the members of the panel and revising the storyboards until there was agreement that the probability of success in conveying the meanings, if put on film, was high. Then, and only then, would I request the large amounts of money necessary for film production.

The official told me that the bureau would welcome the proposal. I flew back to Amherst encouraged. In the next several weeks I wrote the proposal. Over fifty pages long, it stated the problem with copious documentation. To solve it, the storyboards would be created utilizing every trick of sophisticated filmmaking. The fundamental technique would be combining live action and animation, and to illustrate what I meant I included a small portion of my storyboard for "to," drawn by someone who could draw much better than I. The portion was for the sentence "Throw the ball to me." The first frame was an establishing shot of a father and son in a backyard, with the boy throwing a ball to his father. Then, a from-the-waist-up shot of the boy telling the father "Throw the ball to me." This "telling" sequence would have to be filmed two ways. One way would be for the boy to "tell" in sign language. The second way would be for oral schools for the deaf which do not permit their students to use sign language. For oral schools the boy would mouth the words. In both instances, the sentence would come on the screen as a caption to be read. The next camera shot, as the father begins to throw the ball, showed him in the distance and the boy in the foreground near the camera. The father throws in slow motion and as the ball leaves his hand, the word "to" pops on next to the ball and travels with it toward the boy and camera. This slow motion, shown in a sequence of several frames, was intended to give time for the ball and the word to be seen together as they gradually loom larger coming through the air toward the camera. As the boy's hands catch the ball, the word "to" pops off and the word "me" pops on, superimposed on the boy.

This short storyboard sequence was clear. The pictures were continuous and easy to "read." By including it, I hoped to make my proposal understandable to the bureau's review panel, even if its members were not familiar with storyboards and their use. Before it was sent to Washington, I found out that it was clear to the associate dean for research who had to approve all proposals on behalf of the university. He was critical of the School of Education, as were many others in the university, and I was told that he considered mine a superior proposal.

I had requested funds of $67,957. When the university's indirect costs were added, the amount came to $104,715. Most of the money, to be spent over a two-year period, was budgeted for employing a graphic artist and three graduate assistants, plus consultancy fees for the members of my panel of experts. To guard against the kind of misunderstanding I encountered with many students who automatically concluded that a course in creating film meant film *production*, I took the precaution of stating several times in the body of my proposal: "No money is requested at this time for film production." This precaution was in addition to showing no amounts of money for film production in my proposed budget.

The bureau rejected my proposal. With its notification of rejection came what appeared to be verbatim reasons from two members of the review panel. One was: "Damerell is very naive if he thinks he can produce film for only $104,715." The other read: "This proposal is noncompetitive. It duplicates what has already been done." The first reason no doubt came from a panel member with an Ed.D. in media. Despite knowing how closed-minded were the members of the media specialty, each fresh example nevertheless came as a surprise. The second reason had to come from a panel member with a doctorate in the education of the handicapped, and his statement just was not true. No motion picture films to convey the meanings of prepositions and conjunctions to the deaf existed.

I thought of filing a protest with the Bureau of Education of the Handicapped but knew it would be futile, a waste of emotional energy. Instead, I directed my attention to other concerns I had begun to investigate.

One was the problem of television. So many contradictory notions existed about television that it was an educational problem of some enormity. At one extreme, all the blame was heaped on it for the decline in reading and verbal scores, as well as the general decline in the quality of literacy. At the other, television was regarded as the greatest and most democratic educational medium ever invented, capable of teaching even reading skills, an attitude summed up in the name "educational television." Some said that television had created a visual culture, and may have affected the brain, producing an altered state of consciousness.

Tantalizing to me, having grown up prior to television and been among the first to write commercials for it, was the question of why it had so rapidly become universal. In the single decade of the 1950s, starting almost from scratch, television sets became almost ubiquitous. The average time spent watching them per household had climbed to over four hours a day and was still climbing. Why was the television audience so undifferentiated? Why was "what's on" watched by almost all, regardless of age, sex, income level, ethnic group membership, locale lived in, or level of education?

Where to look for an answer came to me one day in class. I was in the middle of introducing visual events that students seldom "saw" while watching films and television. I had given them a list of frequently used visual changes—cuts, dissolves, wipes, zooms, pans, dollies, and freeze frames—each precisely defined. We had discussed them, and I was pointing out examples of the changes in a videotape of a Barbra Streisand special, recorded off the air. We were watching it on a TV monitor with the sound turned off to concentrate exclusively on the visuals.

All at once I had a deeper realization of the significance of all the visual changes we were paying attention to. No camera image remained on the screen for more than a few seconds. Among the four or five cameras used to record the special, switching among them was frequent. One camera was on a boom and from time to time swooped down over and sometimes seemingly through the orchestra. The sets in which Streisand sang totally changed instantly a number of times. The seated orchestra became a marching band in the blink of the eye. Streisand's costumes changed instantly on her. The pace was frenetic compared to a Judy Garland special of the late 1950s. Garland sang in one setting and in the same clothes throughout. Visual changes were limited to an occasional slow dissolve from one camera to another. Visually, Garland's special was as static as Streisand's was frenetic. In the years between the two specials, the medium had progressively added more and more kinds of visual changes and made them more and more frequently.

Part of this insight was remembering what a Hollywood-trained ad agency producer once told me. In Hollywood's heyday of mass producing B movies, the dull ones were doctored by adding more cuts to make them seem livelier and faster paced. Even so, the time considered minimal then for establishing an image was three seconds. Current television had reduced that minimum to below one second.

The reason why frequent visual changes apparently increased everyone's willingness to watch "what's on," was unknown, a rule of thumb without a theory. I became convinced that the reason the rule of thumb worked could be found only in something as fundamental and universal as human biology, and specifically the eye and brain. One of the first books I looked into had that very title: *Eye and Brain* by R. L. Gregory. I also read Gregory's other works and those of authors dealing with visual perception, eye movements, and cognitive psychology. Within a year, I had found out why visual change played a large part in holding viewers' attentions.

First of all, the back of the human eye is lined with a kind of curved, three-dimensional screen called the retina that is sensitive to light. The retina registers images, reduced in size by the refraction of light from the surface of the cornea and by the lens. To register in sharp focus, the image or portion of an image must fall on the tiny spot in the center of the retina called the fovea. Portions of images registering outside the fovea in the surrounding retina are indistinct and a blur. What is seen sharply in the fovea subtends a narrow angle of only about four degrees. Very little of the visual field at any instant is in sharp focus which, if not taken into account, gives rise to confusion about seeing. As Arthur Koestler expressed it:

> Most people with normal eyesight tend to the flattering belief that they see the world around them at any time in sharp focus; in fact, however, they see a blur. Only a minute fraction of the visual field—about one thousandth of it—is seen distinctly; outside of this centre vision becomes increasingly vague and hazy. If you gaze fixedly at a single word in the centre of the page you are reading, and try to prevent your gaze from straying along the line (which is not easy because reading is an automatized skill), you will see only about a couple of words sharp in focus, the rest of the line on both sides trails off into a haze.[9]

Similarly, at any one instant, only a tiny portion of the television screen is seen in sharp focus: if the viewer is four feet from the screen, the portion is only about one square inch; at eight feet, only about four square inches. If the screen is typical in size, nineteen inches measured diagonally, its area is roughly 171 square inches. The portion seen in sharp focus from four feet away is only 0.6 percent; at eight feet, 2.4 percent. This can become noticeable, however, only by placing a spot of adhesive on the screen as a reference point and gazing fixedly at it, preventing the gaze from being "pulled" off—which is not easy because scanning pictures is also automatic, although not a skill. Only the tiny area of the image around the spot of adhesive is seen in sharp focus. The rest of the picture is a blur to us.

We nevertheless extract information from the blur. If we are staring fixedly at the reference point spot and the blur to one side is a lifesize face, we can tell that it is a face. If it is known to us we may recognize it. But we want to know more. We want to know the person's emotions and intentions. To find out, we must see the expressive portions of the face in sharp focus, chiefly the eyes and lips. The brain calculates the direction and distance the viewer's eyes must move to fixate the eyes or lips on the screen. It then issues orders, much as bearing and range are given to artillery crews. The resulting eye movement is, in fact, termed ballistic by neuropsychologists. The eyes do not wander or search. They go unerringly to the predetermined target. And for each successive eye fixation, the way we normally scan a picture, the brain makes new calculations and issues new orders, up to a maximum of five per second.

In possession of these biological facts, it became obvious to me why the television medium has progressively added more visual change and more frequently. Each new camera image as it comes on the TV screen of typical size is more than 90 percent blur at any instant. The brain decides where in the blur the new center of maximum information is located, calculates direction and distance the eyes must move to fixate it, and issues orders so that the eyes go unerringly to it. A major part of television's ability to sustain attention is keeping the brain continuously reacting to visual changes. This is a low order of brain activity. It is not a skill, but an innate reaction wired-in to the brain. Everybody does it effortlessly. We hear much of reading disabilities but we have yet to hear of a television-viewing disability.

Unlike the printed page, the television medium takes advantage of the primitive aspect of our visual system.

> . . . moving from the centre of the human retina [where the fovea is located] to its periphery, we travel back in evolutionary time; from the most highly organized structure, to a primitive eye which does little more than detect movements of shadows. The very edge of the human retina . . . merely initiates a reflex to direct the eyes to the source of movement, so that we can see it with our developed foveal eye.[10]

Our "primitive eye" within is similar to the eyes in lower animals such as frogs, which see nothing that remains static, only that which moves or otherwise changes. The frog's eyes enable it to catch flying insects for food, but it can starve to death in the presence of a pile of dead insects in front of it. Television, by adding as much visual change as possible, takes advantage of the more primitive portion of the human eye and visual processing system.

Having arrived at a theory for the longstanding rule of thumb of film and television producers of adding visual change, I wanted to publish it. Recognizing that I would stand a better chance if I quantified some evidence, I undertook the tedious labor of analyzing samples of television in order to include some numbers. I recorded off the air 172 unduplicated 30-second and 60-second commercials that all together added up to more than an hour and a half. After counting the camera image changes in them by type, I arrived at the average of a change every 3.3 seconds. I also analyzed two intros or billboards to TV programs where the average was one every second. Included in my sample, too, were three teaching segments from *Sesame Street* totaling 3 minutes and 34 seconds in which changes in camera image occurred on the average of every 4 seconds. I arranged these in a chart which I included in my paper. I elaborated on each step in my reasoning, providing authoritative quotes and footnotes. I submitted it to *AV Communications Review* that was supposed to be the scholarly quarterly, the "referee journal" of the educational technology specialty. I did so mindful that my paper tended to undermine at least some of the specialty's assumptions.

Subsequent to this paper, I collected data showing that in television viewing, the human brain gives more credence to what the eyes look at than to language that enters the ears. I started with Marshall McLuhan's observation: ". . . the radio listener to the Kennedy-Nixon debates [in 1960] obtained an impression of decided dominance of Richard M. Nixon over John F. Kennedy. Mr. Nixon's legal skills showed to great advantage over Mr. Kennedy. On the other hand [on television], Mr. Kennedy's charisma outshone Mr. Nixon in an eminent way . . ."[11]

Similar evidence was given me by a graduate student who was head of a state chapter of the American Civil Liberties Union. As such, he was frequently called on by local radio and TV news reporters to comment on civil rights cases. His comments were audio recorded for radio and videotaped for TV. He noticed over a period of time that people who heard him on radio invariably reacted strongly, either in agreement or disagreement. People who saw him say the same things on television, however, did not react to what he said. They commented, instead, on how he "handled himself," his poise and demeanor. People "hear" less well when they watch television.

Evidence exists for believing the human visual processing system is much older in evolutionary time, having been wired-in to the brain before the ability to process language evolved.

". . . the primates have a diminished sense of smell but need a highly developed eyesight to survive in their arboreal environment, where they must be able to climb, swing and jump. Humans, descended from the primate, have a similarly well-developed visual cortex."[12]

With respect to language, on the other hand, the chimpanzee has shown the capacity to construct simple sentences by manipulating signs and symbols to express thoughts, but has biological limitations for spoken language. It does not have suitable vocal cords "nor, it seems, is its auditory system capable of analyzing complex sounds."[13] In the beginning was vision, then came the word.

Hard evidence for believing this comes from controlled experiments conducted by two British psychologists who published their findings in *Nature*, under the intriguing title of "Hearing lips and seeing voices." It reports the results of tests with a film showing a speaker pronouncing English syllables with lip movements that did not agree with the sounds appearing to emanate from them.

> . . . on being shown a film of a young woman's talking head, in which repeated utterances of the syllable [ba] had been dubbed on to lip movements for [ga], normal adults reported hearing [da]. With the reverse dubbing process, a majority reported hearing [bagba] or [gaba]. When these subjects listened to the sound track from the film, without visual input, or when they watched untreated film, they reported the syllables accurately as repetitions of [ba] or [ga]. Subsequent replications confirm the reliability of these findings . . .[14]

In other words, when there was a discrepancy between observed lip movements and what was heard, the brain changed what was heard to more nearly conform to what was seen. This occurred for the majority of a wide age-span of experimental subjects, from preschool children to adults. The psychologists referred to "the powerful nature of the illusions": "We ourselves have experienced these effects on many hundreds of trials; they do not habituate over time, despite objective knowledge of the illusion involved. By merely closing the eyes, a previously heard [da] becomes [ba] only to revert to [da] when the eyes are open again."[15] The brain, knowing the sound it should perceive, cannot correct its perception to conform to actuality. "Seeing is believing" is wired-in to it.

The results of the above pure research are consistent with the findings of the applied research done on TV commercials by Ted Bates, my former advertising agency. It coined the term "vampire video" to describe visuals that suck away the message spoken in the soundtrack.[16]

Television is not an educative medium; rather, it is a regressive one. Its pictorial aspects are primitive in that they convey little information compared to language, yet they dominate to the point of muffling language spoken on camera or off camera. Hyped-up with frequent visual changes, it keeps the brain reacting at a low, primitive level.

Television's inherent regressiveness would have been recognized by schools and departments of education, if educationists had had even the merest beginnings of a body of pedagogical knowledge. Instead of embracing television with open arms, educationists could have taken steps to make sure that teachers and school administrators adjusted curricula and teaching methods to offset its regressive effects. Advanced warnings were plentiful and eloquent. The following appeared in 1935, more than a decade before the first television sets went on sale to the public:

> Television is a new, hard test of our wisdom. If we succeed in mastering the new medium it will enrich us. But it can also put our mind to sleep. We must not forget that in the past the inability to transport immediate experience and to convey it to others made the use of language necessary and this compelled the human mind to develop concepts. For in order to describe things one must draw the general from the specific; one must select, compare, think. When communication can be achieved by pointing with the finger, however, the mouth grows silent, the writing hand stops, and the mind shrinks.[17]

6

"Illiterates with Doctorates"

"Illiterates with Doctorates" is the title of an article published by Peter H. Wagschal, associate professor of education at the University of Massachusetts. It is a prediction of things to come in the not too distant future when: "America can be a society in which knowledge, ability, and wisdom are exceedingly widespread in a population that is substantially illiterate."

Among the illiterates will be those with doctorates, hence Wagschal's title. So confirmed was he in his prophecy that he illustrated it by referring to his own son: "We are witnessing the demise of the written word as our primary means of storing and communicating information. By the time my four-year-old son reaches adulthood [twenty-one in 1995], there will be hardly any compelling reason for him to be able to read, write, and do arithmetic."[1]

Wagschal acknowledged that the public was clamoring for a return to basic education and a far greater emphasis on the 3Rs. He, nevertheless, recommends "placing *less* emphasis on those skills." (Wagschal's italics)

I first came across the article in the main corridor of the school, displayed in the showcase just outside the offices of Dean Mario Fantini and his associate deans. It was from the August 1978 issue of *The Futurist*, a publication of the World Futures Society in Washington, D.C. The article was illustrated by a drawing of a doctoral diploma made to look like the work of a dyslexic. The recipient's first name is misspelled and the initial letter of the last name is reversed. The effect of the diploma was of belittlement.

A few months later, John Simon in his monthly column in *Esquire* magazine wrote a scathing denunciation of the Wagschal article, which had been sent to him by one of his readers. Simon began: "Hardly do I get through telling you about the dangerous shenanigans of one influential academic when my mail is bulging with matching horror stories."[2] He treated "Illiterates with Doctorates" as a horror story.

When I next came across the article, it was in the February 1980 issue of the school's *Alumni Newsletter*. Although I had given up on the school by now, the blatancy of publishing it after John Simon's public criticism shocked me anew. It was one thing for *The Futurist* to publish "Illiterates with Doctorates," and quite another for the school. By reprinting the article the school placed its imprimatur on it. I could imagine the thousands of alumni who were schoolteachers, assistant principals, principals, curriculum coordinators, media specialists, guidance counselors, superintendents of schools, professors of education, and administrators in state and federal education agencies whose eyes would be caught by "Illiterates with Doctorates: The Future of Education in an Electronic Age." To use the behavioristic psychology term, they would be "reinforced" in their miseducations.

The publication of Wagschal's article by the school was consistent with its other policies—disregarding GRE scores in admitting students to master's and doctoral programs, even when, as in Mary's case, they were in the lowest percentiles; and accepting as education majors, undergraduates with "cums" of only 2.50. Publishing Wagschal's prediction of the demise of the 3Rs in the *Alumni Newsletter* was just one more piece of evidence of the school's attitude, and I made it my business to get extra copies.

This undermining of the basics that are necessary for learning academic subjects was made, moreover, in a black context. Announced in the same issue was the establishment of the Horace Mann Bond Center for Equal Education. It's "primary emphasis," said the announcement, was to be "on the black child." On the front cover, too, was the face of Julian Bond,

State Senator of Georgia. But any black person's face on a publication of the school of education also served as a cover of another sort, a shield against criticism.

I sent copies of the *Alumni Newsletter* to six professors in the English, history, and math departments, with notes calling their attentions to the Wagschal article. I wanted them to know how extreme the school was in undermining what their departments taught and stood for. More than that, I hoped for some movement toward getting the university administration to clamp down on the school's indefensible policies and practices.

I was alert, too, for any reaction to "Illiterates with Doctorates" from any of the school's ninety or so fulltime faculty. Among them were half a dozen individuals whom I liked and, to some degree, respected. I was certain that none of them agreed with it. Two of them constituted the reading program. They should be opposed to it for reasons of self-respect, as well as self-interest. I knew better than to be direct and openly ask any faculty member for his or her reaction. I realized by now that any fundamental talk about education was taboo. I was alert to another instance of what was to me, still, an unbelievable, eerie silence in the face of nonsense.

Were a reporter or researcher to interview each faculty member privately, he or she might find that the majority of the faculty disagreed with Wagschal's assertions. But to learn that, he or she would have to read minds. A guarantee of anonymity, except for those who agreed with Wagschal, would loosen not one tongue. No faculty member would answer a reporter's or researcher's single question out of fear of further questions. Were anyone to admit to disagreeing with Wagschal, he or she would invite follow-up questions such as: "Since you disagree with Wagschal's notions, why do you not speak out against them?" "Are you not tenured?" "Does not tenure guarantee academic freedom?" "Why are you afraid to use your intelligence?"

To be faced with answering such questions would be too threatening to the person questioned. Facing up to one piece of nonsense might lead to facing up to all of the nonsense. Carried to the logical extreme, it could mean the field's disappearance; tantamount to throwing away the only job for which he or she has credentials. Moreover, it was a well-paying job, virtually guaranteed for a working lifetime, and with a handsome pension to follow. The motive for keeping silent was the same for each and every faculty member. In the age of Esalen, Arica, Scientology, Primal Scream, and "Take your finger off the repress button," each faculty member had his or her finger pressed down hard on the button marked "repress intelligence."

My colleagues, it seemed to me, belonged in one of three groups: those who were simply stupid and undereducated; those who were bright but accommodating; and those who cynically used the nonsense for personal advancement. That some of the faculty had intelligence to repress or use cynically is beyond a doubt. The graduate degrees of the majority of the faculty were considered among the nation's best. Harvard's School of Education, all by itself, had provided the faculty with 21 graduate degrees, 12 of them Ed.D. degrees, including Dean Mario Fantini's; Stanford was next with 11 graduate degrees, 7 of them doctorates; Chicago 8 graduate degrees, 5 of them doctorates; and Boston 8 graduate degrees, 4 of them doctorates. Universities that had provided 3 doctorates apiece were California at Berkeley; Illinois; and Michigan State. Those providing 2 doctorates apiece were Teachers College, Columbia; Cornell; Florida; New York University; Ohio State; Wayne State; Wisconsin; and Toronto.

Before coming to the school I had been told that Dwight Allen was bringing in faculty from outside of education, and this proved to be correct. Besides Rutstein and me, a dozen or so had Ph.D.s in respected disciplines. They included economic history, English, history, law, linguistics, physics, and statistical analysis. A few of the faculty were also graduates of prestigious liberal arts colleges. Harvard College had contributed B.A. degrees to 3 of them, one being Peter Wagschal; Amherst College 3; Williams 2; and one apiece from Cornell, Dartmouth, Duke, Smith, and Radcliffe. I took pleasure in being the only graduate of Columbia College, and I was not staying.

To a man and to a woman, as I expected, the faculty kept silent about Wagschal's "Illiterates with Doctorates." It was an Orwellian silence, imposed not from above by "Big Brother" but from within by each individual. And it was no less a conspiracy for having been arrived at individually than collectively. The motive for each individual was the same no matter which of the fifty-seven colleges and universities he or she had received degrees, whether in education or a discipline, and whether possessing bachelor degrees in education or liberal arts. Harvard or Georgia Teachers College, Yale or Arkansas State, California or Emporia State Teachers College, it was all the same. Such silence in the face of nonsense, however, was hardly of recent origin or unique. Views as extreme as Wagschal's had been published by educationists for generations. The following is from a paper published in the *Bulletin* of the National Association of Secondary-School Principals in 1951:

> We've built a sort of halo around reading, writing and arithmetic. We've said they were for everybody . . . rich and poor, brilliant and not-so-mentally endowed, ones who liked them and those who failed to go for them. Teacher has said that these were something "everybody should learn." The principal has remarked, "All educated people know how to write, spell and read." When some child declared a dislike for a sacred subject, he was warned that, if he failed to master it, he would grow up to be a so-and-so.
>
> The Three R's for All Children, and All Children for the Three R's! That was it.[3]

That was the slogan when Yiddish-speaking Abraham Lass entered school in 1913 to be taught by "Miss McDonalds." It was equal *opportunity* for all. The paper goes on:

> We've made some progress in getting rid of that slogan. But every now and then some mother with a Phi Beta Kappa award or some employer who has hired a girl who can't spell stirs up a fuss about the schools . . . and ground is lost. . . .
>
> If and when we are able to convince a few folks that mastery of reading, writing and arithmetic is not the one road leading to happy, successful living, the next step is to cut down the amount of time and attention devoted to these areas in general junior and high-school courses.[4]

This view was anathema to many parents and teachers in 1951 and came under heavy criticism. The criticism slowed implementation for a time but educationists eventually had their way. Continuing right into the 1980s, much of the curriculum in junior and senior high schools was watered down everywhere, from large city school systems like San Francisco to regional systems like Amherst. Students got "weeds and wild flowers" instead of botany; general science instead of chemistry and physics; general math instead of algebra and trigonometry; social issues instead of history; film study and group dynamics instead of English. Some schools even worked to undermine parental authority with units such as "What can I do with my old-fashioned parents?"

The point to be made, however, is the similarity between the passage quoted above from the National Association of Secondary-School Principals *Bulletin* in 1951 and Wagschal's "Illiterates with Doctorates" published in 1978. Both disparage the 3Rs and consequently all other subject matter, a disparagement that runs through all educationists' literature regardless of the current educationist fad. Although essentially the same, both give different reasons, reflecting different circumstances in 1951 and 1978.

1951 Reasons for Deemphasizing the 3Rs

Life Adjustment was the educationist fad in 1951, closely related to the prior fad of progressive education. It had started in the U.S. Office of Education in 1947 when it appointed a commission in Life Adjustment Education for Youths. Mortimer Smith, a critic writing in 1953, commented:

> In one respect the statement of the Commission is a milestone in the history of American education for it implies baldly that the majority of American high school students are incapable either of being prepared for college or trained for vocations. The original resolution which suggested a life adjustment program states that twenty per cent of the high school population can be prepared for college and another twenty per cent trained vocationally but for the remaining sixty per cent administrators must devise a new program. "College preparation or training for skilled occupations is neither feasible nor appropriate" for this group, says the Commission.[5]

In 1951, it was not the custom of the Office of Education, education commissions, and other educationists to make mention of black students. Presumably, they would be lumped in with the 60 percent to receive a watered-down education designed to "adjust" them better to the places they were destined to occupy. Blacks would be among those to get less instruction in the 3Rs and the subject matter based on them.

1978 Reasons for Deemphasizing the 3Rs

The first of Wagschal's several reasons is this one: "Increasingly sophisticated audio, video, and computer technologies will soon replace the three R's as the basic tools of communication. Hence, the citizen of the future may be knowledgeable and effective— but largely illiterate".[6]

Except for the inclusion of computers, this is the same claim that the educational technologists made soon after World War II and still prevails among educationists. Wagschal is just as wrong about computers. One group considered by the university's computer science department to be excellent candidates for graduate study are English majors with a GRE score in verbal of 650 or better—English being no less a coded information system than computer languages. Would illiterates be able to make any score on GRE tests given orally? How would they remember the questions and multiple choice answers? How would they remember math problems, let alone be able to solve them in their heads? Wagschal's first reason is idiotic and so is his next, based on talking computers: "The present generation of computers can store more information in less space and communicate more quickly and reliably than any form of printed matter. And the next generations of computers will be still faster, lighter, cheaper . . . call up information instantly in response to the spoken word."[7]

John Simon's comment on this was: "In Wagschal's computerized dystopia even the spoken word may be in serious trouble . . ."[8] It would be in trouble. How would an illiterate understand the computer speaking with written language's attributes of precision and completeness which, of necessity, it would have to speak to convey information of any complexity?

Wagschal went on to belittle books: ". . . books can offer only words and still photographs, which together convey only a paltry fraction of what human beings have to communicate to one another. How much more would we know Freud's thought and work if we had videotapes of his therapy sessions instead of only his books"?[9]

John Simon commented:

Since Freud's sessions, alas, have not been taped, are we going to make tapes in which an actor or a computer impersonates Freud? And assuming even that a later generation of computers can, if not resurrect, at least enact Sigmund Freud in mid-therapy, what good would watching this do the future ignoramus—say, young Wagschal Jr.—playing with his mini- or microcomputer? Someone has to interpret for him what is happening, and that is just what books have been doing all along.[10]

Probably the major reason for Wagschal's article and the chief reason the school reprinted it in its *Alumni Newsletter* is this:

The three R's are, by their very nature, tools of the affluent and elite. They are time-consuming modes of communication and inherently difficult to learn. The illiteracy of the majority of the globe's population has never been a reflection of species-wide stupidity, but rather of the limited and limiting nature of print as a medium. Only a minority of the globe's population can afford the time and resources required to learn and use the three R's.[11]

Wagschal and the school are on the side of Third World peoples and against the affluent and the elite. Wagschal practically congratulated the Third World on its acumen in not succumbing to literacy. It was not worth the effort because soon, Wagschal predicted, "electronic media will make everything there is to know universally accessible to all of the globe."[12]

The world map of hunger as well as illiteracy overlap and cover major portions of Third World countries, and the two are not unrelated. Eight hundred million Third World people, soon to approach one billion, live at subsistence levels of food consumption. As this population expands, prodigious efforts are necessary for them just to remain at subsistence levels. Nations once called emerging and developing are now recognizably failing to do so even with the help of Western science and technology, Western loans and aid, and literacy programs that have largely failed. What is not recognized generally is that their cultures have inherent barriers within them to borrowing and using new ideas from other cultures.

Wagschal's—and the school's—gross misrepresentation of the Third World shows a powerful intent at work. The gross misrepresentation was in keeping with a self-serving purpose typical of the way in which educationists have come to use blacks and other minorities.

Since the early 1950s educationists and the public schools that implement their notions have felt increasingly threatened as criticism grew and public confidence eroded. In 1952 there had been Arthur E. Bestor's *Educational Wasteland*; in 1954, *The Diminished Mind: A Study of Planned Mediocrity in Our Public Schools* by Mortimer Smith; in 1963, *The Miseducation of American Teachers* by James D. Koerner; and in 1970, Charles E. Silberman's *Crisis in the Classroom.*

Educationists still had enough credibility in the early 1950s to shrug off criticism as they hid behind their Big E—Education. It and they were up on a pedestal out of reach. They could successfully fend off criticism as "attacks on our schools." While ceasing to use terms that offended such as life adjustment, they clandestinely carried on with their own purposes. They counterattacked with name-calling. One Harvard professor of education said that laymen who criticized the schools were "among the emotionally least stable members of the community. They are likely to be the ones who have had family difficulties of their own, who have had trouble rearing their own children."[13] Another Harvard education professor said that critical parents "are practically always honest and sincere but nearly always have no factual basis."[14] A critic of the schools was either emotionally imbalanced or a sincere ignoramus.

But handling criticism by name-calling this way was not adequate to ward off mounting criticisms in the 1960s, including numerous accusations of bigotry. Unable to reform themselves, educationists needed something to add to their Big E—education on a pedestal—behind which to hide. They found it in blacks and other minorities. They could fend off criticisms by accusing critics of being guilty of racism.

Wagschal's "Illiterates with Doctorates" represents a degeneration from the 1951 attitude toward the 3Rs quoted on page 71. That attitude could be called elitist, to use the favorite term of today's educationists, in that it recognized the importance of the 3Rs but *only for those bound for college or skilled occupations*. For the other 60 percent of students, most blacks presumably among them, the 3Rs were considered unimportant. By the 1970s, educationists downgraded the 3Rs to being unimportant for 100 percent of students. This made blacks, despite their persistently lower scores on all kinds of standardized tests, equal to whites. Many black organizations claim that standardized tests are unfair and should be eliminated because they are culturally biased, and besides, test nothing important. The National Education Association (NEA), with its membership of 1.7 million teachers, adopted the same position. The NEA came out for the elimination of standardized tests. Referring to SAT tests in 1977, the president of the NEA, John Ryor, said: "Tests of this kind don't serve students, parents, or teachers. They do not measure what is being taught and what is happening to our students. They ought to be dispensed with, once and for all."[15]

This NEA view is in perfect keeping with the views of the Association of Black Psychologists. One of its members who was also the dean of the school of education at San Francisco State University stated: "The history of their use is bad. If only S.A.T's are used for admissions, you miss all kinds of talented black students, because the questions asked do not give them the opportunity to reveal their potential. The problem with standardization is the standardization of non-standard things: they assume a model culture."[16]

The NEA positioned itself alongside blacks, at least those who were outspoken against trying to measure literacy and numeracy. Anyone who criticized schools and teachers could be called elitist at best and racist at worst, although the first often serves educationists as a code word for the second.

Educationists made blacks and other minorities their stalking horses, hiding behind them, using them as camouflage for self-protection. Part of their method was to make their easy degrees readily available to blacks, hire more of them than most academic departments combined, and almost immediately put them in visible administrative positions. In giving blacks a significant stake they protected their own stakes.

The reprinting of "Illiterates with Doctorates" in an official publication of the school is an arrogant expression of the oneness of white and black educationists intent on job security and expanded budgets, while delivering no pedagogic knowledge and undermining all academic knowledge.

7

The Damage
to Reading Instruction

Decades of outright attacks on the 3Rs by educationists have affected and continue to affect *all* public school teachers, including many who know better. Most affected are the teachers in the nation's 62,000 public elementary schools. They were the education majors. Little difference did it make that not *all* of their education professors shared the views of the attackers of literacy and numeracy. But those professors kept silent. By keeping silent they contributed to the diminished importance of the 3Rs.

Most education majors had little reason to resist the diminution. They had reason to welcome it. They were generally drawn from the dregs of the college population, the least literate and numerate, and their education professors did little or nothing to correct their academic deficiencies. What education majors valued was getting teacher certification.

Depending on the state, required certification courses range from the specific to the general. Some are specified by course titles; others only by general intent. Often the intent is stated as promoting "the needs of students," referring to the children and youths in public schools. So open to interpretation is "needs" as to mean almost anything and hence nothing. A field without a body of pedagogical knowledge cannot, of course, be specific about substance and the degree of it. No attempt, for instance, is made to specify the degree of literacy a prospective teacher should attain in order to be certified. Standards are up to the schools of education. A required course taught by one professor when taught by another can be very different. Education schools can, nevertheless, say that a course fulfills a state requirement. Departments of certification, usually located in the state capital, have no firm standards other than number of credits.

In the case of the twenty-two new teacher preparation programs that I promoted in the campus newspaper during my first year in the school, some had no semester-length courses whatsoever. For these innovative programs, the school negotiated with the state education department in Boston to accept them as equivalent to required courses for certification. State requirements can mean just about anything that schools of education say they mean.

Many of the professors who teach them are little better prepared academically than their students. The better educated professors, like my colleagues from prestigious liberal arts colleges with Ph.D.s in academic disciplines, accommodate themselves to the lesser educated faculty and gear their teaching to the ill-prepared students enrolled in their courses. They also acquiesce to a low priority for reading instruction.

When I joined the school, of the approximately three hundred courses being offered in it, only two or three were in reading instruction. A year or so later, the school hired a reading specialist, and in subsequent years another. Nevertheless, a reading course was not required of all education majors. Neither did the school make the ability to speak, read, and write well a requirement for graduation. Few schools of education do.

Reading Instruction in the Local Elementary School

Were we to look at elementary schools that produce the poorest readers, observations would presumably be complicated by considerations of low income and cultural differences. We will eliminate such presumptions by looking at middle- to upper-middle-class schools where reading ability is comparatively high.

Parents whose children attend reputedly good schools believe that the instruction in them is superior. Parents believed it in the Whittier School District of Teaneck, New Jersey, when my daughters attended it. They make the same mistake as parents in similar districts all over the nation. They credit the school with what they should chiefly credit to themselves.

Whittier parents lived exclusively in single family homes. A high percent could afford a cleaning woman once or twice a week; a few, fulltime help. The heads of families were owners of companies, executives, or professionals. Their high average income correlated with their children's high average achievement, as in similar school districts everywhere.

As our system of education exists, it is the parents who make the chief difference, not the teachers, the principal, and the rest of the education apparatus. Were all parents and local circumstances everywhere the same, the sameness of the nation's sixty-two thousand elementary schools would be apparent, reflecting the sameness of schools of education.

The elementary school's prime function should be to turn children into fluent readers and fluent users of arithmetic, giving them the foundation necessary for all future academic learning. In affluent school districts like Whittier, some of the criticial aspects of this function are performed in the home. Many of the children enter school knowing how to read or on the verge of it, and without having been taught "reading skills."

The frequency with which this happens is greatly underestimated by the education establishment. Each of my three daughters began school without their teachers' recognizing that they could already read all of the first reading materials presented to them. The ability of children to learn on their own is, in general, grossly underestimated. They are born knowing how to learn and are proficient at it. Were this not so, children would not learn their native language, which they all do without exception, even the severely mentally retarded. As Frank Smith, one of the world's authorities on the cognitive aspects of language, puts it: "Spoken language is literally self-taught, to a degree far beyond the appreciation of most parents and many specialists in child development. Not even the most accomplished linguists know enough about language to teach a child how to talk, let alone the average parent.[1]

Linguists, nevertheless, know that in teaching themselves to talk, children learn the rules of their native language from the speech they hear. Chinese children learn the rules of Chinese speech, American children learn the rules of English from

American speech, Norwegian children learn from Norwegian, and so forth. Using the rules, children generate sentences that are partly predictable and partly unpredictable. The rules permit children—and adults—to generate an infinite number of sentences from a limited number of words. The sentences are original with them, not copies of someone else's sentences.

An example is in order. While showing my eldest daughter, who was somewhat more than two at the time, a full moon in a wintry sky, a dense black cloud passed in front of the moon and obliterated it, whereupon she said: "The moon has gone home to her mother." It was not a sentence any adult would say. My daughter could not have heard it from anyone else. It was not a copy but an original. She alone generated it. At an age when children make no distinction between animate and inanimate objects, all things had homes and mothers as she had. She generated a sentence that was partly predictable in that it obeyed the rules of English grammar and partly unpredictable in that it conveyed her own meaning.

What is mysterious about young children learning the rules of language, and therefore perhaps difficult to accept, is that the rules remain unconscious. Adults, too, are unaware of the grammatical rules they use in speaking and writing. As Jeremy Campbell, an authority on information science, says in *Grammatical Man*:

> A speaker's knowledge of the rules of grammar is not conscious, and this means it is extremely difficult to make rules explicit in a theory of language. Large aspects of English grammar, in the full sense of the term, are still *terra incognita* for the linguist. The reason why it is so hard to describe this unconscious system of rules is that they are not logical, but psychological. They are peculiar to the human mind.[2]

At a time when we tend to be in awe of computers and robots, we must remember that the human mind created them. It is our brains that we should hold in awe, and especially those of young children. Medical science has reason to believe that the human brain's capacity to learn is optimum at the age of six. At this age, "the young child has a more complex set of connections among the nerve cells of the cerebral cortex than it will ever have in later life."[3]

Learning to read may be considered less natural than learning to speak. All groups of peoples everywhere in the world have a spoken language, and information science regards language as the primary information system found in nature. Only a minority of the world's peoples, however, invented written forms for their languages. Nevertheless, nearly all children can learn to read as readily as they learn to talk. Most fail to learn as readily because they lack reasons for making the effort.

Personal Reasons for Learning to Read

Every child, regardless of the culture, has personal reasons for wanting to learn how to talk. From the first days of infancy, a child hears the speech of parents, siblings, relatives, visitors, and those on radio and television. The child sees that language makes things happen between people, that it has meaning. Being human, the child needs to find out the meaning, make sense of it, learn its rules, and become a talker like everybody else. Because the reasons are intensely personal, they are enormously powerful.

The environment of print, however, is not comparable. Even in highly literate homes reading is less frequent than speaking. Seeing a parent or sibling silently reading, the child may notice the staring at pages and turning them but sees no consequence, although his or her curiosity may be piqued. In homes with few books, magazines, or newspapers, where reading is infrequent, such curiosity is hardly possible. It is true that print is everywhere around us in the form of labels: on cans and packages of foods and drinks, store and street signs, titles on TV programs, captions in commercials, and words and phrases on Sesame Street. The vast exposure to print as labels is apparently insufficient by itself, however, to kindle a desire to learn to read. Labels are read silently in a glance by adults hardly detectable by a young child. He or she has no way of knowing that reading is taking place and has consequences, as in deciding which avenue to drive down or how fast to drive in a speed zone. Children who are insufficiently exposed to meaningful print must rely on their local schools for acquiring the necessary personal motives, insights, and reading opportunities.

Preschoolers who are richly exposed to printed language that means something to them, on the other hand, gain the personal reasons they need in order to want to learn to read. Frank Smith, the author of *Understanding Reading*, states that for children to make the effort they must have two fundamental insights. One is that *print is meaningful* and the other that *written language is different from speech*. The second insight, he says, can be acquired only in one way: "by hearing written language read aloud."[4]

Reading became part of the bedtime ritual for our three daughters from the time that each of them was about two and a half. Freshly bathed and pajamaed, snuggled in their beds, they listened to the traditional fairy tales and poems. My wife and I always read to each individually from her own books. Often the children chose the stories and poems they knew well and wanted to hear again, perhaps for the fiftieth time. One result was that each of them started kindergarten at the Whittier school reading at approximately the first-grade level, and not because we planned it that way. Our youngest credits her sister, thirty-one months older, with teaching her. With only a little help from us and sisters, each taught herself to read. Each connected the fascinating stories and poems they heard to the print in their books, which was different from anything heard in everyday speech, on television, or anywhere else. At an early age they learned to appreciate literary quality without knowing the term.

Many children in affluent school districts like Whittier acquire the necessary insights about written language at home, as our children did, before entering school. They teach themselves to read with only a little help, although that little help is critical. Cases have been documented, too, of children from educationally impoverished homes who have similarly taught themselves to read.[5]

Two eminent authorities on reading from two different schools of psychology—Frank Smith from the cognitive and Bruno Bettelheim from the psychoanalytical—are in agreement that children do, indeed, teach themselves to read, and they agree on the circumstances necessary for this learning to occur. Children must have the insight that written language is meaningful, which requires that the materials from which they learn to read be meaningful.

When many children easily learn to read on their own at home, with only a little help from parents and siblings, why do millions of other children fail to learn to read well in school? Are the nation's sixty-two thousand elementary schools making it difficult for children to use their innate ability to learn? Are they failing to provide them with the necessary insights, meaningful reading materials, and opportunities to learn?

All sixty-two thousand schools rely heavily on instructional reading programs that they purchase from one or more schoolbook publishers. Some twenty-two states, including Texas and California, have schoolbook selection committees. Only those programs approved by the state are used in its public schools. In other states, the selection of reading programs is left to each school district. Within each reading program selected is a series of primers and readers, each one "graded" in difficulty—the word "graded" in quotes because the grading is based on dubious assumptions.

Both Frank Smith and Bruno Bettelheim find that the books specially tailored for children in widely used reading programs are not meaningful to children. Unlike the storybooks read to them at home, they make little sense and are an obstacle to learning to read as fluently as children can. Bettelheim puts it this way:

> Children who acquire a great interest in reading in their homes have an easy time in school, and they form the overwhelming majority of those who later become the good readers. The educational establishment points to them as demonstrating that the methods used to teach reading in school are successful. But it is not these methods that turned them into good readers and eventually literate persons. . . . Were it not so, why should the children of more highly educated parents have such an advantage in educational achievement over the children of less well educated parents who are of equal intelligence? Why would so many children who come from culturally disadvantaged homes not become literate persons, although they have acquired the necessary skills for reading in school? One major difference between the children who teach themselves to read at home and those who learn it only in school is that the first group learn to read from texts that fascinate them, while the second learn to read by being drilled in skills of decoding and word recognition

from texts devoid of meaningful content that are demeaning
to the child's intelligence.[6]

This is one of the conclusions reached by Bettelheim and his
coauthor Karen Zelan in *On Learning to Read*. Their book is
based on a four-year study conducted in eight elementary schools
located in three cities in California and two in Massachusetts.

The study was done in classrooms. From my own experience
and others, I know that such a study is difficult to arrange.
Classroom teachers are apt to feel uneasy and insecure if
observed by outsiders. The authors apparently ran into such
difficulty because they say: "Observation was continued only in
those classes where teachers responded positively to the project."
Bettelheim and Zelan conducted observations mainly in schools
that were considered "the best in their respective systems,
according to school administrators and knowledgeable members
of their communities . . . and, further, only in what each school
considered its best classrooms, taught by its best teachers."
Three of the school systems were in towns dominated by a
leading university, and were accustomed to educational research
being conducted in them. Only one is identified, Berkeley, and
the authors say that quite a few of the children observed were
those of university faculty members. The authors point out that
"the best teachers are also those who are interested in educational
problems," and tend to be the most cooperative.[7]

The classes were far from typical. Many of the students were
probably much like those in the Whittier school my children
attended, and those in Amherst schools where university and
college faculty children are enrolled. The aim of the authors,
nevertheless, was to answer the vexing question: "Why do so
many children fail to learn to read as well as they could?" Using
their psychoanalytical orientation, they tried to "concentrate on
the child's concerns rather than those of the teacher and the
educational system." They studied "children's responses to being
taught reading." Any shortcomings discovered would be much
greater, of course, in classes chiefly of children from educationally impoverished homes.

The chief and most serious shortcoming that Bettelheim and
Zelan found was the meaninglessness of the primers and readers
used, as evidenced by the children's reactions to them—bore-

dom, inattention, shame, resentment, or anger, depending on the child. These were not reactions that children expressed to their teachers. Children were afraid to criticize what they were reading for fear of appearing to criticize the teacher, or the school in general. Bettelheim and Zelan point out: "One must take into account the great insecurity of the beginning reader in intellectual matters. If he cannot keep himself interested in an assigned text, he tends to think that there is something wrong with him: *it takes considerable self-confidence to conclude that the shortcoming resides in the reading matter.*" [Italics added][8]

What bothered children greatly was the vacuity of the texts they were required to read. Containing a tiny vocabulary that was endlessly repeated, their emotional reactions to the texts often led them into what teachers considered errors in reading when in actuality they were well acquainted with the words they misread. Because the children could see that Bettelheim and Zelan were not so interested in their reading errors as in their motives for making the errors, they revealed feelings to them that they would never express to teachers.

One first grader, on reading "sticks" for "chicks" as he had previously done several times, corrected himself without help and angrily blurted out: "Fill in the blanks, that's all I get! Witch, witch, witch . . . ditch, ditch, ditch . . . stick, stick, stick . . . chick, chick, chick!" He then refused to read any more that day.

This same boy, another time, was urged to read a story considered advanced for his age. He read the beginning of it with interest, confidently and flawlessly. But he suddenly substituted "defective" for "detective" in the reading of: "He's in the barn. This is it! Hand me the detective kit." Earlier, the boy had read "detective" correctly. That was before it became apparent that the "detective kit" served no real purpose in the story. By substituting "defective" he was commenting on and venting his displeasure at its meaninglessness.

> A few days later, once more this boy's workbook required him to read a list of words out of context which, when read one after the other, made no sense. He then read "dump" for "jump." Responding to the feelings this misreading expressed, we asked "Who wants to dump this?" referring to the workbook. The boy immediately reread "jump" correctly. He

nodded a pleased assent to our remark that it seemed he wanted to dump the workbook. And when we asked him why he wanted to dump it, his unhesitating reply was " 'Cause it's garbage."[9]

This first grader was confident in his ability to read well. He had to be in order to refuse to read any more in the first instance, call a story "defective" in the second instance and his workbook "garbage" in the third. He was being required to do things that were beneath his ability and he resented and resisted it.

My eldest daughter resisted similar nonsense in quite another way. On seeing her with a *Dick and Jane* reader, I asked her:

"Karen, doesn't your teacher know that you are reading much more advanced books than *that* on your own at home?"

"No," she answered.

"Why not?"

"Because I can't answer the questions at the back," she replied.

Having looked through the book and seen that it contained nothing but nonsense, I knew Karen had judged it the same way. Nonsense is difficult to remember. It can be memorized but I did not urge Karen to do so, and she marked time in reading until the school no longer required her to read nonsense.

Dick and Jane of the 1960s has been supplanted by the *Janet and Mark* series but which is essentially unchanged. It was in wide use in the late 1970s when Bettelheim and Zelan made their study. This is a sample of it: "Janet and Mark. Come, Mark, come. Come here, Mark. Come here. Come here, Mark, come and jump. Come and jump, jump, jump. Here I come, Janet. Here I come. Jump, jump, jump."

In the 177 lines of the *Janet and Mark* text, "come here" is repeated twenty-four times and the simpler command "come," or statements that someone is obeying their command, appear forty-three times. The girl Janet and the boy Mark are asked to "see" something, at which they are already looking, thirty-nine times. A typical first preprimer like *Janet and Mark* contains only twenty or so different words. No way exists to make so few words say anything meaningful to children whose speaking vocabularies at this time consist of around 4,000 words.[10]

Each further book in a reading program adds only a few

words of vocabulary at a time. Books considered appropriate for first, second, and third grades are so limited in different words that they suffer from the same restrictions and arouse the same reactions in children. Bettelheim and Zelan summed up the spontaneous reactions of first and second graders this way:

> The children were unanimous in not liking any of the stories, said that they read them only because they had to, and that on their own they would never read such "junk." Their reasons were that "It's all impossible!" Asked why, they answered: "Because none of them are real!", referring to the people in the stories. "They aren't shy!", "They aren't afraid!", "They aren't angry!", "They aren't upset!" When one explained "They aren't anything!", they all agreed that this summed it up perfectly and that there was nothing more to be said.[11]

These children gave their frank opinions only after Bettelheim and Zelan had spent many months visiting their classrooms, and after talking about a wide variety of topics. When the children saw that they were genuinely interested in their opinions, and the subject of primers and readers was introduced, out poured their angry criticisms.

These children, it should be remembered, were in the best classrooms with the best teachers. What made them best, of course, were the children themselves. Most were good readers, having taught themselves to read either before or after entering school, and had retained their insights that print is meaningful and different from speech, in spite of the reading programs they were subjected to. Obviously, they had the self-confidence to blame the primers and readers for being "stupid" rather than themselves. But most schoolchildren, particularly those of the poor, do not have such self-confidence. They may learn what teachers regard as reading skills and be able to "decode" print but they do not become fluent readers because the first books they are exposed to are the wrong books. They may acquire a low level of literacy, be functionally literate, but they do not become literate persons. Most do poorly academically, although grade inflation, low standards, and social promotion mask the degree of their low academic performance.

Bettelheim and Zelan found reasons other than anger and resentment for students' errors in reading. Some were due to children's attempts to make the stories make more sense, others to being misled by incongruent pictures, and in a few cases to personal reasons, such as the errors one boy made in reading about a dog because his own dog which he cared for greatly had recently been run over by a car.

Teachers, too, are affected by the extreme vacuity of the readers. Because they have no intrinsic interest, the only way a teacher can keep up his or her interest in the children's reading is in making sure that they read the words exactly as printed.

The findings of Bettelheim and Zelan that widely used reading programs discourage children from becoming readers is in accord with Frank Smith's findings in his *Understanding Reading*. Smith states:

> Children may learn to recite such print, but there is no evidence that it will make them readers. Any insight they might have in advance about the nature of written language is likely to be undermined, and worse, they might become persuaded that the print which they first experience in school is a model for all the written language that they will meet throughout their lives—a conviction that would be as discouraging as it is misleading.[12]

With respect to "misleading," when the cry among blacks and educationists was for "relevancy," there was a movement to use reading materials in ghetto schools depicting black children in situations reflecting their ghetto lives. The intent was to get away from the language and situations of the white middle-class. No one pointed out that the language in primers and early readers was never used by the white middle-class or by anyone else. Such language, says Smith, is strictly "school language."[13]

How Reading Programs Became Meaningless

Reading programs began to change for the worse in two fundamental respects in the 1920s. At the time, the second generation of professors were replacing the first. The first generation, the original members of schools of education when they were established, had been trained as academicians. Members of the second generation had not, and were further removed from the academic disciplines and subject matter.

Publishers of reading programs hired members of the second generation as consultants to write, guide, and approve of their programs. Publishers do not decide what constitutes desirable reading instruction. Professors of education do that. In order to sell reading programs to public school systems, the publishers must make their programs in accord with what the professors are teaching the future teachers and school administrators, and what they are recommending to school systems.

Under the guidance of the consulting professors, publishers of reading programs began to reduce the vocabulary of the primers and readers. Decade after decade, they cut down the number of different words in them. One study shows that first readers in the 1920s contained on the average 645 different words; in the 1930s, about 460 words; in the 1940s and 1950s, about 350 words.[14] Another study compared five successive editions of a widely used first-grade reader. From containing a high of 425 different words in 1920, each subsequent edition contained fewer and fewer to reach a low of 153 in 1962. The number of pictures in them, on the other hand, nearly doubled—went from less than one per 100 running words in 1920 to nearly two in 1962.[15] Bettelheim points out that in the 1920s few children went to kindergarten and few preschool children were given reading instruction. In the 1970s when many children attended kindergarten and reading was quite consistently taught there, primers contained only 28 percent of the vocabulary presented to their counterparts of fifty years ago.

The deliberate reduction of vocabulary brings to mind the destruction of English in George Orwell's *1984*. "We're destroying words—scores of them, hundreds of them. . . . Every year fewer and fewer words, and the range of consciousness always a little smaller."[16] Linking the reduction of vocabulary in schoolbooks to the destruction of English in *1984* might be tenuous but for other Orwellian characteristics of educationists. Already noted is the collective silence in the face of nonsense, of which the mute acquiescence of Wagschal's fellow professors to his attacks on the 3Rs is one example. A lingering adherence to the psychology of behaviorism, applying operant conditioning to children, is another.

Behaviorism assumes that children have no inner life, emotional or intellectual. It assumes no personal reasons for wanting to learn, that they must be motivated and "conditioned" by others. It assumes that behavior can be broken down into separate steps and "shaped" into one continuous sequence that produces the desired "behavior," which from time to time needs to be "reinforced." Most primers and readers reflect this behaviorism, assume that the repetition of a few words over and over again, adding new ones occasionally, will eventually produce the habit of reading in the child. Primers and readers became meaningless largely due to professors of education and their assumptions of behavioristic psychology derived from experiments with rats and pigeons. To them, meaning has no importance because meaning is not part of observable behavior.

The reduction of vocabulary by professors of education in reading materials is the first fundamental reason that reading programs changed for the worse. The second is that the education professors began in the 1920s, too, to concentrate on "methods" which has come to be known as "the wasteland of teacher education."[17] In reading instruction, they turned their attention to two different methods. One was the "whole word" or "look-say" method; another was the "phonics" or "decoding" method. Professors advocated one or the other and split into two separate camps. Reflecting them, all reading programs purchased by school systems were, and still are, based on one or the other. Both methods fail, however, to treat reading as one whole. Both break down reading into what is claimed to be "reading skills." This may be logical but it is not *psychological*. It is not the way the human mind works.

The performance of a skill is observable. One can see a boy riding a bicycle, hear a girl reading aloud. But although we recognize the *performance* of the skill, we cannot see the skill itself or put it into words. We can talk around a skill. We can say that bicycling requires balance, muscle coordination, and so forth. But such talk does not produce the skill, nor do sets of separate balancing and muscle coordination exercises.

Like any complex skill, reading is a totality that cannot be divided into subskills. But that is what educationists attempt to do. Both of their methods attempt to teach reading skills, which is very different from teaching reading.

In widest use since the 1920s in the United States is the

"whole word" or "look-say" method. Most currently used reading programs are based on it. Teachers' guides come with these programs and are very specific in holding teachers to the method. For example, a series of instructional pages of a program I examined concentrated a page at a time on a single word. The word is at the top of the page. The teacher could call students' attention to it by saying "Look at the word at the top of the page," or by spelling the word. But the teachers' guide tells the teacher to do something quite different.

Next to each word is a prominent picture which the teachers' guide uses as a pointer. Next to the word "are," for example, is a drawing of a monkey. The teachers' guide directs the teacher to tell the students to look, not at the word, but at the monkey and then to say: "The monkey is looking at a word. It thinks if it looks very carefully at the word it will be able to read it. Let's give the monkey a little help. Monkey, this word is *are.*"

When children learn a sufficient number of words, the method assumes that students will then recognize sentences. Again, this is logical but it is not *psychological.* The human mind seeks meaning and the word "are" by itself means nothing. When young children are learning to talk, they never hear "are" by itself. Children who teach themselves to read at home never see "are" isolated from other words.

Lower down on the instructional page is a picture of a boy removing cupcakes from a baking pan on a table. The drawing occupies ten times the amount of space of the sentence next to it: "The cakes *are* on the table." But as if the large picture is insufficient to clue the meaning of the sentence, above the word "cakes" is a tiny drawing of two cupcakes, and above "table," a tiny drawing of a table. No pictures are above the words "the," "are," and "on," since they have no visual equivalents.

All the widely used reading programs based on the whole word or look-say method rely heavily on pictures. Students can read them instead of the words. Carried to extremes, which teachers' guides tend to do, the method avoids spelling and does not teach the alphabet, which is why the teachers' guide in the above example has the teacher point to words with pictures rather than spelling them.

Many people in the job market in the early 1980s do not know the alphabet. Employment agencies that supply temporary office help to corporations find it necessary to give job applicants a test, one part of which is on the alphabet. The test is an expense that the agencies would rather not incur, but they know from experience that they cannot risk sending applicants to jobs where they might have to do filing. Failing this part of the test, not to mention the arithmetical portion, is a daily occurrence.

The swing in reading methods in the 1980s is away from the whole word to phonics and decoding, probably because of the intense dissatisfaction of the public with schooling in general. It is time to try the other method. But the phonics method, too, attempts to teach reading skills rather than reading. The phonics method assumes that reading is a matter of decoding written language to sound, of translating the letters of words into their supposedly equivalent speech. Phonics assumes that *meaning* cannot be gleaned directly from the printed page, that it first must be decoded, which is utter nonsense. Mute Helen Keller, who became deaf and blind before she learned to talk, learned language without being able to decode it to speech. The Chinese and Japanese have nonalphabetical writing that has no sound correspondences, yet Chinese and Japanese children learn to read. Frank Smith points out:

> The Chinese ideographic system can be read by people from all over China, even though they might speak languages that are mutually unintelligible. If a Cantonese speaker cannot understand what a Mandarin speaker says, they can write their conversation down in the nonalphabetic writing system they both share and be mutually comprehensible.[18]

Written Chinese does not correspond to spoken Chinese in any way but *meaning*. If decoding from the written form to the spoken form were necessary, nobody could learn to read it. Certain aspects of phonics are highly useful for some things but are not necessary or even a help in learning to read English because, like the Chinese, we too learn to read by seeking *meaning*.

Phonics, as practiced in many classrooms, often is the means of destroying *meaning* for students. Bettelheim and Zelan observed children who, after years of phonics instruction, did not attempt to make sense of what they were required to read. Reading aloud had become for them an exercise in looking for little words in big ones, which is what their teachers had told them to do. A third-grader, who was a better reader than his teacher realized, had lost all interest in comprehending what he was reading aloud. He would read "jo" and "in" for "join," and the article "a" separate from "sleep" for "asleep." In laboriously looking for little words in big words, or paying attention to each and every syllable, he lost the thread of meaning which led him into other reading errors. It turned out that he was deliberately carrying the teacher's instructions to extremes as a way of protesting the lack of sense in what was expected of him. It demonstrated reading skills, but not reading.

Although both the phonics and whole-word methods are misconceived, they are the two on which educationists have concentrated and over which they have debated endlessly and fruitlessly. It is a debate that appeals to them. It permits much research, which creates numbers and statistics with their aura of science, and many claims and counterclaims. Little did it matter that their research omitted too much of critical importance to have value. Cognitive psychologists Eleanor J. Gibson and Harry Levin, referring to the multitude of studies conducted between 1920 and 1960, state:

> Regretfully, it seems fair to say that the results of these 40 years of research test out poorly. We are in no better position to say that one method is superior to another. For every study that indicated the efficacy of one method, an equal number of studies reported results in favor of some contrasting method. The results tend to be interpreted with statements like "It all depends on the teacher."[19]

Today's teachers, including many considered the best, fail to recognize the consequences of using meaningless primers and readers and closely following their teachers' guides. In some of the classrooms observed by Bettelheim and Zelan, the teachers admitted that they, too, found the reading materials boring and meaningless. Nevertheless, many of them "firmly asserted" that the content did not matter, a view accurately reflecting their training. These best teachers accepted the reading programs as having been put together and selected for them by experts. They "did not question the teaching of reading by means of content that they themselves considered irrelevant, if not obnoxious. . . ."[20] They assumed that their students would learn reading skills and become literate in higher grades, an assumption contradicted by all the evidence. Students at every level beyond the early grades score lower in standardized tests in verbal ability than their counterparts in previous decades; and the higher the grade, the lower the comparative score.

A large number of today's elementary schoolteachers are not literate persons. They are not readers; do not read for enjoyment or for knowledge of any complexity. They have reading skills, can recognize words and decode print well enough to follow the simple and simplistic directions of teachers' guides, but have little understanding of what they are doing. If they did, they could not adhere slavishly to the directions in teachers' guides. How can teachers who are not literate persons, not good readers themselves, teach children? Only a good reader has the necessary intrinsic understanding.

Intrinsic knowledge—what we know implicitly yet often cannot put into words—is no less knowledge for being unconscious. When my daughters were small I was still in advertising. I had never thought about how children learn to read and had no opinions about it. Yet, as it turned out, my wife and I, as literate parents often do, created nearly ideal circumstances for our daughters to teach themselves to read, and to go on to become the literate adults that they are today. In reading to them nightly and answering their occasional questions about the stories and poems, my wife and I were not making a conscious effort to be good parents. We had been lifelong readers and read to our daughters because we and they enjoyed it.

A literate person who is also a teacher has an *implicit knowledge* of reading. He or she uses that knowledge to some degree in every decision made in the classroom. But if implicit knowledge is insufficient, as it is in the majority of the nation's elementary-school teachers, he or she is unable to help children become fluent readers.

A further elaboration on "implicit knowledge" may be necessary. The pioneering cognitive psychologist George Miller of Princeton reports that he taught himself to juggle from words and pictures in a book. "Now I can juggle," he said. "I know I have learned something, but I don't know what I have learned." Whatever it is, he said, it is not propositional and not in pictures."[21] The knowledge learned is unconscious and implicit.

I have used a typewriter most of my life and probably type faster and more accurately than the average secretary. Yet, I cannot write down or otherwise replicate the typewriter keyboard. I cannot consciously remember the positions of the letters, punctuation marks, etc. But when I type my fingers remember, or rather my brain draws on its knowledge to direct my fingers which keys to touch. At a time when "consciousness raising" is still in vogue, it is well to remember that what the human mind does best it does unconsciously. "The mind goes to work *away from consciousness*, retrieving the necessary information to put together complicated behavior—and nobody has ever seen what the mind is doing then."[22]

Reading, speaking, and writing are complicated acts—far more complicated than either juggling or typing—based on implicit knowledge of language. But there is a great range in how well people read, speak, and write. Obviously, the more literate person draws on a larger store of unconscious knowledge than one who is less literate.

Can an *explicit* knowledge of some of what must happen when we read make up for an insufficient implicit knowledge? A lucid exposition of what reading is about has existed for the enlightenment of teachers since 1971—Frank Smith's *Understanding Reading*, now in its third edition. His excellent book is not a description of reading ability itself, which is not directly knowable. But it presents some of the things that can be reliably inferred to happen when we read. Smith combines the findings of information science with what cognitive psychology has demonstrated, to formulate the clearest understanding we have available. So cogently are the concepts presented and linked that most people who are literate can nod their heads as they read Smith, even if disagreeing with some of his degrees of emphasis.

I first learned of Frank Smith's work from one of my best graduate students, who was taking a course in the school's reading program. Its two faculty members were admirers and users of his *Understanding Reading*. A year or so later, however, when I inquired if it was still in use, the answer was "No, students find it too difficult." Evidence that education majors in other schools of education also found it too difficult came in

1978 with the publication of Smith's *Reading Without Nonsense*. It was essentially the same as *Understanding Reading*, rewritten in simplified form in an attempt to make the same material understandable to education majors. With "nonsense" in the title, by implication polemical, it had more appeal for them. Then, too, everything about the book's appearance made it *look* easier to read. The type was larger and more widely spaced; the number of lines on the page were fewer, notes eliminated, and the bulk of the book far less. This simplified version for teachers in training is, appropriately, published by Teachers College Press.

Frank Smith is first and foremost a writer. Before becoming a professor he was a published novelist, newspaper reporter, and editor. Being a professional writer contributed as much to his books, if not more, than his studies in cognitive psychology under George Miller. He put into his books what he already knew *implicitly* before studying cognitive psychology. He fitted the new explicit knowledge into an already existing, though unconscious, mental structure.

Having used Frank Smith's *Understanding Reading* and his *Comprehension and Learning* in courses, I know what gives present and future school teachers and administrators difficulty. My graduate students understood his words and sentences readily enough up to a point. They had what educationists call the reading skills of word recognition and decoding. What gave them insurmountable difficulty is the connections between paragraphs and chapters. Although the book's ideas were skillfully linked by Smith, what were disparate ideas to my students remained disparate. They could not maintain the connections Smith made between the limitations of short-term memory, what is known about how fast the brain processes information, how the eyes scan lines of type and so forth, let alone the many aspects of language. My students could talk about some of the ideas separately, repeat them, but they could not join them together in anything approaching wholes. It was as if their minds were divided into exceedingly small compartments without doors or windows into other compartments. The exceptions were those who were sufficiently literate. Only they could recognize and maintain the connections. Smith himself states in his introduction to *Comprehension and Learning* that many of the so-called learning problems that teachers presume to see in children are fundamentally "language problems."[23]

The failure of teachers to possess an adequate implicit knowledge of language cuts them off from gaining the explicit knowledge of some important aspects of reading that Smith discusses. They are forced in the classroom to slavishly rely on the methods of reading programs and their materials that Frank Smith says cannot succeed:

> The question of what is the best method for teaching reading has, I think, not been answered because it is not the appropriate question; children do not learn because of reading programs, but because teachers succeed in making their instruction meaningful to children, with or without formal programs. It is the wisdom and intuition of teachers that must be trusted, provided that teachers have the basic understanding necessary for the classroom decisions that only they should make.[24]

But what is lacking in most elementary school teachers is precisely "the basic understanding necessary for the classroom decisions that only they should make." It is also lacking in most school administrators, including those at the very apex of the enormous education pyramid.

8

"The Right to Fail"

The man behind the enormous desk with clusters of papers on it smoked a cigar while he was being interviewed by Joseph Lelyveld of *The New York Times*. Lelyveld would write that the cigar together with "his long sideburns made him look more like a cardsharp in a nineteen thirties Western than a fashionably hirsute executive."[1] The reason for the interview was that he was "one of the most powerful men in American education." He presided over 65,000 teachers, nearly 4,000 principals, superintendents and other administrators in 916 schools in which no less than 1 million students were enrolled. Man and desk were in the northeast corner office on the tenth floor of 110 Livingston Street in Brooklyn, headquarters of the New York City public school system. Lettering on the outer door to his suite of offices announced that he was the Chancellor, the new title for the system's new chief administrator. He was Harvey B. Scribner.

A further reason for the interview was that Scribner made interesting copy. The nine-thousand word article for *The New York Times Magazine* that Lelyveld was writing would cover his first six months in office. From the beginning, his controversial stands made front page news. He had offended the city's power blocs, and raised hopes that New York City had hired an educational leader with the courage to improve the schools despite the obstacles. Editorials had supported and praised

Scribner for being "feisty," "combative," and "courageous." After five and a half months, however, editorial support had abruptly ceased. Editorials became negatively critical and his continuance as chancellor was in doubt.

Lelyveld's article would say that Scribner was in trouble because he was "a victim largely of his own political naiveté."[2] The deeper reason was something else, something unthinkable and unprintable although Lelyveld would come close to saying it. From what Scribner revealed of himself to Lelyveld, it was more than possible to suspect that the head of the nation's largest school system was educationally impoverished—not a literate person.

Legions of school administrators and teachers throughout the nation were poor students when they attended public school. Among those legions was Harvey Scribner. He told Lelyveld that he had graduated from high school the last in his class, had come "the closest you could get to failure and still get through."[3] He told the same thing to other interviewers, including me. "I was a failure in school, a total failure!" This admission was not pried from Scribner. He volunteered it, proud to show how far he had come. "I didn't become an A student," he said, "until I was a doctoral candidate."[4] Along with others, I had assumed that his B.A. and M.A. in education and Ed.D. degree made up for what he had failed to learn in elementary and high school. No assumption was ever more wrong.

Harvey Scribner retained his last-in-the class academic deficiencies from the bottom of his career ladder to the top. He had started to climb in 1935 when he dropped out of Castine Normal School to become the teacher in a one-room schoolhouse in Unity, Maine,[5] not far from his hometown. A duty each morning was to start the fire in the single classroom's potbellied stove. His next job was teacher-principal in a four-room school teaching grades 5 through 8, and driving the school bus. After 8 years as an elementary school teacher he moved up to teaching high school. During these years he attended Farmington State Teachers College part time, where at the age of 32 he got a B.A. degree.[6] State teachers colleges have the lowest standards of all degree granting institutions. It would have been difficult, moreover, for a teachers college to deny a degree to one who had been a schoolteacher for twelve years. In another couple of years, having become a high school principal in the meantime, Scribner became superintendent of schools in Eastport, Maine.

While Eastport's superintendent, he applied for graduate study in education at the University of Maine. He had difficulty getting accepted due to his poor grades. But no college or university department of education wants to offend a superintendent of a school district. Professors of education need cooperating school districts in which their students can do practice teaching and, after graduation, get jobs. Then, too, professors like to be hired by school systems as consultants. They also need enrollments for their graduate courses. Self-interest dictates quid pro quo relations. Even when academic deficiencies are recognized, which they often are not, a key school administrator must be allowed a degree.

Armed with his new M.A. in education, Harvey Scribner left Maine for superintendencies in more affluent school districts in Massachusetts. His first was Wareham, near the Cape Cod Canal; his next, Dedham, a middle-class suburb of Boston. While Dedham's superintendent, he became a doctoral candidate at Boston University. The professor of education who was to be Scribner's dissertation chairman had a grant from the U.S. Office of Education to do research on students teaching one another. The professor needed cooperating school districts in which to conduct the research, and Scribner needed an Ed.D. degree for further moves up the career ladder, another not uncommon quid pro quo situation. As superintendent, Scribner arranged for Dedham schools to be part of the experiment, one of four school districts in which federal money was spent and research data collected. Then, the findings were incorporated in doctoral dissertations, one of them being Scribner's. That is how he came to possess his Ed.D. degree.

Newly entitled to put "doctor" before his name, Scribner soon moved on to become superintendent of schools in Teaneck, New Jersey. There in 1966 he received national recognition for his role in integrating Teaneck's six elementary schools. The National Education Association (NEA) gave Scribner its Pacemaker Award—"pacemaker," like intern and diagnostic, was borrowed from the medical profession. Scribner immediately looked around for a bigger job. This surprised Teaneck's residents, particularly blacks. It never occurred to them that

Scribner would leave, that his committment to integration did not include staying to make sure it worked well. They were nevertheless understanding when they heard he was in line for the superintendency of the city of New Rochelle. Its black population was larger than Teaneck's, segregated schools existed for Scribner to integrate, and the job paid $10,000 more a year. Blacks did not blame him for wanting to capitalize on his reputation and use it to do good elsewhere. When he turned down that job, however, and went instead to Vermont as state commissioner of education for a $2,300 cut in salary, where blacks were less than one-quarter of one percent of the population, they were dismayed.

Much of Scribner's rhetoric consisted of doing things "for kids" and during the fight over integration, for "black kids." When people reminded him that there were few black kids in Vermont, he answered that there were pockets of poverty there and he would have the chance to help "poor kids." Yet his every move had been toward affluence, not poverty. There were sixteen thousand superintendents of schools in the United States and only fifty state commissioners of education. Scribner wanted to be one of the few.

Throughout his adult life Scribner had worked for status and respectability. He had had neither as a child and adolescent. In his small hometown of Albion, Maine, where everybody knew everyone else, he and his family had been lowest in the economic and social scale. His father was a failed farmer, his parents divorced, and he had spent periods of his childhood in foster homes. Scribner had overheard mothers warn their children not to play with "that Scribner boy."[7] His escape from poverty and low social status had been slow. During his first dozen or more years as a teacher, Scribner had supplemented his pay during summers, weekends, and nights working as dimestore floorwalker, grocery clerk, truckdriver, and factory hand.

Through sheer singleminded dogged determination, Scribner had done all of the right things to climb the educationist ladder, attain status, and become respectable. Not only did he get an Ed.D. degree, in Dedham he was also president of its Rotary Club, a member of the board of deacons of his Congregational church, the president of the alumni association of Boston University, and a registered Republican.

When Scribner arrived in Teaneck from Dedham late in 1961 the winds of social change were blowing and the town, though more affluent, was quite different. With twice Dedham's population, a bedroom suburb of New York City, Teaneck's residents were ethnically diverse and more liberal. The change in towns and upsurge in the civil rights movement made standards for status and respectability different from those Scribner had adhered to in Dedham and were more to his liking. He was freer to express the bitterness he still felt for having been looked down upon as a child. The town and the times presented opportunities for becoming the underdog's champion.

Scribner never before had a school district with a sizable Jewish community. It was no underdog in any economic or cultural sense. But anti-Semitism existed in Teaneck and, soon after Scribner's arrival, was marshaled to defeat the school budget for the first time in the town's history. It was called a Jewish budget by those who fought it and their campaign literature referred to Jews as "big spenders."[8]

Within the year, Scribner won the Jewish community's approbation by promulgating new regulations to deemphasize Christmas observances in the schools and practices connected with them. He moved so quickly that one of the three Jewish members of the Board of Education warned him: "What's your hurry? We're not pushing you. You might get into trouble."[9] Scribner also had a few angry words with one or two superintendents in neighboring school districts over the scheduling of interscholastic athletic events on Jewish holidays.

Scribner quickly became the champion of Teaneck's black residents who were also of the middle-class. The enrollment of black students in one of the town's six elementary schools was about 33 percent at the time and growing. In another couple of years it might go over 50 percent, which was a concern to several Board of Education members before hiring Scribner.

The first time I ever saw Scribner was in the Whittier school where my eldest daughter attended kindergarten. The date was December 9, 1963, not many days after the assassination of President Kennedy. The Whittier auditorium was overflowing with parents and teachers. Scribner was there to answer questions about the mandatory integration plans that the Board of Education had announced it was considering. My first impression was negative for his poor use of language. In reply to why more blacks had not taken advantage of the voluntary transfer plan that was in effect that year, Scribner said that they did not want the "responsibility." I thought to myself. "What's wrong with responsibility?" Only after further questions and answers did it become clear what Scribner meant to say. Subsequently, in writing my book on Teaneck, I corrected Scribner's language and quoted him as saying that the voluntary plan put "the onus of responsibility" on Negroes when the problem was not theirs alone but the community's.[10]

Scribner did not make a favorable impression the second time I saw him. A meeting between us had been arranged for the purpose of my getting information from him on I.Q. testing. At the outset, however, Scribner said he did not want to talk about I.Q. tests, that he did not believe in them. He told me that he had had access to his children's I.Q. scores when they were small and because they were "nothing special," he had been disappointed, which may have affected his attitude. My impatience probably showed as I reminded him that I was not there to hear about the merits of I.Q. testing, but to get information to put into a publicity release intended to help the election of the three pro-integration candidates to the Board of Education. The release was to offset the unfounded charge that if they were elected, Teaneck would follow New York City in eliminating I.Q. tests. Scribner had lost sight of the purpose of the meeting.

But my initial negative impressions were offset following the victory in the integration referendum when I interviewed Scribner in gathering information for my book on Teaneck. It was then that I first heard about his childhood and background that he would later tell to Lelyveld of the *Times* and others. Scribner told all the same details right down to the green wood[11] his family burned for fuel that gave off little heat. As Lelyveld would note, Scribner was a "good storyteller in the Down East tradition," and his Yankee accent charmed. His presentation of himself, the poor boy who made good, aroused admiration. Admitting to being at the bottom of his high school graduating class made him appear exceptionally frank, and added to the obstacles he had supposedly overcome in acquiring his three education degrees.

Scribner took pride in his degrees, knowing no better. He was wholly a product of the field in which he was thriving. Never having known a body of knowledge, he missed none. In his climb up the educationist ladder, he never exposed himself to knowledge. He read only articles and books on education, written almost solely by educationists. In what must be the understatement of the twentieth century, Nicholas Murray Butler, president of Columbia University, said that educationist literature "is not nutritious as a steady diet."[12] Most of it reads like editorials on the side of good against evil—the evil usually being something called "traditional."

Scribner had never read any genre of good writing—not novels, poetry, plays, histories, humor, biographies, essays, detective stories, or science fiction. It would not occur to him to read a Russell Baker or William Safire column, unless the word "education" or "school" in a heading caught his eye. He would surely cease reading the instant he recognized that the writing was not educationese. Scribner recognized no intellectual or artistic authority—not Newton, Einstein, Shakespeare, Dickens, Balzac, Tolstoy, or Eliot—most certainly not George Eliot. I have seen Scribner's face contort into a grimace of disgust pronouncing Silas Marner. Being wholly an educationist, Scribner saw no value in reading anything that he could not relate directly to his career.

Scribner rarely strayed beyond narrow recreational limits. He seldom saw a movie, did not attend plays, concerts, art exhibitions, or sporting events. Although he could afford trips abroad, he had no desire to see foreign countries. He had no inclination to eat in fine restaurants. His attention to political news was chiefly as it affected his field, and whether a candidate for office was liberal or conservative. From Teaneck days on, his attention was caught by news pertaining to rights and social issues involving underdogs. Scribner's sole criterion for relevance was himself.

The one aspect of not being a literate person that Scribner recognized about himself was his inability to write coherently. While still the superintendent of schools in Teaneck, he showed me a proposal he had written. We were seated on the front porch of his home at the time. When he saw the look of puzzlement on my face as I read the first page without being able to make the least sense of it, Scribner took it back, saying: "I should know better than to ever show anything of mine to a writer." As he got up to go inside, he muttered that writing was a problem that had plagued him all of his life.

Scribner knew that others could write about school topics better than he. After the appearance in the local press of the publicity release I wrote on I.Q. testing, that Scribner had at first refused to talk about, he telephoned and thanked me for it. "You wrote that better than we could have done," he said. Scribner could have done better with his utterances as state commissioner of education in Vermont. Whenever he had something to say, the news media were on the spot, including television cameras, to report it. Some of the things he said got him into trouble. Well-written press releases probably would have helped him. On accepting the chancellorship in New York, Scribner anticipated similarly being in the public eye, including making speeches. Within his first few days he set about hiring a writer to do all of his writing for him.

Because Diane Divoky had interviewed Scribner in Vermont and said flattering things about him in a *Saturday Review* article,[13] Scribner asked her to recommend a writer. He turned out to be Leonard B. Stevens who, until a couple of months before, had been the executive editor of *Change* magazine. Previously, he had been with *Education News*, and before that was the education reporter for the Providence *Journal*. Scribner read a few of Stevens's articles and recognized the same educationist writing he had been reading all of his life. He also saw that Stevens was in the same liberal camp as himself. He hired Stevens with the official job title of speechwriter although he had never written a speech.

Scribner left Stevens pretty much to himself. Under the pressure of daily crises in the school system, and attending meetings with members of the Board of Education three and four days a week, Scribner made little time to confer with his writer. Stevens would tell me after a year and a half with Scribner that his longest private conversation with him had been his job interview. Stevens would write a speech for an upcoming speaking engagement and Scribner would make some small changes in it. Essentially, what Stevens wrote Scribner delivered. Not being a literate person, Scribner could hardly do otherwise. He had no understanding of rhetoric—the art of persuading others. He did not know that the same information or viewpoint can be written in many ways, each with a different emphasis and tone to produce a different effect. Scribner had no inkling that even a good writer can sometimes be wrong— fail to convey what is intended, or say what is inappropriate. Experienced, conscientious writers invariably want their writing criticized by others as a check on themselves. Although Scribner had acquired a personal staff of a dozen people, most of whom he trusted, he did not send them copies of a speech beforehand for their comments, or gather a few in his office to try a speech out on them. Indeed, Scribner and Stevens had little conversation between them. They did not ask: What do we want to accomplish with this next audience? What effect do we want the speech to have on it? What will be the consequences of talking about this or that? Scribner's lack of sufficient literacy to weigh his own words led directly to his loss of editorial support among New York City newspapers. It also provided Lelyveld with more evidence of his ineptness as chancellor, and permanently damaged his already bad relations with the school system's teachers and administrators.

On St. Valentine's Day, 1971, Scribner was the guest speaker of the Council of Supervisory Associations (CSA) at its annual convention at a luxury hotel in Freeport, Grand Bahama Island, in the Caribbean. The CSA represented the system's various associations of elementary school principals and high school principals. Altogether, the CSA represented nearly four thousand school administrators. Guests other than Scribner included Albert Shanker, the head of the teachers' union, and reporters from the city's newspapers. Chancellor Scribner was the afterdinner speaker. When he finished his speech, a few scattered hand claps accentuated an icy silence. The negative reactions of the CSA and Albert Shanker were reported the next day in the city's newspapers, and for the first time, editorials were adversely critical of Scribner. Each member of Scribner's personal staff, except Stevens, believed the speech to be a horrendous mistake.

Scribner was more than surprised. He was staggered by the negative reactions. He said that he had thought it one of his better speeches, and even scholarly. Leonard Stevens, for his part, said that he had expected the reactions to be negative.

Stevens was not sharing his prescience with Scribner, not pointing out beforehand the probable effects of his speeches. Early
in his tenure, Scribner had said that his role as chancellor was
to lead the system by setting a "tone" for it, but he was tone
deaf to the utterances Stevens wrote for him.

Inherent in being a literate person is the ability to distance
oneself from a situation, to see it in its context. This was
something Scribner could not do. He did not see that his
invitation from the CSA to speak was a peace offering, part of
a ceasefire that had been arranged two months before, and that
his speech amounted to renewing hostilities.

Hostilities had begun with the CSA in Scribner's sixth week
on the job, shortly after the NAACP had brought suit against
the school system. The suit charged that the tests given to select
principals and other supervisory personnel discriminated against
blacks and Puerto Ricans, and failed to measure "fitness and
merit." New York City's school district was one of two in the
state (the other being Buffalo) that went beyond state certification
in licensing school personnel. Its licensing agency was the Board
of Examiners, which had been established around the turn of
the century in order to remove school jobs as plums in a corrupt
patronage system, and to set competitive standards. It was
autonomous—not under the Board of Education—and its four
members were appointed for life, as are the justices of the U.S.
Supreme Court.

The basis for the suit was the unequal rates at which blacks
and Puerto Ricans passed examinations for supervisors compared to the rates for whites—white Puerto Ricans were presumably factored out by means of their Hispanic surnames.
Overall, in recent years, examinations had been passed by
minority groups at the rate of 31.4 percent while the whites
passed at the rate of 44.3 percent. The discrepancy was much
larger at the assistant principal level, which established the pool
that could take the tests for principal. Among test-takers for
assistant principal of junior high schools, blacks and Puerto
Ricans passed at nearly one-half the rate for whites. These and
other figures were given by the NAACP to substantiate the
charge that the tests were racially biased. Also pointed out in
connection with the suit was that the Chicago, Los Angeles,
Philadelphia, and Detroit school systems—where no competency

tests were given—had at least five times as many black and Hispanic school administrators as the New York City system.

Named as defendents in the NAACP suit were the Board of Examiners, which administered the tests, the Board of Education, which made appointments to the Board of Examiners when vacancies occurred, and the chancellor, who recommended personnel to the Board of Education for appointment. In the normal course of such a suit, the city's corporation counsel would defend all of them together. Most of the burden of adducing evidence for the defense would fall on the Board of Examiners.

Scribner, however, in private meetings with the members of the Board of Education, urged that they and he take a stance of no defense. Scribner made it plain that he wanted to get rid of the Board of Examiners. Of the five Board of Education members, one was black and one Puerto Rican and these two favored Scribner's position. The three members who formed the majority, however, strongly disagreed. They defended the licensing system, saying that to do away with it would lead to a lowering of standards. They also pointed out that the method of personnel selection the NAACP suit challenged was the same issue that created the Ocean Hill–Brownsville confrontation of two years before when three citywide teachers' strikes had racked the schools for months on end. The issue had amounted to a black-Jewish confrontation with black and Puerto Rican community groups insisting on appointing teachers and administrators of their own choosing, and Jewish teachers and administrators fighting to maintain the legal licensing system. The new decentralization law enacted the year before had presumably settled the issue by retaining the Board of Examiners and its testing procedures. Scribner was warned that black-Jewish relations were at their lowest ebb, that the stand he wanted would exacerbate an already dangerous situation.

Lawsuits take much time, and Scribner could have studied the situation before committing himself. The court judgment, moreover, would not necessarily be influenced by a stand of his for or against. Instead of postponing a decision until he got to know the system better, Scribner wanted to make his stand immediately public. He put it in a confidential memorandum to the Board of Education that was so poorly written that

Leonard Stevens would not let me see its first page at all. The rest of it was disjointed and fuzzy in that it went beyond the scope of the NAACP suit. The suit did not challenge the licensing of teachers; Scribner's memo did. He recommended that the thirty-two community school boards in the newly decentralized system be permitted to use state certification as the sole basis for selecting school administrators *and teachers*. Scribner's stand on supervisors might influence the outcome of the NAACP suit, but attacking the method of licensing teachers could have no effect. That could only be changed by the state legislature.

As Scribner knew beforehand, one of the two minority members of the Board of Education would leak his memo to the press. The next day Scribner's stand made front-page headlines. He had gone out of his way to offend most of the system's school administrators and teachers. He added insult to injury a few days later in appointing a black principal to a Harlem high school who was not on the Board of Examiners list of eligible principals.

Predictably, Albert Shanker and the head of the CSA accused Scribner of making "cynical" and "destructive" attacks on the system, of trying to establish "a quota system" of black principals for black high schools, and encouraging racial confrontation. The Elementary School Principals Association asked the state commissioner of education to investigate Scribner and remove him from office. Shanker and others considered that Scribner's efforts were illegal. Scribner's responses to them also made headlines. One read: SCRIBNER TELLS CRITICS HE WON'T BACK OFF OR QUIT. Shanker charged him with bringing the morale of school personnel "to an all-time low" and threatened a citywide teachers' strike if Scribner did not change his ways.

Much of the early editorial support for Scribner was in terms of giving the new chancellor a chance. A *Daily News* editorial said: "It ill becomes local educators . . . to take out after the Scribner scalp so indecently soon. How about public opinion backing Dr. Scribner at least for now." The majority members of the Board of Education, too, could not be critical of the man it had just hired. Everyone was nevertheless aghast at the open fight between the head of the system and the heads of the teachers' and the supervisors' unions. One newspaper called it "The Battle of the Bigs." School personnel said that the captain of the ship had mutinied against his crew. How was anything to be accomplished when the leader was at odds with those whom he was supposed to lead?

Repeated efforts were made to get Scribner to meet with Shanker to end the fighting, without success. One such effort was made in a large private meeting in which Scribner and Shanker were both present. Board of Education member Seymour Lachman, who was chiefly responsible for bringing Scribner to New York, leaned over to Scribner, put a hand on his arm and whispered that he should meet with Shanker following the meeting. Scribner's response was to angrily remove Lachman's hand saying "I will *not* meet with Shanker!"

Since Scribner would not cooperate, the same board member persuaded Shanker to take the first step to end the fighting. All of a sudden, early in December, Shanker appeared to reverse himself. He publicly stated that Scribner "must succeed," and that "if he fails there's trouble ahead." Shanker followed up by having Scribner appear before the UFT's assembly of delegates. In introducing Scribner, Shanker noted that it was the very first time that a chief administrator had appeared before the assembly and "should give us great hope that we can work together and avoid conflicts."

But Scribner and his closest aides misread Shanker's peace overtures. When I visited the chancellor's office in January, the euphoric feeling was that Scribner had defeated Shanker, made him back down. One of his aides said that Scribner was a political genius and spoke of him as the next U.S. Commissioner of Education. Scribner and his closest aides were from outside of the school system and from outside of the city. Only from Murray Polner, one of the insiders on Scribner's staff, did I get a different view. Polner had been a high school teacher, UFT chapter chairman, and most recently the executive aide of board member Seymour Lachman. Polner said that Scribner would have to work with Shanker to accomplish anything. "The union, after all, is the most powerful political force in the city of New York," said Polner. "Anyone who doesn't recognize that is blind—suffers from a severe case of galloping myopia," implying that that was what Scribner was suffering from.

Scribner could have spared himself the shock of surprise at the negative reactions to his speech, had he shown it beforehand to Murray Polner or another insider. What angered Albert Shanker and the CSA members after their peace efforts was that Scribner came right back at them with another attack on the licensing system. The speech contained the notion that high school students, as well as parents, teachers, and other supervisors, should have an advisory role in selecting high school principals. The rest of the speech, full of generalities, seemed to justify giving students an advisory role by citing student disruptions in high schools across the nation.

When I next visited the chancellor's offices shortly after the publication of Joseph Lelyveld's article in the *New York Times Magazine* on March 21st, the mood had changed from euphoria to pessimism about Scribner's future. Some of Scribner's worried personal aides were blaming his writer Leonard Stevens for trying to "out-Scribner Scribner," and had told him so. They had debated the CSA speech with him. While the debate was in progress Scribner happened along. After listening to it, Scribner said that if he had it to do over again he would give the same speech.

One of the typical characteristics of a literate person is curiosity. Scribner was not curious even about his own surprise. He did not ask himself what he had failed to see or understand to cause him to be surprised at the negative reactions to his speech.

The Lelyveld article, by itself, was a staggering blow. Scribner looked inept in it, although he denied that the article was anything but "fair" to him, to quote his own word for it. To a friend who called and told Scribner that it made him look like a country bumpkin, he responded: "That's the way I'm playing it." One of his daughters telephoned and asked: "What are they doing to my father?" Board of Education member Murray Bergtraum told Scribner that the article made him look weak.

My research included interviewing a few people outside of the school system who had an interest in the chancellor. One was a Wall Street lawyer and talent searcher in the Kennedy administration, William Josephson, who had performed a similar function for the Board of Education. He considered Scribner guilty of "hubris," a passionate pride in his own rightness that would be his downfall. Another opinion was that of Charles Silberman, although I heard it from Marion Taylor of the

Vermont Board of Education. She reported that Silberman had remarked to her that he did not think Scribner was up to the job intellectually. Lelyveld had likened Scribner to "Bunyan's Pilgrim passing through the Valley of Humiliation."[14]

His next humiliation came in connection with a charge made by the first Puerto Rican superintendent of one of the decentralized districts. He charged that the city's three special high schools were the most racially imbalanced in the system, and that the tests for admission to them were culturally biased. The three were Stuyvesant, Bronx High School of Science, and Brooklyn Tech. When I graduated from Stuyvesant in 1938, it was known as a school for the academically talented. But as student achievement dropped precipitously over the years in the city's other high schools, with a few notable exceptions, achievement in these three was maintained and even increased. They became known as elite schools, among educationists an invidious term.

Students at Stuyvesant and Bronx High School of Science routinely won more Regents scholarships than those of other high schools. A survey by the Health, Education and Welfare Department had found that Stuyvesant and Bronx High School of Science were the two leading high schools in the nation in the production of graduates who later earned Ph.D. degrees and other doctorates. Prominent blacks were among them.

The two-hour admission examination to them was half mathematics and half verbal, with three out of the four reading selections in the verbal portion on scientific subjects. Places in the schools were awarded to the top scorers, and the examination was the sole basis for admission until 1965 when a Discovery Program was added. Minority students who scored just below those accepted were also admitted and given extra academic help over the summer. The fall previous to the Puerto Rican superintendent's charge, 3,484 students had been admitted to the special schools on a competitive basis plus 352 minority students on a Discovery Program basis.[15] The Stuyvesant student body consisted of 4.2 percent Hispanic, 6.0 percent Oriental, 10.3 percent black and 79.4 percent white.[16] The percent for whites was disproportionate to the city's school population but not nearly so disproportionate as the percent for Orientals.

New York City high schools were among the best and the

worst in the nation. When the charges of racial discrimination were brought, the chancellor could have decided that with achievement exceedingly low in the overwhelming majority of high schools, he was not going to tamper with those considered the nation's best. Scribner announced, however, that after investigation and careful consideration, he found there were "serious questions" about the admissions policies of the special schools and that they deserved a "hard look" by a committee that he was going to appoint.[17]

Scribner had been accused by his critics of "shooting from the hip." Characteristically, Scribner ordered that the notices to students accepted by the special schools for the coming fall not be mailed. As any insider could foretell, parents of students waiting for the notices immediately protested. And then they helped do much more. They and the parent organizations of the special schools, plus the extensive and politically powerful alumni of them, organized themselves into a lobbying group. Due to their efforts, the state legislature passed by a better than 3 to 1 majority a bill that specifically forbade the chancellor from making any changes in the admissions policies of the three special schools. The twenty-four member committee that Scribner in the meantime had appointed to study them was left high and dry.

Once again, Scribner was surprised. He had ignored charges that he was intent on wrecking the special schools, of trying to destroy their academic excellence, and of being a "leveler." The speed and power with which his hands were manacled shocked and embittered him. Those who put on the handcuffs were 100 percent correct. Having never come close to academic excellence himself, Scribner was tampering with the special schools without any idea of what he might destroy.

In most of the city's schools, student achievement was vastly lower than in the city's best. Of all seventh graders at the time, 70 percent of them read too poorly to do seventh grade work. Only 30 percent of high school students—chiefly whites in a system that was 60 percent black and Puerto Rican—successfully completed the ordinary curriculum.[18] But in none of Scribner's speeches, public utterances, and actions did he address these specific problems. I never heard him address them in private. He indulged in generalities. As Lelyveld observed, Scribner was "never one to shrink from a platitude."[19] His most specific reference was to the "learning needs" of children, "Whatever that means or can be made to mean," wrote Lelyveld.[20] Like many another school administrator who was a low achiever in school, achievement meant little to Scribner.

While state education commissioner of Vermont, Scribner recalled that he had desegregated a predominantly black school in 1952, two years before the Brown Supreme Court decision. It was in the Wareham Unified District near Cape Cod, Massachusetts. An NAACP lawyer had called his attention to a school attended by the children of cranberry pickers where achievement was extremely low. Scribner had closed it and put the children into another school. It pleased Scribner immensely to recall this. It did not occur to him, or to me at the time, to wonder why, as the superintendent, he had been unaware of a low-achieving school.

Scribner's academic deficiencies severely limited his initatives and decisions as New York City's chancellor. His limitations were especially apparent in his political choices. Most of the people with whom he came in contact were better educated than he. One was Seymour Lachman, with whom he had the most friction. Another was Charles E. Silberman, whose *Crisis in the Classroom* had just been published. In Silberman's foreword he had thanked Scribner for supplying information for his book when commissioner in Vermont.[21] Silberman invited the Scribners to his home for dinner, and had telephoned Scribner a number of times to urge him to work with Albert Shanker. According to Scribner, his response had been, "Charlie, you *write* about reform. I've got to *do* it." When Silberman told him that he did not understand teachers' unions, Scribner replied, "I don't *want* to understand teachers' unions."

Usually when I was visiting him and his staff, I merely observed and asked questions for information. One time, however, I wanted to point out the foolishness of a phrase that he and Dwight Allen, dean of the U. Mass School of Education, were using at the time. Both Scribner and Allen were claiming "the right to fail." Who would undergo surgery with a surgeon or fly with an airline pilot who claimed such a "right"? Thinking to put it in terms of Scribner's own life, I pointed out that what he had risked as a young man in Maine was not failure but success.

"By your own account, Harvey, you were a failure," I reminded him. "You didn't have to do anything to fail. All you had to do was stay where you were. What you risked in trying to better yourself was *success*. Instead of the right to fail, shouldn't you be claiming the right to *succeed*?"

Scribner looked fixedly at me for a moment, before answering. "You have thought more about that than I have," he said and turned away.

Scribner was most comfortable with blacks and Hispanics. They failed to make Scribner feel uncomfortable even when they went to extremes in putting pressure on him. During a public meeting of the Board of Education, a group from Ocean Hill–Brownsville raised signs saying HARVEY SCRIBNER CHICKEN because he had not removed the corrupt community board chairman, Sam Wright, who was politically powerful. One of its members marched to the front of the hall carrying a shopping bag, placed it down on a table in front of Scribner, and ripped it open to reveal a live chicken. In the expectant pause that followed, all eyes on Scribner, he put his head back and laughed loudly. Another member of the group stood in front of him, hands thrust forward in coat pockets as if holding handguns and about to shoot him. No public official should be so menaced, but Scribner made not a murmur of complaint at the time or later.

His forbearance did not extend to school personnel, particularly high school principals and superintendents. With them he was quick to take offense. In a meeting with the executive committee of the High School Principals Association, when its members were critical of him, Scribner announced, "I'll not stay here and take any more of this crap!" and walked out. Scribner cut off the high school principals and refused to meet with Shanker for the same reason he cut off Charles Silberman and Seymour Lachman. They were better educated than he.

Almost all had entered New York City schools in the 1920s, '30s, and '40s when the system was recognized as superior throughout the nation. Many had attended City College of New York when, because of its high standards and excellence, it was known as "the poor man's Harvard." Some had graduated as chemists, engineers, and architects, during the depression of the 1930s and, unable to find work in their fields, became teachers. The majority who were Jewish remembered the overt and widespread anti-Semitism of the years before World War II and the quotas by which many were kept out of colleges, professions, and corporations. But all Scribner sensed was that they were better educated than he and cut them off. He did not discuss "the roots of their dissatisfactions" and try to allay their "fears, real and imaginary," which *The New York Times* editorial, following his CSA speech, blamed Scribner for failing to do.

The difference in Scribner's treatment of representatives of supervisory personnel and black and Puerto Rican groups was well-known. A retiring superintendent wrote that there was disillusionment among his fellow professionals. They had to stand outside Scribner's office without being able to see him, while a community group with a complaint could barge right in. A great put-down was going on, said the professionals, and they were the ones being put down. But the more Scribner was criticized, the more he dug in his heels to remain as he was.

He nevertheless felt increasingly anxious about being fired as chancellor, and retreated to the high moral ground of doing what was "best for kids." Disclaimed Scribner: "*Somebody* needs to stand for kids, and forget his job. Just forget the whole goddam thing, and say, look, for once, though my voice may be weak, I'm going to stand for these kids in this system and go down with them." Scribner's anxiety about possibly being fired intensified toward the end of the school year. His personal staff increasingly heard from the bureaucrats at 110 Livingston Street that Scribner was not a good administrator, the reason given for firing the only previous outsider to head up the school system, Calvin Gross. Scribner kept nervously asking aides: "How long did Calvin Gross last?" He had trouble falling asleep at night, breaking out in a cold sweat for fear of not getting enough rest to get through the next day. Early in June, every now and again Scribner wished aloud: "If only we can get through the next few weeks!" He worried that some act of violence or student disruption would take place before the schools closed for the summer and be used against him.

The five members of the Board of Education took one-year turns presiding as president and on July 1 the rotation came to Isaiah Robinson. Scribner's aides predicted Scribner's relations with the board would be better with a black president. But one of Robinson's aides told Scribner to his face: "If *you* go down, *we* will not go down with you." The board was the only paid board of education in the United States, with each member enjoying the perks of a chauffeur-driven car, a personal support staff of aides, and a suite of offices on the floor above Scribner's. The board's first priority was its own survival.

Scribner's anxiety was alleviated later that month when the decision was handed down in the suit brought by the NAACP— *Chance and Mercado* v. *Board of Examiners et al.* The decision by U.S. District Court Judge Walter R. Mansfield virtually abolished the Board of Examiners for an indefinite period with respect to testing and licensing school administrators. Scribner had, indeed, influenced the decision. In Mansfield's written opinion he said: "Having in mind that the existing examination system is not believed by the Chancellor of the New York City District to be a workable one, we do not envisage any great harm to the public as a result of preliminary relief."

Like everyone else at the time, I did not recognize what the decision in the NAACP suit really exposed—the lack of a body of pedagogical knowledge by all of the parties involved. Scribner's lack could be seen in the Lelyveld *Times* article. When Lelyveld asked for the source of his views on education, Scribner did not mention the work he had done for his Ed.D. degree, or anything learned in his many education courses. Scribner instead talked of:

> . . . the first superintendent for whom he worked in Maine, one W. H. Phinney, who taught him, he says, "to get out of the way of children so they could learn once in a while."
>
> Sometimes . . . Phinney would yank him out of school while classes were still in session and lead him to a nearby stream. "He'd have a couple of fishing poles there backed into the bank with cork stoppers on them and he'd philosophize with me, you know, and I learned a great deal from him."[22]

Scribner had told me exactly the same thing when I interviewed him for my book on Teaneck. I did not include it because I did not think that getting out of the way of children and going fishing amounted to an educational philosophy. Moreover, I did not think Scribner could mean it the way it sounded. His telling the same thing to Lelyveld confirmed that he meant it in all seriousness. Judge Mansfield quoted nothing stronger from Scribner in his written opinion than that the existing examination system was not "believed" by him to be workable. Scribner gave no rationale for his belief which, in private, he called a "gut decision."

The NAACP, for its part, would never have brought suit if blacks and Puerto Ricans had passed the examinations at the same rate as whites. It would never have raised the issue of relevance, the job relatedness of the tests. The NAACP suit was a class action about jobs—not about quality of instruction and student learning. At stake at the time were the jobs of 168 black and Puerto Rican acting principals and assistant principals who were not eligible for permanent appointments because they had not taken or had not passed the appropriate Board of Examiners' tests.

The Board of Examiners, too, had no body of pedagogical knowledge. A portion of its examinations for administrators consisted of the type of material taught in graduate courses in educational administration, required for state certification. Possession of state certification was first necessary to be eligible to take the appropriate Board of Examiners' tests. In attacking the tests, Scribner was attacking his own field but that was too complex a connection for him to make, and was not made by anyone else. The material taught in such courses is so vague and general as to be immemorable without resorting to memory techniques, such as the following cited in the NAACP's brief:

> *PERT CAGES* for Improved School Discipline
>
> Planning of standards and rules   Conferences
> Environment, improvement of   Analysis of difficulties
> Routines, training in   Guidance procedures
> Teaching, improvement of   Evaluation and follow-up
>   Self-control emphasis

This memory device aided the recall of the topics listed so that they could be included in essay-type answers. Presumably, a candidate for a principal's license should have the opportunity to demonstrate that he or she can write coherently. But having to incorporate all of the generalizations in such as the list above resulted in educationists' typical, impenetrable jargon. Judge Mansfield wrote, "The ability to memorize and regurgitate laundry lists of bad answers is not, we hope, a true test of a candidate's qualifications for a supervisory position." The "bad answers" belonged to the field, not just to the Board of Examiners.

Most hurtful to the defense of the Board of Examiners was its inability to show a correlation between passing its examinations and success in becoming a competent school administrator. This, too, reflected the field's belief in educational research, on which millions in federal and state money is spent annually but which rarely enlightens. Much of what the field pretends to be able to measure cannot be measured for cause and effect. Judge Mansfield, of course, had to decide on the merits of the suit before him, not on the weaknesses of the educationist field.

What could be said in support of the Board of Examiners, and was said by its defenders, was that the licensing system had been in place for nearly three-quarters of a century. Indeed, it had been in place longer than most schools of education. It had replaced a spoils system, to which the system could revert. The licensing system had served the schools well in helping make them superior to schools in other systems.

The superiority was in part due to portions of the Board of Examiners' tests that were quite traditional, and more demanding than the requirements for state certification. One part was a test of general knowledge, which those who were readers had the best chance of passing. Assistant principals and principals had also passed the board's tests for teachers, which included an oral test. Teachers had to express themselves well, were failed for using bad grammar in speaking, or for having a speech impediment. Prospective teachers who were Jewish sometimes failed the oral portion for having Yiddish pronunciations, which most corrected before taking the test again. In 1970, the Board of Examiners was still the means of promoting the most well-spoken, knowledgeable candidates available.

Scribner's stance of "no defense" in the NAACP lawsuit had forced the Board of Education into a "passive defense," further weakening the Board of Examiners' position. It had to retain separate counsel and stand alone in its "active defense." Scribner had contributed mightily to the court's granting "preliminary relief." He followed up what he considered a personal triumph that fall by getting the Board of Education to pass a resolution permitting appointment of acting and permanent school administrators on the basis of state certification alone.

The impact on the school system was enormous. During the 1971–72 school year, over five hundred administrators would retire, double the number of any previous year. Among them were one-third of the high school principals. The Mansfield decision was not the only cause, but a major one. Many of the administrators retired complaining bitterly of the "deterioration" of the schools, of Scribner's "permissiveness," and an increasing climate of fear of violence in the schools.

Board of Education statistics showed a marked increase in assaults on students and teachers, muggings, robberies, vandalism, and so forth. A resurgence of street gangs was taking place and a proliferation of cheap handguns known as "Saturday night specials." High school principals, in particular, blamed Scribner for encouraging violence in schools and not doing enough to stop and prevent it. The principals were essentially correct about the tone and spirit of Scribner's administration. He expressed overt sympathy for students, was protective of their "rights," and wanted schools to adjust to disaffected students by becoming more "relevant" to their "needs." Concern for the welfare of teachers and principals was hardly equal.

Abraham H. Lass, whose tribute to his "Miss McDonald" teachers was quoted in Chapter 3, wrote a letter to the editor of the *Times* in which he ridiculed Scribner's "relevancy":

> Mr. Scribner and others seem inclined to the current notion that the junkies are pushing dope, the rapists are raping, the molesters are molesting, the arsonists are setting fires in the schools, the vandals are smashing hundreds of thousands of school windows, the disoriented youngsters are running amok because they find their courses of study not relevant. So, give the curriculum more contemporary zing. Let the children take what they want. And the mayhem will cease.[23]

Lass was answered by an official of the New York City Civil Liberties Union (NYCCLU), active in the defense of student rights, who referred to "the rage of those thousands of students who enter high school every year and can *barely read or write*." (Emphasis added.)[24] Scribner himself was not without a similar rage and for a similar reason. Not being a literate person, not being able to represent situations coherently to himself, he was often bewildered by much of what was going on around him. As Lelyveld noted, he expressed surprise in private that many of his critics were Jewish. He protested, "In Teaneck my strongest supporters were Jewish." But 75 percent of all New York City administrators were Jewish at the time and Scribner had attacked them and all they stood for in the system, without regard for them as school personnel or as Jews with their traditions and historical circumstances. Although they had made peace overtures to him, he had made none in return.

Early in 1972 his Jewish critics put on a campaign to drive Scribner from office on the issue of school violence. He survived their efforts and other crises that made newspaper headlines. Much of what he did in the final year of his contract was determined by a desire for an extension of it, a desire frustrated by the Board of Education's refusal to extend it.

Scribner's chancellorship was a disaster for the education of "the kids" in the New York City public schools. As is typical of educationists, however, Scribner turned disaster into personal success. To cap his career, he received and accepted an offer from the U. Mass School of Education to join it as a full professor with tenure. U. Mass was not the only ed school to offer him a professorship. He had other offers—one from the then chancellor of the College of the City of New York, who Scribner said came to his office to make the offer. One of the reasons Scribner chose the U. Mass ed school was that he already had many years in the Massachusetts retirement system and could "buy into" it for the years he was out of state.

Two of Scribner's personal staff and others from the city school system would follow Scribner to Amherst to become doctoral candidates—one, his speech writer Leonard Stevens. Scribner was the chairman of their doctoral committees. Scribner, in fact, would chair many more doctoral committees each year than most U. Mass professors. He would also teach courses in "school administration," although by his own assertion as chancellor in New York he was a poor administrator. Having little wisdom or practicality to pass on, he encouraged students to engage chiefly in "discussions."

One of Scribner's last acts as chancellor in New York would directly depress student achievement there for the rest of the decade. It was an act that Scribner said he was particularly proud of. Shortly before he left, Scribner got the Board of Education to replace the three different high school diplomas students earned—academic, general, or vocational—with a single diploma for all that made no distinctions. Gene Maeroff of the *Times* observed, "The single diploma was adopted as an egalitarian device, supposedly eradicating the stigma of the less prestigious diplomas."[25] As it turned out, the single diploma encouraged many students, including some relatively high achievers, to take easier courses. At Brooklyn Tech, one of the three selective academic high schools, students with three years of math at the end of the junior year plummeted from 95.1 percent in 1973 to 77.2 percent in 1978.[26] For the same five–year period, all of the City University's colleges reported receiving students who were more poorly prepared than their counterparts of previous years. The single diploma resulted in fewer courses being taken in English, math, chemistry, biology, physics, history, and foreign languages.[27]

> In 1972, nearly half of the 36,782 graduating students had 10 Regents credits required for an academic diploma, the most rigorous of the three certificates then offered. . . . In 1979, only 33.7 percent earned a Regents endorsed diploma, the closest thing to the academic certificate . . . eliminated [at Scribner's urging].[28]

In 1973, high school students who completed three years of English by the end of the junior year amounted to 66.3 percent. By 1978, that figure had declined to 53.2 percent. For the same years, the percent of high school seniors who had completed algebra and geometry dropped from 40 to 33 percent; those with two years of science dropped from 62.9 to 51.0 percent.[29]

The above citywide figures are nevertheless inflated. They do not reflect the dozen or more of the city's 109 high schools that were in such a chaotic state that they supplied no figures or none that were usable.[30] Neither do the above figures reflect the tens of thousands of low achieving students who dropped out of high school before the end of their junior year.

Scribner's critics had charged him with being a "do-nothing Chancellor." Albert Shanker said: "He leaves all the problems alone." Although empowered to set standards for the elementary schools in the thirty-two decentralized districts, Scribner had left the districts alone. He said he expected reforms and educational innovations to "bubble up" in them with the help of parents. With his Ed.D. degree and thirty-five years of school experience, Scribner had relied on parents. In the words of historian Diane Ravitch: "The professionals had failed, so why not turn the system over to the parents who at least really care about the kids."[31]

Her quote is from a study in 1980 by *The New York Times* that evaluated the first decade of decentralization, the compromise structure that grew out of the fight by black and Puerto Rican groups for community control. The *Times* study showed that it produced no better education for the children of these groups than the old structure. Enrollment of minority students in the ten years had risen from 59.7 to 71.3 percent.[32] Despite hundreds of millions of dollars in federal and state funds spent on compensatory education, the average citywide achievement remained years behind students in small cities and suburbs in the rest of the state, where student achievement had also declined. The *Times* study quoted Dr. Kenneth Clark as saying ". . . the minority community was not prepared to cope even with diluted decentralization . . . because parents themselves are victims of inadequate education and didn't have the experience or the training in organizing their own destiny."[33]

Much of what had happened in the ten years had been predicted by Scribner's critics. One article in the *Times* study was headed: POLITICS AND PATRONAGE DOMINATE COMMUNITY-RUN SCHOOL DISTRICTS. There was also corruption. Community schoolboard chairman Sam Wright had been convicted of soliciting a bribe from a supplier of educational materials; Scribner had been called "chicken" for not removing him. Three school-board members in a Harlem district were convicted of conspiracy to misuse public funds in their board election campaigns. Mismanagement as well as corruption played a role in keeping student achievement low. Millions of dollars were misspent.[34]

Another article of the *Times* study was headed: LOCALLY RUN SCHOOLS DISAPPOINT MINORITY EDUCATORS AND PARENTS. Although the percent of minority superintendents, principals, assistant principals, teachers, and paraprofessional teachers' aides had greatly increased, and minority students had many more "role models," that did not help achievement. Parents complained of getting the same excuses from them that they had gotten from white administrators and teachers.[35]

One of the five authors of the *Times* report, Gene Maeroff, used a phrase reminiscent of Scribner's "right to fail." He wrote: "Inherent in decentralization's license to experiment is the freedom to fail. . . ." He went on: "A result has been turbulence and instability in places like Central Harlem's District 5, where the school board has dismissed more than a half dozen super-intendents in 10 years."[36] Yet in Harlem in the 1930s, there had been success, as Dr. Kenneth Clark attested: "I went to schools in Harlem. I know what good teachers can do. I didn't know whether the school system was centralized or decentral-ized."[37]

If there is anything that parents do not want, it is "freedom to fail" with *their* children. Parents who can manage it in New York City send their children to private or parochial schools, unless they live in one of the few decentralized school districts still considered good. The Public Education Association esti-mated in 1983 that 25 percent of the city's school age children were not attending public schools.[38] In 1984, the Urban League reported that 13 percent of black children and 33 percent of white children were in private and parochial schools.[39]

The decline in student achievement in New York City is, of course, the same as the decline in other large cities, suburbs, small cities, towns, and rural areas, and for similar reasons. In addition to the year-to-year declines, there is also a national pattern of decline grade by grade.

Reading test scores are given in terms of grade level, the national average or norm for each particular grade. In New York City and elsewhere, reading scores remain at or near grade level through the first four grades. In the fifth grade, however, a split occurs and continues through all remaining grades. One group of students continues to score at, near, or above grade level through the twelfth grade. Another large group slips below grade level from the fifth grade on, with the gap widening progressively in each grade thereafter.[40] Reading instruction in this group failed to take. Students in it did not become readers; cannot read in order to learn; cannot make progress in academic subjects. They become in-school illiterates.

On arriving in high school many of them drop out. The dropout rate in 1982 was estimated to be 44 percent in New York City; 48 percent in Boston; 56 percent in Chicago; and nearly 70 percent in Detroit.[41] The Urban League in 1984 reported that a catastrophic 78 percent of New York City's black children do not complete high school.[42]

Yet standards are so low that students can graduate from high school in New York City with only an eighth grade reading level, remembering that standards for each grade are lower than formerly. Many who go on to college cannot be said to be readers, though some of them may acquire college degrees.

People who never become readers remain educationally impoverished all of their lives, though they attain high positions in education. Far from being unique, Harvey B. Scribner is typical of a high percent of those with education degrees, including doctorates. They are deans of schools of education, professors of education, federal and state education officials, superintendents of schools, and other school administrators, as well as teachers. This, more than any other factor, is the nation's education problem and has been since long before publication of the following in 1963: "It is an indecorous thing to say and obviously offensive to most educationists, but it is the truth and it should be said: the inferior intellectual quality of the Education faculty is *the* fundamental limitation of the field.[43]

This truth, from *The Miseducation of American Teachers* by James B. Koerner, remains true.

9

To Make Up
Your Mind Anew

"Why do schools everywhere do a poor job of teaching math?"

A graduate student who was an experienced classroom teacher answered me flatly: "The culture doesn't support it."

My question was triggered by reactions of students to my criticisms of their storyboards, which we had just gone over. None had adequately carried out the assignment, which was to teach the concept of pi. All had failed to make explicit that pi was the ratio of the circumference of a circle to its diameter, an invariant for all circles. Several students protested that they had never been taught the concept. All they had been told, they said, was that pi was 3.14 or 22/7. Their example of inadequate teaching prompted my question.

That the culture did not support math instruction was nevertheless the only answer I could elicit and I let it stand without comment until the class' next meeting. Then, having brought in the help wanted section of the Boston *Globe*—most of the students being from the Boston area, where many high tech companies were located—I confronted them with it. I showed pages of classified ads seeking people with math skills. Holding up the pages, I asked: "Isn't the world of jobs part of the culture? Doesn't it support the teaching of math?" The graduate student who had said that it did not, looked sullen. He remained silent and so did the rest of the students, their faces empty of agreement.

Education students have a unique solidarity. Had I asked my questions in a noneducation course I might have received a variety of answers. Most college students could have told of having math teachers who knew little math. Each of my daughters, in the reputedly good Amherst school system, had had more than one whose knowledge was grossly deficient. Education students, too, have had such math teachers. But teachers-to-be are not free to say so. Having attended public schools for twelve or more years, future teachers—unlike future engineers, police officers, and business people—have a firsthand knowledge of their field before they enter it. Consciously or unconsciously, they know it discourages criticism, and hence thinking.

I have in mind Hannah Arendt's meaning of thinking: "Practically [speaking], thinking means that each time you are confronted with a difficulty in life you have to make up your mind anew."[1]

In showing the help wanted section of the Boston *Globe* to my students I had presented them with a difficulty. If the culture, of which technology is a vital part, cannot be blamed for poor math instruction, the cause must lay elsewhere. But were any in the class to consider that the cause might be schools of education, his or her self-interest would be threatened. The School of Education did not check the math ability of future teachers and school administrators before admitting them, taught no math in its courses, never tested their math competence before sending them out to practice teach in schools or granting them B.A., M.Ed., and Ed.D. degrees. Were my students to think about why the nation's schools do a poor job of teaching math, they might have to make up their minds anew that it was due to teacher ignorance.

Unable to say anything against their own interests, my students maintained an embarrassed silence. They regarded me, I suspected, as an oddity at best, or suicidal and traitorous at worst, for undermining my position in the education field as well as theirs.

I had not always disturbed students with disquieting questions. During my first years in the school, although I always gave subject matter assignments, I permitted them to do storyboards that chiefly attempted to entertain rather than instruct, like most of the so-called educational films and television programs they saw. As time passed, I felt ashamed at how grateful I had felt when students put effort into their storyboards no matter how ill they treated the subject matter. I was a poor teacher then, though students gave my courses good evaluations which personnel committees cited in recommending me for reappointments.

It was never my intention to teach math, science, or language. Film techniques are complicated enough for the uninitiated without trying to teach them subject matter at the same time. But as I kept explaining to students, the real challenge was to use film techniques to call attention to the subject matter. In the case of the pi assignment, for the simplest example, flowing a circle onto the screen instead of presenting it already whole was the better technique. The lengthening arc engaged the eye's involuntary motion detection system—as motion does in even the lowest animals—to focus attention autonomically. Entertainment qualities could be added, if necessary, after the subject matter had been made central and understandable.

I assigned easy subject matter, no higher in difficulty than the seventh grade so that all would be able to do it. I wanted to spend class time on the film techniques, including how to use words and pictures together. Nevertheless, most students found the subject matter difficult. They gave little evidence, moreover, of feeling responsible for knowing, or learning for the first time, what they should have learned in junior high school.

One such assignment was to present in visuals and words that an object immersed in water displaces a volume of water equal to the volume of the object. If the weight of the displaced water is greater than the weight of the object, it floats; if less, it sinks. To introduce this assignment I showed a videotape recorded off the air from educational television. Although it failed miserably to convey the principle, it reminded students of what equipment they might show in their storyboards and permitted us to discuss how and why it failed.

In one class when I finished showing the tape, a doctoral candidate eagerly volunteered: "I know that. That's Archimedes' Principle. I remember because I saw an animated film about it. An Archimedes character jumped out of the water yelling 'Eureka! Eureka!' " This doctoral candidate was on the faculty of Mount Wachusetts Community College. He was a professor of communications media and his claim of remembering was more a claim for his specialty than for knowing the principle. When the assignment was due the following week he complained that he had had difficulty doing it because science was not his specialty. He had had to get help, he said, from the professor at his community college who taught science. Even so, he got the principle wrong and the errors within his storyboard were inconsistent.

It was an effort at times to keep from exclaiming that although I had spent twenty years in the advertising business before becoming a professor, I was able to remember most of what I had learned in school. I remembered math and science well enough to recall with the aid of an encyclopedia. I urged students to resort to one too, but suspected that few were able to glean the knowledge they needed from the printed page.

Two doctoral candidates assigned to me claimed an inability to read due to dyslexia. One was on the faculty of Fitchburg State College where she taught film and photography. She acted as if her degree work could consist of independent study, done mostly in the dark room. The other self-described dyslexic, during a conference, pointed to an open book on my desk and said: "Print is just lines on the page to me." Yet, she sometimes carried in her tote bag books on photography's most technical aspects—the speeds of films and lenses. I believed she could read those books. Her dyslexia, it seemed, could be turned on and off, a contradiction. But most of the graduate students and faculty in the school were little bothered by contradictions. One professor offered a course entitled: "Operationalizing Fuzzy Concepts."

Having initially joined the school to create instructional materials in the visual media, I became its defender of language. My colleagues preferred to speak of nonverbal communication, even in faculty meetings.

In one such meeting, a protest against the mindless term welled up within me like nausea and was out of my mouth before I knew it. The occasion was a crisis meeting in the school. Chairing the meeting was my fellow professor of education, Kenneth Blanchard—the coauthor of the 1983 bestseller *The One Minute Manager*. Blanchard was speaking to the forty-or-so faculty and graduate students present when a secretary entered the room and told Dean Dwight Allen that he was wanted on the telephone. The moment Allen was out the door, Blanchard said to the rest of us:

"I'm a student of nonverbal communication. What the dean's leaving tells me is that he's not interested in the opinions of the faculty."

"But if he'd stayed," I blurted out, "you could have said it meant that he didn't trust the faculty to deliberate *alone*. As Dostoevsky said, psychology is a two-edged sword. It cuts *both* ways."

A murmur went through the room at my mention of Dostoevsky, particularly among the graduate students. I had committed the unpardonable sin of citing authority. Before and after the murmur was silence. Blanchard looked straight ahead, as still as in a freeze frame. After what always seemed minutes instead of seconds in such circumstances, he continued on as if uninterrupted.

In other meetings, similar eruptions of mine were greeted with the same silence. Under discussion in one was the method of having questionnaires filled out by students. An objection raised to it was that students would be able to see each other's replies and be influenced by them. A senior professor, ever anxious to curry favor with students, responded, "I don't think students are influenced by each other's answers."

"Don't you know how doctors test pain-killing drugs?" I erupted. "They use a double-blind test. Neither the one administering the tablet or the subject taking it knows whether it is the drug or a placebo. Even then the placebo works almost as well as the drug. That's how easily people are influenced."

The senior professor stared at me blankly, then continued without acknowledging that I had spoken. Such colleagues' silences were the same as those of my students when I asked them disquieting questions; the same as the faculty's silence at the inclusion of "Illiterates with Doctorates" in a school publication; the same as in my daughter's seventh grade math class when the teacher, halving the distances she paced off to the classroom door, ended up with her feet against the door after saying that she would never reach it. Everyone in the field—ed school professors, their students, and teachers—maintained or imposed silence as a way of covering up their own and their field's idiocies. They prohibited real criticism, questioning and inquiry.

I continued to try to get students in courses to think—to make up their minds anew. They were not innately stupid, just terribly miseducated. My chief opportunity was in media theory, a course required for state certification for media specialists but taken largely by others. Before I began teaching the course, it had been taught as behaviorism, what Arthur Koestler referred to as "ratomorphism." I taught it as comparative media, in which I showed that all of the visual media are inferior to print in conveying most types of useful information and knowledge. The only superiority of the visual media was in showing surfaces—the looks of things. Slides of paintings and sculptures are necessary in a course in art history. Even then, more can be "seen" by the literate than the semiliterate. This went against the grain of what students generally believed, or "felt," to use their word. Only by presenting them with difficulties could I hope to disabuse them of their "feelings."

A prevalent feeling was that all media are equal, that what a child fails to learn from print can be learned from another medium. This notion had been picked up while attending public school as well as in the School of Education. Most of the widely used reading materials were largely pictures. It was said that they helped teach reading, that television children related better to pictures. In countering such notions I used the services of a Chinese graduate student from Taiwan. Having traced on the blackboard before class a typical picture used in materials to teach reading, I asked her to write a Chinese sentence next to it that could be said to go with it. The only sentence I forbade her to write was the all-too-familiar "The cat is sitting on the mat." The result was the following:

貓
的
眼
睛
張
著

I told the class: "Pictures are commonly said to clue the sentences next to them. That's the rationale given. But since we can't read Chinese, we in this instance are like the young child who can't read English. I ask you, does the picture clue this Chinese sentence? If so, what is it?"

I waited for responses. I hoped that someone would object that "The cat is sitting on the mat" is what most children give for this picture, that in practice in the classroom the picture "works" regardless of what I was trying to show. Responding to students' objections is more effective than just lecturing. Taking student objections into account while explaining fully also tells students that the instructor permits disagreement. I wanted disagreement as a way of getting their resistance out in the open where I could deal with it.

I was ready to show why pictures appear to work in the classroom. They are arranged in obvious patterns. The human mind excels at recognizing patterns. The young child can "read" the pictures by the pattern, as is obvious from the following drawings and sentences found in a typical reading primer, which I was ready to show to my class.

The lion is holding a letter.

The lion is holding a leaf.

The lion is holding a ladder.

Once the teacher or another child says aloud, "The lion is holding . . .", what any child naturally does is note the objects held in the pictures. But that is not the same as reading written language and does not lead, necessarily, to learning to read. Even single pictures by themselves usually follow the same pattern as in the foregoing series—a dominant object doing something to a lesser object, the lion and the cat being animate and dominant. Recognizing the pattern, the young child can usually give what the reading materials call for.

No student in the class raised an objection to my use of the cat-on-the-mat picture with the Chinese sentence, so I was forced to lecture. Before doing that, I asked for sentences that could be said to go with the picture. The very vagueness of "go with the picture"—there is no other way to say it—indicates how unrelated are words and visuals.

One student reluctantly offered: "The cat is waiting for its dinner." After a period of silence, another volunteered: "The cat is watching for a mouse." Following another pause, "It is a fat cat." Half a dozen sentences were slow in coming, and to each one the student from Taiwan indicated that that was not the Chinese sentence she had written. It was: "The cat's eyes are open."

Seldom did I see the smile of recognition that sometimes lights up the faces of learners, although I did succeed with some students. My media colleague, Patrick Sullivan, reported that one told him: "It finally dawned on me what Reg is trying to do. He's trying to get us to think."

I offered the media theory course every other semester. Not knowing if a Chinese student would be enrolled in it again, I took the precaution of asking the young woman from Taiwan to write her sentence next to the cat-on-the-mat picture and I used it every year thereafter. I also composed fifty-seven possible English sentences for it, to show how grossly ambiguous are pictures; in the language of information theory, how utterly they fail to reduce uncertainty about the words placed next to them. The only unambiguous use of pictures are those of single objects that are labeled, as in the case of a line drawing of a generic book with the word "book" next to it.

I also showed my classes examples of the absurd use of

pictures in instructional materials other than those for reading. One was a whole geometry textbook, put out by a well-known textbook publisher, foisted on my youngest daughter in the ninth grade in the Amherst junior high school. In it, the following drawing was at the head of the lesson entitled: "Theorems about Right Angles."[2]

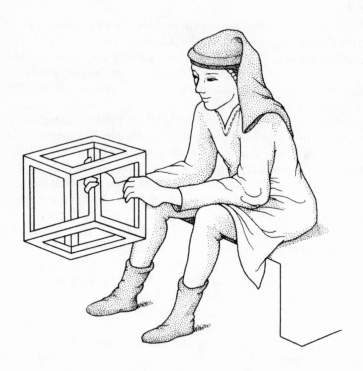

Anomalies fascinated those in my media theory course, graduate students all. One of their favorites was "The sound of one hand clapping." The drawing of the cubelike figure above attracted because it is impossible. The artist Escher drew it on paper but what he drew cannot be constructed in the physical world. Anomalies hardly belong in a textbook on precise, logical geometry. They confuse, lead the minds of ninth graders in all directions at once, or in none at all. They increase uncertainty instead of reducing it.

The text that followed the above figure did not make clear that it was impossible. To the contrary, confusion was compounded by showing another such figure, this one a doctored photograph. It had been taken of a wooden crate, then doctored to show the slats farthest from the camera passing in front of the slats nearest to the camera. The text told the student to assume that the photograph had *not* been doctored and to explain "how such a crate could be built."[3] The text about it ended there, without clarification. Even if the student looked for enlightenment in the answers section at the back of the textbook, he or she could find no reference to this impossible photograph. The student remained mystified about what was expected unless sufficiently self-confident in geometry to dismiss the textbook as absurd, something the administrators who selected and the teachers who used it were incapable of doing or unwilling to do.

Even more mindless, the lesson's theorems about right angles were stated imprecisely. Omitted were qualifying words necessary to limit the theorems. The statements of them relied, instead, on other drawings. Only teachers grossly deficient in geometry *and language* could possibly use such a textbook.

How many other schools systems were using it I had no way of knowing. But no publisher puts out a textbook expecting to sell it to only a few. Why it was published was apparent to me. All of its confusing drawings, photographs, pictorial advertisements, comic strips, and cartoons, which fought the very idea of geometry, were the result of "visual literacy," "today's students learn better from pictures," and all of the other expressions of this false notion that millions of teacher trainers, teachers, and school administrators believed.

I used the impossible cubelike Escher drawing only once in my media theory course and dropped it in subsequent years. My students, like the Amherst teachers who used the textbook, did not know enough geometry and language to follow my logic and see it as a gross misuse of pictures.

It was much easier to demonstrate how uninstructive and confusing were the visuals in educational films and television. Before showing students examples videotaped from broadcasts on public television *during school hours for schools,* I would remind them that in these media (though not in physical reality), what is seen dominates what is heard, and often changes it. The visuals in them, therefore, must be crystal clear. My students readily agreed with my reminder because it seemingly confirmed their notion that visuals are more powerful than language. I then played a sample with the sound on the video monitor turned off, and asked what specific instruction was being attempted. To their surprise, none of their guesses were ever correct. When I replayed the same tapes with the sound on, they had to accept that the visuals did not work. Moreover, only a few who had taken my course in planning film and television on storyboards could suggest the techniques that would make the visuals clear, although all of them saw the techniques daily on television.

Among the many false notions perpetrated by educationists and broadcasted in schools by the teachers trained by them, is that the television generation learns more readily from pictures. To the contrary, *raw visual data is the hardest kind of data from which to learn.* It took painters twenty thousand years to learn perspective. That is the length of time humans were drawing pictures before perspective was "discovered" by the artists of the Renaissance, although the laws of optics guarantee that all humans and lower animals were seeing the world in perspective throughout evolutionary time. The abstractions of language and mathematics are the prime means of acquiring knowledge, not the apparentness of pictures. Educationists' unfounded rhetoric about things visual had taught students everywhere less than nothing about pictures. Worse, it had undermined the primacy of language.

My students were conscious of being the first generation raised from infancy with television. More than one told me "We're the first nonprint generation." I was even told "I don't trust words. They lie but pictures don't." They felt television and its video offshoots to be their medium. They might have lectured me about television had they not known that I worked in it. Their attitude, nevertheless, was not due just to the historical accident of having been born when TV sets became ubiquitous. It had been inculcated by their schools and teachers. Their teachers had told them that they were the first TV generation, that visuals were their "natural language," that their literacy was "visual literacy." It was in schools that they heard the disparaging term "nonprint"; in which there were media and resource centers rather than libraries. Some of their teachers had required reports on films instead of the books on which they were loosely based. Some had their students make what they called films and slide shows in lieu of writing papers.

Many teachers and librarians resisted the efforts to undermine literacy, of course. But schools had ways of attacking their resistance. The most common was to disparage them as old-fashioned and traditional. In at least one school system in the Amherst area, part of the annual evaluation of teachers was whether or not they used media in their class-rooms, judged by whether or not they checked out media equipment.

I had observed firsthand some of what went on in schools. In my early years as a professor, I was curious to see the use of media in them, particularly the software they used. To find out, I concocted a course to give in an elementary school. "Concocted" has the right deprecatory tone. At the time, I knew little more about what I was doing than my colleagues. The course was not really a course but a module. It met once a week for five weeks and I called it Evaluating School Media Software, hardly real-izing then that what criteria students possessed was sure to be entirely wrong. I met my module of twenty-five undergraduates in the Amherst Fort River elementary school at the end of its school day, when the children and most of the teachers were gone. We met in the Resource Center that was surrounded by "quads" instead of classrooms. The school was brand-new and conformed in construction to the latest of the never-ending series of fads spawned by the notions of progressive education of the 1920s, the "open classroom." The quads were open spaces to hold the equivalent of two or more classes. I got staff members to show me and my students how they used media in that school.

One was its media specialist, Gary Whitman. First he showed his TV studio equipment, letting some of the students use the cameras. He also demonstrated the school's capacity for recording educational programs off the air and piping them to video monitors in the quads. A piece of equipment or system that he seemed especially proud of was a network of wires or antennas imbedded out of sight in the ceiling, whereby instructions could be broadcast to a child below wearing a receiving headset covering both ears. The instruction recorded on a cassette by a teacher told the child what to do at work stations. It seems not to have occurred to anyone who contributed to the decisions governing the construction of the school, that this narrow, closed system contradicted the "openness" of the open classroom. But it did not matter. Whitman said that the system had not been used because teachers had no time to plan the work stations and make the recordings to tell children what to do at them. Though spared subjection to this particular equipment, I am sure the pupils were not spared its spirit—treating them as objects of behavioral objectives.

Unlike elementary schools built in earlier decades, the Fort River school did not have to convert a library into a resource center. It opened with one designed as such. It had its own media equipment of teaching machines at which pupils punched buttons and word cards popped up. Rows and rows of carrels had electrical outlets in each to plug in filmstrip viewers, audio-cassette players, and movie projectors. Shelves were spacious with many nonprint materials integrated among the books.

Nonprint materials were purchased for the Amherst elementary schools by a special administrative staff housed in the old, former elementary school on East Street. Here the director of instructional support services, Billie Howes, explained her operation to me and the students in my module. During her presentation she made snide remarks about teachers who thought that the only way for children to learn was from books. She demonstrated a new filmstrip being considered for purchase from a commercial supplier. Part of the filmstrip package was an audio cassette, and each time a "ping" was heard in its sound track Billie Howes advanced the picture on the viewer manually. At one point she turned to us and said very deliberately: "For students, turning the knob on the viewer is *involving*." Had I not been her guest I might have blurted out: "That's damning with faint justification."

The remaining three meetings of my module were spent in the Fort River school resource center, examining nonprint software, most of which was horrendously uninstructive and aesthetically gross. For each piece of software examined, I had students write a description and an evaluation. None was as succinct and to the point as the one I got from my daughter Diane, then thirteen, when I asked her if she had ever used any nonprint materials in the junior high school. "I looked at a math filmstrip once," she replied. "But it was the same as in a book and a book is easier to use." Had school administrators and teachers the common sense of a thirteen-year-old, tens of billions of dollars wasted on media in the United States could have been better spent.

Each time I faced my media theory graduate students, I was painfully aware of how they had acquired their notions. Most, it was true, had attended public school systems not nearly as affluent in media equipment as the Amherst schools. Nevertheless, they had been exposed to all the same language about it. Contrary to their notions, language acts so powerfully in the brain that nonexistent things can be given names and people insufficiently literate to recognize a nominalistic fallacy when they hear or see one treat the name as if it stood for something real. The chief business of schools of education is naming things that do not exist and perpetuating them in every conceivable manner, including publishing such travesties of thought as "Illiterates with Doctorates."

In order to disabuse students of their false notions, I presented my media theory students with difficulties. The greatest difficulty for them was trying to write the three short papers I required a term of two thousand words each, or five typewritten pages. The books of the course were *Comprehension and Learning* by Frank Smith, and portions of *Eye and Brain* by R. L. Gregory, and *Media and Symbols* edited by David R. Olson. They were lucidly written books that threw light on learning and media. The papers I required had to deal with ideas in them and/or class demonstrations. But over a six-year period more than half the papers turned in contained no ideas whatsoever. The majority of papers read like editorials, a string of the accepted opinions of the field, regurgitated unexamined. I wrote on such papers, "You could have written this without taking the course," and added that I could not accept the paper. With each successive year, feeling more embarrassed at having to do it, I elaborated at greater length that I required papers to be on the work of the course. I gave students, graduate students all, written instructions and included a dozen sample topics for papers, each precisely worded to show that it was on some portion of the work of the course. I permitted students to choose their own topics but warned them to reread my instructions before beginning their papers because I would not accept any that were not on the work of the course. I told them that they could come to my office and talk about a topic beforehand to make sure it would be acceptable but none ever did. Nor did any write on any of the sample topics I gave them. Despite reiterating the requirement time and again, to the very last I continued to get papers without a single idea that had been presented, read about, and discussed in the course.

One of the last was that of a Puerto Rican doctoral candidate who had taught in the New York City school system. She nevertheless insisted that her paper was on the course work, although she could not point, as I urged her to do, to a single relevant sentence in it. She had taught in a decentralized district in the Bronx, where ethnic politics has everything to do with the appointment of teachers and administrators. As she disputed with me, her attitude was one of I-dare-you-to-turn-down-the-paper-of-a-minority-student. Well aware of the ethnic politics of the school, she was unafraid that anything I could do would prevent her from getting an Ed.D. degree.

My standards for writing were low. They had to be. I even accepted papers that quoted a sentence or two from a text, although what came before and after the quote were unconnected to it. It was there, I knew, to point to as being on the work of the course. But this had become my minimum requirement. So unable were students to handle ideas in writing that it was impossible that they could learn to do so in my course. They were even incapable of paraphrasing portions of texts. I nevertheless wrote copious comments on their papers, often rewriting sentences and saying that my rewrites were what I *thought* they were trying to say, hoping they would think about what made them different and spark a concern for language. When any portion of a paper was adequate, I also made a point of praising it.

The chief exceptions to excruciatingly poor papers were those of the foreign students—from the West Indies, Canada, Ireland, Taiwan, and mainland China, but excluding those from Indonesia and Guyana. Each year, I had two or three foreign students in my courses. Most had been sent to the school by their governments or came on scholarship money. Some were undoubtedly exceptionally good teachers or students in their own countries. For me to compare my domestic students unfavorably with them was unfair. Yet, one student from mainland China wrote adequate papers even though she could not speak or understand spoken English. In my TV Workshop, I could allow her only to observe, not participate. But in my media theory course this nonspeaker of English read and wrote better than most of my domestic students. She was able to deal with the ideas of the course, probably because she was literate in her native language. Despite mistakes in idiomatic English, her meaning was clear. She connected ideas logically, as written language demands, to show something of what she had learned.

Of the foreign students, the one from Taiwan who wrote the Chinese sentence for me; Linda Best from Trinity College, Dublin; Ashley Hibbert from the West Indies; and Joan Schell from Western Canada were so superior to the domestic students that I was embarrassed that they had come so far to be in such inferior company. The low quality was recognized by them and other foreign students, not only in my media theory course but in the other courses in the school. Some adopted a "when in Rome . . ." attitude. Conscientious in everything they did at first, they soon became less so. Their first papers were the best and their last, the least. I understood, of course, that being in the United States was vacation-like for them. Working to lower standards gave them more time to enjoy the country. The outstanding exception was the teacher from mainland China, possibly because of her inadequate understanding of spoken English. She was conscientious throughout and it showed in the progressive improvement of her papers.

Over the years, only a tiny minority of the domestic students had sufficient "mind" to make up anew. One of the exceptional few was a librarian of a small school system in the area who, at the end of my media theory course said, with a touch of awe in her voice, "I didn't realize that language is so important." She was in her forties, however. She had started school when teachers were more literate and the importance of language was taken for granted. She had witnessed the change from libraries to resource centers and may have taken my course to learn the reasons for the change, only to have me confirm that language in all its forms, of necessity, is the prime tool of instruction. Most gratifying to me were the several students who, coming to the school to study media, either changed to studying language or decided not to work for a doctorate at all.

Perhaps my most subversive effort was a course I offered for undergraduates to which I gave the title, Media Teaching Tools. I knew what would happen. Students would sign up for it expecting a course in equipment operation. They might not if they read the course description carefully, but I knew that few students ever did that. In effect, I would lure them into taking the course in order to demolish their false notions. I conceived it as an undergraduate version of my media theory course, with less reading, no papers to write, but a final examination to pass. I was determined that they would not go into the classroom as teachers innocent of ideas that contradicted the notions of the field.

Unlike most School of Education courses that met once a week in the late afternoons so that local school personnel could also enroll in them, my Media Teaching Tools course met three times a week in the mornings. A dozen undergraduates enrolled and on the first day I assigned the first chapter in Gregory's *Eye and Brain*. This surprised them but none protested until the next meeting when I started a discussion of the ideas in it. The typical protest was an outraged: "But this is *biology*!" Years of exposure to teachers talking and practicing "relevance" had never developed ability to relate anything to anything else. They should have been able to glean just from the first part of the second paragraph in the book that it *might* shed light on the media of photography and television:

> The eye is often described as like a camera, but it is the quite uncamera-like features of perception which are most

interesting. How is information from the eyes coded into neural terms, into the language of the brain, and reconstituted in experience of surrounding objects? The task of the eye and brain is quite different from either a photographic or television camera converting objects merely into images. There is a temptation, which must be avoided, to say that the eyes produce pictures in the brain. A picture in the brain suggests the need of some kind of internal eye to see it—but this would need a further eye to see *its* picture . . . and so on in an endless regress of eyes and pictures. This is absurd.[4]

I patiently explained to students that they could not begin to use good judgment about media as teachers if they knew nothing of the workings of the eyes and brain. I assured them that the reading was indeed relevant to the course. I could see that I did not succeed in satisfying them. Two students subsequently dropped the course but I managed to hold on to the others through the first six class meetings, past the deadline for adding and dropping courses. This was the moment I waited for when I could expose with full force the course's intent.

During the seventh meeting of the class, I announced to my students that I sensed they were dissatisfied with the course. I then passed out blank sheets of paper and asked them to write down what they thought the course was about when they signed up for it. When they were finished, I immediately read aloud most of their statements. Each of them had said that they expected the course to be on media equipment. "Equipment teaches nothing," I said vehemently. Pulling the overhead projector out from its place in the corner of the front of the classroom, I said, "See this? This is a *machine*!" Raising my voice, I shouted, *"Machines teach nothing!"* And I gave it a swift, hard kick. Though allowing myself to be angry, I enjoyed the shock on their faces. It was a moment I hoped they would not forget. "In this course, you are going to learn that the chief media teaching tool is *language*! Language, too, is a medium and a powerful *technology*." I paused to let this sink in. In a lowered voice, I added, "You don't have to accept anything just because I say it is so. You can argue all you want but when you do, I insist on *rational* arguments based on some evidence, not just asserted opinions."

I could not have been so vehement if I thought for a moment

that these students were atypical. They were alike as peas in a pod to each other and other students throughout the school. All had the same false notions about media, inextricably tied to the depreciation and derogation of language in all its forms.

During the academic year 1975–76, the special education program wanted me to supervise the making of a slide/audio tape production about their program. They were impressed with the one I had done for the Massachusetts Hospital School in Canton, near Boston. They wanted one like it of their program and provided a graduate assistantship to get it done, which I split into two half assistantships, one for a photographer and one for a writer. I advertised the half assistantships in the school bulletin and other places. Many students applied for the photographer's but none for the writer's half-assistantship, although a full waiver of tuition went with each. With the stipend, each was worth about $3,000. Graduate students in education—future school administrators, state and federal officials and professors of education—are no more able to write than the former chancellor of the New York City public school system, Harvey Scribner. Unable to obtain a student from anywhere within the school to write a simple slide presentation, I had to rely on the recommendation of Professor Leheny in the English department.

The students in my Media Teaching Tools course could tell that I had no dislike of equipment per se. They saw me use the overhead projector and the videotape player and monitor. But I used them in a noneducationist way. They became invisible when I used them, as invisible as the blackboard on which there are words and numbers written. We attend not to blackboards but to the meanings on them. Educationists reverse this. They attend to blackboards.

My students did not forgive me for tricking them into addressing ideas that were contrary to their notions. When I mentioned in the office of the head of my division, Byrd Jones, how I had fooled the students into taking my course, he replied: "I know. They were all in here complaining." Jones was a tenured full professor, a graduate of Williams, and had a Ph.D. in economic history from Yale. The look on his face said that I had made a serious error, but he asked no questions of me and volunteered no information about what the students said to him or what his reply was to them. Although not trained as an educationist, he risked no more talk about anything fundamental than any who were.

My students were chiefly sophomores and consequently unsophisticated about how to get their way in the school. They could easily have gotten out of my course if they had known how. They were also white, chiefly of Irish extraction from the Boston area. Had they been black or Hispanic, they would have gotten out regardless of university regulations. During the rest of the term I gave them ample opportunity to disagree and argue against anything in the readings or presented in class, but none ever did.

Ten days before the final exam, I gave them a set of questions from which I would select those that would make up the exam. All of the questions required answers in essay form. Specifically and inherently, they had to contradict what the students believed when they signed up for the course. Several questions required articulating that *language* is the prime teaching tool. Whether any of the students had made up their minds anew during the course or would merely write what I wanted to hear, I had no way of knowing. I was certain, however, that in order for them to prepare appropriate answers to my questions they had to understand, to some degree, the readings, class demonstrations and discussions. I was at least making them address the work of the course as I had not succeeded in doing with most of my graduate students. When I went to the academic affairs office to pick up bluebooks for the examination, the administrative assistant there expressed surprise. My course was one of only two in the school, she told me, giving a final exam.

Grading the exam was a pleasant surprise. I found I was able to give two students grades of A. By this time, the school permitted professors to give letter grades if the intent to do so was announced at the beginning of the term, although most continued to grade pass/fail. One of the students whose examination I had given a grade of C, which became her grade for the course, came to my office afterwards to protest it. She told me that all in the class had studied for the exam together, and all knew the work equally, including her. "I know I know the work," she insisted. "I just can't express it." With this statement alone, she told me that she had missed one of the course's most important principles. For teachers, no useful distinction can be made between knowledge and its expression. How could she expect to convey knowledge to future students, even the knowledge of what she wanted them to do on a homework assignment, if she could not *express* it?

10

Third World Within

I had arrived at the School of Education of the University of Massachusetts in Amherst with a full head of hair, only slightly receded from where it had been in my youth. All of a sudden, in the middle of my first semester as a faculty member, it began coming out by the combful. I was soon also without eyebrows, eyelashes, and facial hair to shave. All my hair vanished within two weeks. The dermatologist I was referred to diagnosed my condition as *alopecia universalis.* "We don't know what causes it," he said, "and there is no treatment for it. The hair follicles in the skin are not dead. They are alive and in some cases the hair grows back. It's believed to be emotional in origin."

I had sensed the cause was emotional and something to do with my new circumstances. I realized that I would have kept my hair had I remained on Madison Avenue. But this insight was too shallow and general to help. It had not stopped my hair from falling out; nor did it lead to it growing back. Not until seven years later, a year after I served on Bill Cosby's dissertation committee and about the time that I plotted my Media Teaching Tools course to fool the students who would enroll in it, did I identify the specific emotional cause. I at last admitted to myself that I had recognized from the very beginning that the school, in its entirety, was unredeemed mindlessness. I had repressed that knowledge in order to be able to continue as a faculty member. In a word, I had repressed my *intellect.* Repressed knowledge strongly felt seeks expression as surely as the steam in a covered pot of boiling water seeks release. My *alopecia universalis* was the physical manifestation of it, what Freud called "the return of the repressed." It made me look to the world what I was trying to deny to myself. It made me appear the very stereotype of the intellectual, an egghead.

Being six feet two inches tall, my return-of-the-repressed was conspicuous. My naked head stood out. Strangers sometimes stared at me, especially young children. One day as I got out of my car to fill up at the gas station next to the post office in the middle of Amherst, a college student working there pumping gas, stared at me and asked:

"Are you a professor?"

"Yes."

"You *look* like a professor," he said.

"Thank you," I replied.

"You take that as a compliment!" he exclaimed.

"Did you mean it as *other* than a compliment?" I retorted.

His face flushed with embarrassment and he muttered a denial.

The incident showed how I looked to the world. My retort reflected a certain pride that, despite concomitant feelings of shame, did not permit anyone to put me down because of my changed appearance.

Repression of intellect can only result in naiveté. I was profoundly naive as a faculty member during my first four years, notwithstanding occasional bouts of mental nausea. They occurred only when I was caught offguard by something more obviously mindless than usual. The degree of my naiveté was the effort I put into the book length manuscript I wrote about Harvey Scribner showing him in a favorable light as the chancellor of the New York City school system. I allowed no doubts about him to break into consciousness even when his know-nothing views pained me personally. When the admissions tests for the special high schools became an ethnic issue and the New York state legislature passed a bill specifically to prevent Scribner from changing them, I mentioned to him that I had graduated from Stuyvesant. Perhaps my mention was a return-of-the-repressed dig at him. Scribner took it as a dig. He answered petulantly, "Were you one of those up there in Albany lobbying for that bill?"

Most circumstances favored and encouraged my naiveté. Scribner had told me that while the Board of Education was considering him for the chancellorship, each of its five members had received a copy of my *Triumph in a White Suburb* and had been influenced by it. So associated was Scribner with my book that on the day the Board of Education announced its selection of him, NBC News sent a reporter and camera crew to my office on Madison Avenue and interviewed me about him. A portion of the interview was shown on the six o'clock news that evening, together with a full screen closeup of my book. I wanted to believe that it had helped the board select a good chancellor, not one who was a disaster.

In the School of Education, I kept hearing its key members, from the dean down, say that Scribner was doing the right things in New York, particularly his stand with the NAACP in its suit against the Board of Examiners. I also kept hearing Scribner applauded by members of two other widely separated education departments. One was a full professor in the Graduate School of Education of Rutgers in New Brunswick, New Jersey, Maurie Hillson. The other was full professor of education at Lehman College in the Bronx, Archie Lacey. Maurie Hillson was white and Jewish, and Archie Lacy was black. Both lived in Teaneck, were named in my book about it, and I often stayed overnight with one or the other on my trips to 110 Livingston Street to collect information. Scribner was a hero to both of them.

A key member of Scribner's personal staff was a recent Ed.D. graduate of the school, Jack Woodbury. It was he who told me that he had come to consider Scribner a political genius. Woodbury's name was frequently mentioned in the school as its highest paid recent graduate. He had been a member of the school's Urban Education Center and continued to keep in close touch with it.

Urban Education was one of the school's largest centers and had much money in federal grants. Of its faculty at the time, three were black and one was white. Because of my book's prointegration stand and my association with Scribner, they looked on me as a friend of blacks and invited me to their center's monthly meetings, held in a hospitality suite of the Howard Johnson motel on Route 9. The meetings were chiefly social occasions, with the liquor flowing freely and music and dancing. The center's federal funds enabled it to support a large number of graduate students, about half of them black, on assistantships. They, too, knew about me, my book, and my connection with the head of the nation's largest school system. Everybody made me feel a part of the school's "in" group, a flattering circumstance conducive to naiveté.

The school's prime commitment was to "combat racism" and, according to Dean Allen and others, the commitment was best exemplified by the Urban Education Center and its federally funded Careers Opportunity Program. Known colloquially as "cop," its funds were to enable teacher aides in inner city schools to earn bachelor degrees so that they, the disadvantaged, could become teachers. The center ran COP programs in three cities— Worcester and Springfield in Massachusetts, and Brooklyn in New York. Brooklyn was the largest COP program, and the most dramatic. To teach the courses, the program flew instructors there from Amherst once a week. Because the director of the program thought he might find the funds to make a film about the program, he arranged for me to make the trip so that I could begin to plan it.

Eleven of us that day went by campus bus to La Fleur Airport in Northampton, where two light propeller planes were waiting. The larger held eight passengers, the smaller three. I climbed in the smaller because I loved the sensation of flying and the smaller the plane the greater the sensation. (A lifelong regret was that I could not become a pilot in World War II because I wore glasses.) Approaching LaGuardia Airport was exhilarating. The view from inside the tiny plane was unobstructed in all directions. Clearly visible were the commercial jets taking off and those in the sky in holding patterns waiting for their turns to land. On the ground, two limousines carried us from Queens to the Bedford-Stuyvesant section of Brooklyn where block after block of abandoned buildings and empty lots of rubble and decay made it appear a war-torn area. We arrived at the intermediate school just as it was letting out, the entire trip from the campus having taken two hours. Teacher aides assembled for their classes, most of them from other schools in the area. Nearly all were black.

Recognizing that the cost of transporting faculty by planes and limousines had to be high, I asked why Brooklyn COP was not run by one of the many local city colleges that had education departments. I was told it was because of the animosity blacks felt toward Jews since the recent teachers' strikes over the issue of community control in Ocean Hill–Brownsville. Because the percent of Jewish professors was high in the local colleges, the black teacher aides preferred the U. Mass School of Education. Published reports, on the other hand, gave "the lowest bid" as the official reason why the federal government awarded the Brooklyn COP program to U. Mass.[1]

Another question I had was: How could disadvantaged people in their thirties and forties learn much in courses that met only once a week for two and a half hours, for which the instructors arrived just before classes, departed again immediately afterwards, and remained 160 miles away between classes? I refrained from asking for fear of appearing naive, and believing the answer would come as I learned more about the program.

I regarded my acceptance in the Urban Education Center as especially fortunate because my relationship with Nat Rutstein, responsible for bringing me to the School, had deteriorated. Soon after we arrived, he took offense at a column that appeared about me in *The Record,* northern New Jersey's principal newspaper. It had given much space to me and my book when published, my subsequent speaking engagements, and my Urban League Award "for sustained and dedicated leadership in behalf of Negroes and similarly disadvantaged citizens of Bergen County." Because I was newsworthy in the county, Mark Stuart wrote a column on my leaving Madison Avenue for academe. But during Stuart's interview for the column I made the mistake of having Nat Rustein with me. It turned out that he expected the column to be chiefly about him because he was the Media Program Director. But the column was chiefly about me and he was so angry that he wrote a nasty letter to the Managing Editor of *The Record* accusing Stuart of falsely attributing some of his statements to me. Mark Stuart had telephoned to warn me of Rutstein's reaction. "I hope I haven't done you any harm," said Stuart.

Not knowing if I could remain in the media program, I thought it prudent to establish one foot in the Urban Education Center. I arranged for my second course to be under its auspices. I received no more direction and help than with my first course.

What and how to teach were left to me. Since community control was the latest panacea for the ills of inner-city schools at the time and I was experienced in investigating and writing about the community of Teaneck, I offered a graduate course on doing research in communities and writing the findings in reports. Fourteen students attended its first meeting, two white and the rest black. But at the class's second meeting, I was shocked to find that all except the two white students had dropped the course. When I looked into the reason, I was told that they had been put off by my expectations of writing. "You have to keep in mind," I was told, "that they are *nontraditional* students." I did not offer that course again.

The next I gave under the aegis of the Urban Ed Center was one I entitled: Current Educational Leadership. The content of it was the information I had accumulated and was continuing to collect at 110 Livingston Street. I tried to give students a picture of the workings of the apex of the huge school system, including sharing documents I obtained from Scribner's staff— Xerox copies of Scribner's speeches, items voted on by the Board of Education in public meetings, Judge Mansfield's written decision in the NAACP lawsuit, and even confidential memoranda and letters. Although the students enrolled had never seen such documents before, as I had not, I sensed that few if any read these handouts. They never asked for clarification or background information, and never volunteered comments on them, let alone analysis. In providing my information, I was often interrupted before I could give sufficient detail to make it understandable. A graduate student who would soon become a superintendent of schools stopped me in the middle of one explanation. "Hold on," he said. "You're doing all the talking, acting like instructors know everything. You're not giving us a chance to contribute." These were students accustomed to courses dealing with issues rather than knowledge. Typically, the professor presents an issue and then has the class split up into groups of three or four to discuss it. The professor sits apart or wanders around the room, pausing here and there to overhear parts of discussions. Later, a student in each group tells the others the gist of the group's talk. My course was predicated on giving students information about the administration of the nation's largest school system. How could they contribute without learning something about it first?

When I broached the subject of written papers to the class, a black student instantly rejected this form of contribution. "Papers are out!" she declared emphatically, and was echoed by the other students, black and white. They were aware that course work had been downgraded by the dean. Dwight Allen had said publicly that the impromptu rap sessions which took place in the halls were more important than what went on in the classrooms. Written papers, to my students, belonged to the discredited, racist past. They proposed, instead, oral presentations accompanied by slides. I was too numb to resist, although the content of the course—the operations of 110 Livingston Street—could not possibly be pictured on slides. Their presentations consisted of the educationist notions with which they had been indoctrinated, although I was too unsure of myself to see it and tell them so. I had to fake interest and pretend to take their presentations seriously.

With numbness of mind, I floundered from one course to another during my first three or four years. I had to accept what was going on around me whether or not I understood it. Any uneasiness that showed was attributed to my being new to "education." Some relief came in my fourth year. Nat Rutstein resigned from the faculty at the expiration of his three-year appointment, and I went back to being wholly in the media program where my intellect was less inhibited. Through my fourth to seventh year my numbness of mind slowly but surely thawed.

With the thaw, there emerged from the school's ambience patterns of treatment of blacks and black attitudes toward learning, patterns that aroused serious concern about their consequences. When someone like Mary came along, described in Chapter 1 as incapable of learning the simplest things in the TV studio, I recognized the damage to other blacks, and whites, were she to obtain a degree. With it, she might get a position of consequence in a school, community college, government agency, or federal, state, or city program of some kind. But in trying to adhere to the barest common sense standards, I increasingly risked being accused of racism.

Mary accused me of just that to the university ombudsman. The ombudsman at the time, Robert Wellman, passed on the accusation to Norma Jean Anderson, the associate dean for student affairs, who told Wellman that there was nothing to the accusation. Whether Mary made the charge because I had given her an incomplete in a course, or kept her out of the doctoral program, I understood why she felt justified in calling me racist. The school, and by extension the university, in admitting her to the special graduate program, had in effect told her that she was a qualified student. In ignoring her lowest possible GRE score in math and her nearly lowest possible GRE score in verbal, the school had said to Mary that those scores did not matter, as indeed they did not. Mary had obtained a teaching assistantship in the University Communication Skills Center. And she had been given grades of A in some of her education courses. From Mary's point of view, my being an impediment to her must be due to racism.

Other Marys, male and female, some of them Puerto Rican, were in the school. They were probably indistinguishable from other students in most courses because they were never required to do anything to any standards. My media courses, on the other hand, required some performance. Ironically, I often had the poorest students, whites as well as minorities, tell me in so many words that they were poor in anything academic and consequently wanted careers in media. But their academic deficiencies were glaring even in what I considered my Mickey Mouse Educational TV Workshop. Inability to learn the audio controls was the immediate tip-off. In addition to the mechanics of what knobs to twist and switches to flip that controlled various microphones, the tape deck, and videotape sound, all audio changes had to be planned in advance and held in mind. This, the academically impoverished lacked the mind to do. A term production was required of each student's own devising, initially in script form. Usually, at least half the students planned an all-visual production which they claimed needed no script.

Such a claim was made by a black undergraduate whom we will call Vaughn, not his real name. His production was to be a demonstration of how to defend oneself against attack by a mugger. It had nothing to do with education, but were I to make that a requirement, 90 percent of the students would be unable to devise a production. I told Vaughn that his viewers would not see what he was trying to show unless he also told them what to notice; therefore a script was necessary. He appeared not to understand or believe me so I asked rhetorically,

"Why do professional athletic teams have coaches? You've seen the NBA basketball coaches on television. Aren't they always *telling* players what to do? If it were easy to *see* the right thing to do, any player could just watch the best player on his or the opposing team, or a videotape of him, and do what he does. But it doesn't work that way. It is *not* obvious to the eye what the best player does so well, let alone a team. Coaches therefore coach mainly by *telling*."

A week later, still without a script, Vaughn said he could not find the right words. I urged him to act out his demonstration while saying his actions aloud. "For instance," I said, getting up from my desk to act out my words, "if it's necessary for the would-be victim to put his weight on his left foot while his left hand grabs the right wrist of the attacker, say so out loud as you do it, then write it down."

Vaughn was a well-mannered, attractive young man whom I took to be interested in learning. When he still did not write a script, and also because he expressed himself poorly in speaking, I ventured to suggest:

"Vaughn, you have a language problem. You should be taking courses in which you have to read and write."

"I'm taking creative writing now," he said as if in agreement.

"In the English department?"

"In the Black Studies department," he replied.

Another time, I said to him: "My eldest daughter is majoring in English, which I told her is the best preparation for life and any profession she might enter. If I gave different advice to my students than to my daughter, wouldn't I be a racist?" Vaughn did not answer so I continued: "I believe you have a language problem and should be taking courses in the English department."

More than a year later, Vaughn came to my office to get permission to take my graduate media theory course. I warned him that it required considerable reading and the writing of three papers during the term. He had followed my advice and taken English courses, he said, and so I gave him permission. Not until near the end of the course, months late, did I get his first paper. It consisted entirely of paragraphs copied verbatim from two of the texts.

Only one thing about Vaughn was certain. I had passed him

in my TV Workshop though he wrote no script for his "mugger" production. A professor's *actions*, like anyone's else's, speak louder than words. Vaughn could assume that I would also pass him in media theory though he still could not write. But by this time I was not passing anyone who did not do the work of the course. I informed Vaughn that turning in someone else's writing as his own was called plagiarism, rejected his paper, and gave him an incomplete that he would not make up. He would get no credit for the course even if all trace of it was removed from his records, including the grade of F that his incomplete would automatically become, as happened in the case of Mary, who, nevertheless, graduated with an M.Ed. degree.

The assiduousness with which grossly unprepared students pursued degrees without pursuing learning was puzzling. It seemed that degrees were a right because opportunities to acquire them had been denied in the past. I got an inkling of this at the time I was recommended for appointment to associate professor. On the personnel committee making the recommendation was a black graduate student who wanted to speak to me in the privacy of his office. (He was also the administrator for one of the COP programs.) He did not oppose my appointment, just wanted to get something off his chest. *"We,"* he said, "have been kept from getting credentials for so long that it blows my mind that someone can become a professor without a doctorate."

Equally puzzling were the nationally known blacks who wanted Ed.D. degrees. How Bill Cosby got his is described in Chapter 1. Roberta Flack, the famous rhythm and blues singer, and Jesse Jackson, head of an antipoverty program in Chicago at the time, were also doctoral candidates in the school. I saw neither of them on campus, knew they were students only from hearsay. The *Hampshire Gazette* newspaper reported in 1975 that Jesse Jackson's records showed that he had enrolled in four courses, and Roberta Flack's record had one entry for "special problems."[2] Lesser black luminaries were also Ed.D. candidates. From the Children's Television Workshop came Loretta Long who played Susan on *Sesame Street,* and Lutrelle Horne, one of *Sesame Street's* producers. Both Long and Horne received Ed.D. degrees in 1973. The jazz pianist Billy Taylor got an Ed.D. degree in 1975. Bill Cosby's friend Al Freeman, the detective on *One Life to Live,* is mentioned in Chapter Two as an enrolled student.

Perhaps these famous and near-famous blacks, like all people in show business, ever fearful their careers might end, sought education credentials as another career to fall back on. But whites in show business, just as fearful, did not enroll in the school. They were not recruited by it, to be sure. Of all blacks who had bachelor degrees in 1976, one-quarter had them in education; of all with doctorates, 56 percent had them in education.

The importance of credentials in education was impressed on me in my first chairmanship of a dissertation committee. I was asked to chair that of Moshe Giladi from the Kibbutz Mizra in Israel. He was head of teacher training for the kibbutzim at the time. Part of kibbutzim ideology was not giving or acquiring formal credentials, and the ideology covered its teachers and teacher trainers. Moshe had deliberately not taken degrees for which he had done degree work. In the early 1970s, however, the training of teachers for the kibbutzim was going to be absorbed by the University of Haifa. For Moshe to have an equal standing with its professors he now needed a doctorate, and he came from Israel for a year to acquire one. He wrote his dissertation on kibbutz education, about which I knew no more than anyone else in the school. I was asked to be his chairman because I was available. Although a fluent speaker and reader of English, Moshe was not fluent in writing it. That was my principal contribution to his Ed.D. degree, which he received in 1973. Working with him was an enjoyable experience because of what he taught me.

Not all students came to the school merely for degrees. Some came to learn and asked for no special consideration. Included were a few blacks of superior education, and/or experience. Ashley Hibbert from Jamaica, mentioned in Chapter 1, was one of them. He had studied in England, had a master's degree, and his government had sent him to acquire another in media. When I learned that his GRE scores in mathematics approached perfection, 780 out of a possible 800, my impulse was to alert Norma Jean Anderson or another black administrator. Everyone in the school was always talking about making the most of human resources. Ashley was, in their terms, an exceptional black role model in math. But I curbed my impulse. The black administrators, like their white counterparts, were not the least interested in subject matter. Besides, I knew no love was lost between American and West Indian blacks.

Another superior student was Ben Holt. He had been a high school English teacher for decades. In his forties at the time, he became a doctoral candidate in the Urban Education Center straight from Forest Hills High School, one of the few in New York City where achievement remained high. Most of its students were from middle-class Jewish homes in the area and bound for the better four-year colleges. Ben had not taken any courses with me. We happened to become acquainted only because he was a friend of a friend.

One day during his second year, Ben unexpectedly showed up in my office looking frustrated and anxious. He asked me to take over the chairmanship of his dissertation committee. Byrd Jones was his current chairman and Ben said of him: "He's treating me like a nigger. He makes me drive him over to Whitmore [the administration building at the other end of the campus] and wait for him while he attends meetings, as if I were his black chauffeur." Ben also complained that he had been giving Jones chapters of his dissertation to read and had been waiting for months for his guidance on them. Ben was getting frantic because time was running out on his leave of absence from the New York City public school system.

Ben and his wife Ermine had consulted a lawyer to see if he had grounds to bring suit against Jones. The lawyer told them that Ben had no grounds for Jones' not responding to his dissertation chapters. Why Ben asked me rather than another faculty member to be his chairman, I did not know. I recognized that I would probably make an enemy out of a supporter, if I agreed. I was also warned, "Don't mess with Byrd." Although politically inexpedient, I became Ben's chairman.

Byrd Jones, however, had enemies who took his mind off me. Within a year, a faculty member whom Byrd Jones had personally recuited, Robert Suzuki, blew the whistle on the Urban Education Center's fiscal practices[3] which resulted, in 1975, in a scandal of major proportions, leading to the resignation of Dwight Allen as dean. Until then, Jones had been powerful indeed, the sole white professor in the center. A graduate of

Williams with a Ph.D. from Yale in economic history, and a former professor at Cal Tech, Byrd Jones and Robert L. Woodbury, the associate dean, had virtually created the Urban Education Center together. Woodbury, like Jones, had a Ph.D. in history from Yale, awarded the year after Jones' in 1967. They had also been together on the faculty of Cal Tech, from which both had joined the school, and together they had home-grown the initial three black faculty members for the Urban Education Center.

First, there had been Atron Gentry. Before the fiscal scandal, Gentry was a full professor and had taken Woodbury's place as associate dean in charge of special projects. Gentry had known Jones and Woodbury in California and had a B.A. in education from California State College at Los Angeles where his average grade was C.[4] On arriving in the school in 1968, Gentry was made a full-time lecturer while he worked for a doctorate, enrolled in one formal course and took the remainder of his credits in independent study and dissertation preparation.[5] Woodbury was his dissertation chairman and Jones a member of the dissertation committee. He got his Ed.D. in 1970 and was then made an associate professor.

Although Gentry was a voluble talker, I understood little of what he said. It was also true that I seldom understood anything said in meetings of the teacher preparation programs committee. But I never had difficulty understanding the *informal* talk of any of its members as much as I did Gentry's. One of his phrases was "get caught." It was a constant in his speech although what he meant by "get caught" was seldom clear. In one of his rare lucid explanations, he had told me that the key to the Urban Education Center's operations was keeping control of its federal funds. He boasted that he had brought in an experienced "watchdog" to keep administrators from "stealing," from juggling funds from one program to another, and Gentry meant that he could "get caught" short until repaid from another fund.

The "watchdog" Gentry brought in was Cleo Abraham, who had worked in the city manager's office in New Haven, Connecticut. He, too, was hired as a lecturer fulltime while working for a doctorate.[6] He, too, had Robert Woodbury for dissertation committee chairman with Byrd Jones serving as a committee member. In fifteen months, by 1971, he also had an Ed.D.[7] and was made an assistant professor. It was "watchdog" Cleo Abraham who was tried in federal court and found guilty of misappropriating federal funds.

The third black faculty member in the center was Barbara Love, a most physically attractive young woman, with a B.A. from Arkansas State and an M.A. from the University of Arkansas. She did her dissertation on racism in education with Byrd Jones as her chairman, got her Ed.D. in 1972 and also became an assistant professor. Barbara Love would make a career of giving workshops on racism.

Byrd Jones was the Urban Education Center's senior faculty member and chief supporter of the three initial black faculty members. He wrote recommendations for their appointments, reappointments, promotions, and awards of tenure. They were dependent on and beholden to him.

One way in which a department or center builds a reputation is by placing its graduates in key positions elsewhere, which was why Jack Woodbury, the younger brother of Robert Woodbury, was frequently mentioned while he was on Scribner's personal staff. The usual route to a good reputation was to have graduates become professors in other schools of education, a route that Byrd Jones pursued. For a time he was irritated with me because the Rutgers School of Education, where my friend Maurie Hillson was a professor, failed to hire one of Jones' prize Ed.D. graduates, who subsequently joined the faculty of a black college in the South. Jones saw Ben Holt as a future education professor, and had tried to talk Ben into resigning from the New York City public school system. But all Ben wanted to do was to return to it with an Ed.D. degree, and become a high school English department chairman. Jones' harsh treatment of him appeared to be, at least in part, pressure to bend Ben to his will.

Jones' use of his power inevitably made enemies, most notably Bob Suzuki, a Japanese American. Suzuki had a Ph.D. in physics from Cal Tech, and had known Byrd Jones there—used to play tennis with him. Jones recruited Suzuki as a faculty member but he did not stay in the Urban Education Center for long. Suzuki moved out of it and subsequently made charges of misuse of funds by the center that led to investigations by the state attorney general and the F.B.I.

The *Daily Hampshire Gazette* ran a series of articles on the scandal. It reported that "at least $50,000 in COP funds were spent by School of Education personnel on travel and other expenses not directly related to the program." One expenditure was for a weekend retreat in Montreal costing $3,345 for a number of faculty and some spouses. A school telephone bill of $11,000 was paid for out of COP funds.[8] The *Gazette* pointed out how little the instructors who taught the courses in the COP program were paid—$1,050 to $1,200 per semester, in contrast to the $5,230 Byrd Jones received during the summer of 1973 as the administrator of the COP program, which was in addition to his full professor's pay.[9]

The *Gazette* conducted long distance telephone interviews with Brooklyn COP program students, many of whom were angered by the disclosures. One was quoted as saying that the education courses were the "easy" ones and "seemed like a waste of time."[10] The students interviewed nevertheless said that they were grateful for the program, that there was no other way for them to get degrees while taking care of their families and working fulltime as teacher aides.

The then chancellor of the university, Randolph Bromery, tried to lessen the scandal. He said that he believed the fiscal problems of the school to be the result of "poor management" rather than any "intentional wrongdoing."[11] He also said "the taint on the integrity of the School of Education and this institution has to be removed as fast as possible,"[12] and he proposed the usual way of doing it. An outside blue-ribbon panel composed chiefly of educationists would come to the school, collect some documents, ask some questions, and make a report that would, in effect, be a whitewash.

The scandal and the panel's report would change the school hardly at all despite Dean Dwight Allen's resignation. Atron Gentry would remain a full professor but take several years' leave. Norma Jean Anderson would replace Gentry as Bill Cosby's doctoral committee chairperson. Byrd Jones would keep a much lower profile in the years ahead. The *Gazette* had exposed numerous nepotistic conflicts of interest in admitting people to graduate programs. The secretaries of Dean Dwight Allen and Associate Dean Robert Woodbury had received Ed.D. degrees.[13] The next dean, Mario Fantini, nevertheless entered into a more nepotistic conflict of interest. He permitted his wife to work for an M.Ed. degree in the special program for people without bachelor degrees. Although the school had been accused of having low standards, if anything they would go lower.

Noticeably absent from the reports of the *Hampshire Gazette* was any mention of ethnicity. It did not report the scandal in the context of the school's widely publicized commitment to combat racism, which included the hiring and training of more black faculty, as well as recruiting more black students. The *Gazette* named individuals but did not report that those most involved and affected by the fraud and mismanagement uncovered were black—Cleo Abraham, who was forced to resign, Atron Gentry, whom it reported fired as associate dean, half of the graduate students employed in running the COP programs, the onsite administrators of the program in Brooklyn, almost all of the COP students there, and even University Chancellor Bromery, the overseer of what to do about the scandal. The *Gazette* reported in a general way that there were federal and state officials enrolled as doctoral candidates while continuing in their jobs in Washington and Boston.[14] Not mentioned by the *Gazette* was a black federal official who was directly involved in the renewing of COP program contracts while working for his Ed.D. degree in the Urban Education Center.

Any seeming criticism of blacks, no matter how true, reasoned, and well-intentioned, had been inhibited for years. I had nevertheless begun to wonder about the effects of educationists on minorities, and vice versa. In the next couple of years I would recognize that ethnicity and the field of education—involving all from kindergarten teachers to university presidents—had become inextricably entwined. No discussion of the entanglement was possible in universities or the press, except in such terms as "racism," "affirmative action," "integration," and "cultural bias." The education field, once exclusively white, except in the South, in many locations had become heavily black in students, teachers, school administrators, and professors of education. Black educationists now had the same self-interest as white educationists, further inhibiting any free and open discussion of the effects of minorities on education and vice versa. To me, disentangling them appeared central to any educational reform.

No way of writing about it had occurred to me by the time I left U. Mass and returned to live in New York City. But I had a glimmer of an idea of how I might go about disentangling education and ethnicity, and show how the two had affected each other.

Years before leaving U. Mass I had counted the graduates and the black faces among them in my Stuyvesant High School yearbook, and found what I suspected. The percent of black graduates was roughly equal to the percent of blacks in New York City's population at the time. By the 1960s, however, blacks were so underrepresented in Stuyvesant and the other two special high schools that a Discovery Program had been instituted for the purpose of getting more minority students into them. Entrance was decided solely by test score. Those above the cutoff point were admitted; those below it were not. Under the Discovery Program, begun in 1965, any who scored just below the cutoff point and met the criteria for being "disadvantaged" and were recommended by their schools, could take a six-week summer program operated by each respective special school, and be admitted to it in the fall. From 10 percent to 14 percent of the places in the special high schools were reserved for Discovery students. Apparently, however, so few blacks had been helped to gain entrance by this route that it did not appreciably increase their representation, and the exam was challenged by Harvey Scribner in 1971 and by the Civil Rights Commission in 1977 with charges of cultural bias and outright racial discrimination. The charges were unfounded unless discrimination by merit was to be made illegal.

Stuyvesant was one of some two hundred schools in the United States in which student achievement had remained high and even increased, while achievement had declined precipitously in the nation's other twenty thousand high schools. Stuyvesant's curriculum had remained fundamentally the same. Except for updating and improving courses in math and science, adding advanced courses and computers, the curriculum was much the same as when I attended it. In other words, its curriculum had not been affected by ethnic considerations, had not been affected by educationists' fads. Because it had remained fundamentally the same while most of the nation's other high schools had changed drastically, I could use it as a standard spanning five decades. Only the ethnic proportions of New York City's population had changed, had become heavily black and Puerto Rican. To find out what effect this had had on Stuyvesant High School, I spent half a dozen days in its library examining its yearbooks, including counting the size of the graduating classes and the number of black faces in them.

In my era, there were two yearbooks each year called *The Indicator*, one for January graduates and one for those in June. I combined the June black graduates with those in my January graduating class, and they amounted to 4.8 percent of the year's total graduates. I did the same analysis for 32 of the 47 years of graduating classes from 1938–84 and plotted my data, along with New York City's black population as a percent of the whole, on the following graph.

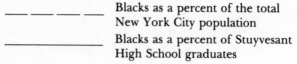

_____ __ ___ __ Blacks as a percent of the total New York City population

_____ Blacks as a percent of Stuyvesant High School graduates

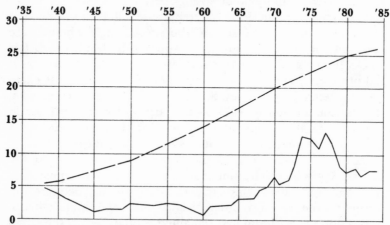

Starting in my year, 1938, the two lines are almost touching, indicating near parity. Thereafter, a gap grows between the percent of the city's black population and the percent of blacks in Stuyvesant graduating classes. The gap kept growing, moreover, even while millions of white families were moving beyond city limits to the suburbs. Only for the period 1973 to 1978 had the gap lessened, then resumed widening. By 1984, black representation had shrunk to less than a third of what it had been in 1938. For black males the disparity was much greater. When Stuyvesant was all-male in 1938, 41 blacks had graduated. In the 1984 class, roughly half female—"roughly" because I did no analysis for gender—the number was about 31. Over the 45-year period, black males had lost ground absolutely as well as relatively. Most ominously, the graph appears to indicate a greater disparity in black representation in the years ahead.

One can see in the graph that the slight increase in percent of the black graduates in the 1968 and subsequent classes might reflect the Discovery Program, initiated three years before. But if the increases were due to it, why was there a marked decrease in black representation from 1979 on?

Females were admitted to Stuyvesant for the first time in 1969, and in the next few years came to make up roughly half of each class. This new factor gave no advantage to any ethnic group. It merely doubled the number of bright test-takers. The admission of females to Stuyvesant had the effect of setting cutoff scores higher than before.

The ever upward curve of blacks as a percentage of New York City's population was the result of the massive immigration of Southern blacks, all of whom were poor and schooled to low Southern standards. One who came at the beginning of that mass migration, who would gain entrance to Stuyvesant, was Thomas Sowell. As he relates it in his autobiographical *Black Education: Myths and Tragedies*, he and his family arrived in Harlem from Charlotte, North Carolina, in 1939. All children entering New York City public schools from the South were automatically put back a grade because of their poorer schooling. Already an iconoclast at the age of nine, however, Sowell held out for being assigned to the fourth grade to which he had been promoted before leaving Charlotte.

His new school and surroundings took some getting used to. The black children in his Harlem school considered kids from the South to be "dumb" and talk "funny," including Sowell at first. From the top of his class in Charlotte, Sowell went to the bottom of his $4A^3$ class and had to struggle to do the work. Fighting among his schoolmates was more frequent and more fierce than in the South, and he joined a gang. Negro schools in the South all had black teachers; in Harlem at the time practically all the teachers were white. Although corporal punishment was not permitted in New York City schools, a white teacher used it on him and in return Sowell kicked him in the belly so hard that the teacher doubled up with pain. That same teacher, nevertheless, promoted him at the end of the term to 5B[1], putting him for the first time with the best students.

The Sowell family moved across school boundaries, and Thomas went to another school in the sixth grade, away from his gang, and he began to enjoy academic success and entertain thoughts of possibly going to college. But from there he was graduated to a junior high that he could see was "too torn by disruption for much teaching or learning." The Sowell family was close enough to a better junior high, J.H.S. 43, to make a case for transferring there. It was integrated and still predominantly white, with students from lower- to upper-middle-class. Sowell says: "Without that transfer, the last door might have been shut on me."

On entering his new junior high, Sowell was placed in the R class for rapid advancement because his IQ score was over 120. His high score was also useful in the ninth grade when a prejudiced counseling teacher tried to dissuade him among others from taking the entrance exam to Stuyvesant. The previous R class had made a poor showing on the entrance exams to the special high schools. Some teachers believed that the R classes, becoming increasingly integrated, were going downhill. Of the ten students in the previous R class who took the entrance exam to Stuyvesant, only one had gained admission. Not wanting a repetition of this low percentage and how it reflected on the school, the counseling teacher was as discouraging as she could be to the R class about trying for the special high schools. Sowell describes her exasperation when he nevertheless said he intended to go to Stuyvesant:

> "Have you been listening to anything I said? What makes you think that *you* can go to Stuyvesant High School?"
>
> "I have a friend who goes there, and he has never seemed to be a better student than I am."
>
> "Oh, really? Let me look at your IQ," and she began digging into the folders with great energy. When she got to my IQ records her sneering expression turned to cold resentment, and she went on to the next student.[15]

Sowell did so well on the entrance exam that he was placed in an advanced section. And contrary to the teacher's fears, all in his R class gained admission to the special high schools. Sowell remarked: "It was an amazing example of mass misjudgment by the teachers and a disquieting indication of what unspoken feelings and fears can do."[16]

I took the entrance exam to Stuyvesant in 1934, ten years before Sowell. Unknown to me at the time, it was the first year in which an examination was required. Founded in 1904 with an emphasis on shops (wood, metal etc.), four years later Dr. Ernest Von Nardorff, a physicist, became its principal. During his twenty-six years as principal, Dr. Von Nardorff established Stuyvesant's reputation for scholarship, particularly in math and science. So many students were attracted that in 1920 it went on double sessions to accommodate them. Even triple sessions were tried, which did not work. Inaugurating the entrance exam was to limit, on a rational basis, the admission of students to the number it could accommodate.

Of the thirteen of us from P.S. 87 who took the exam, twelve were admitted. But what was most significant in the light of the intense competition to gain entrance to it in later years, none of the others who were admitted with me attended Stuyvesant. All eleven of them went to other high schools.

To check my memory of this, the very first thing I did in the library of Stuyvesant was to examine closely each face and name of the 420 in the June 1938 *Indicator*. These were the students with whom I had entered Stuyvesant, although I was not among them because I had graduated the semester before. I did not recognize a single P.S. 87 classmate.

The circumstance that permitted those eleven, and their parents, to turn their backs on Stuyvesant was that most of the New York City high schools were good then. Although Stuyvesant, along with Townsend Harris, was known as the best (Bronx Science would not come into being until 1937), its superiority was not so great as to offset all of its several drawbacks. It was awkward to travel from the West Side to a noisy neighborhood of five-story walkup tenements on the northern fringe of the Lower East Side, an old physical plant with poor athletic facilities, no girls, and on double session. It was still possible to get an adequately good education at other high schools. Dr. Kenneth Clark, the famous black psychologist who attended elementary school in Harlem in the 1920s, for example, graduated from George Washington High School. He did not need to go to Stuyvesant, Townsend Harris, or Brooklyn Tech to get a good start. Neither did United States Senator Daniel Patrick Moynihan. He graduated from Benjamin Franklin High School in East Harlem in 1943 and would later become a Harvard professor. My younger brother graduated from the High School of Commerce in 1941, which I regarded as second-rate. He was very bright, had skipped two half-grades to my one at P.S. 87, and I had argued with my parents that he should go to a better school. He nevertheless learned enough math there to be trained in World War II as a navigator in a night fighter plane. What made most New York City elementary and secondary schools good at the time was that they were still staffed with traditional teachers who were literate and knew their subjects. Equal educational opportunity existed for all, including blacks.

Equality of opportunity is never absolute, of course. Fate, luck, pure accident, play their parts and create inequalities, advantages and disadvantages. They played their parts in Thomas Sowell's somewhat more than a year at Stuyvesant. He became ill for a time, had difficulties with his family and Harlem milieu. He fell behind in his school work, started over again, got discouraged, and dropped out. Writing in 1972, Sowell nevertheless had this to say about his schooling in New York City from 1939 to 1946:

> In one important respect, my educational experience was very different from that of today's black students, and very different from that of most white students as well. Early in my development I learned what the intellectual process was—what was meant by systematic thinking, relevant evidence, and organized writing. Not only in junior high school but even in the "one" classes in the Harlem elementary school, intellectual values and intellectual achievements were promoted, respected, and rewarded—even if not always impartially. At Stuyvesant High School I saw what intellectual excellence meant, even if I was not able to participate in it. In short, I was *oriented* toward the intellectual life, as few American youngsters are in most schools.[17]

Sowell's experiences were much like those of Kenneth Clark's in Harlem schools a generation earlier. His learning of the intellectual process ultimately enabled him to graduate from Harvard, earn an M.A. degree at Columbia, a Ph.D. in economics at Chicago, be employed in business for a time, teach at Howard, Cornell, the University of California, and become a Senior Fellow at the Hoover Institution at Stanford University.

The most fortunate of Sowell's boyhood circumstances was that he arrived in Harlem in 1939 when most of the city's schools were still good. A few years later, they were overwhelmed by the mass immigration of Southern blacks and Puerto Ricans, with which the schools could no longer cope as they had coped with the mass of immigrants from Eastern Europe and Italy before and after the turn of the century. By the 1950s, most of the city's schools, especially in the primary grades, had become overwhelmed, too, by the noxious influences of schools of education through their propagation of fads and the way they miseducated school teachers and administrators.

The deterioration of the city's schools had a tremendous impact on Stuyvesant and the Bronx High School of Science. During the decades in which I and Thomas Sowell attended, and in all previous decades, Stuyvesant's student body was overwhelmingly poor, working class, and first generation Americans. All nationalities and ethnic groups were represented in it, with the overwhelming majority being Jewish with Italians in a distant second place, both groups residing chiefly in the Lower East Side. The assistant editor of my *Indicator* wrote: "It would be no exaggeration to say that well over four-fifths of my acquaintances are not more than one generation removed from the 'old country'." Among the colleges that the graduates in my 1938 *Indicator* said they were going to attend, more gave C.C.N.Y. than any other, followed by Brooklyn and Queens Colleges, Cooper Union, and numerous others within the city. Except for Columbia, which could be attended while living at home, few aimed for Ivy League colleges. But into the 1960s that changed. Competition for entrance into the special schools increased dramatically, so that five times as many students were taking the entrance exams to Stuyvesant and Bronx Science than they could admit. More and more of the aspirants, too, were taking the exams from *private* schools. For a time, the Stuyvesant *Indicator* gave the home addresses for its graduates, and I was struck by how many lived in Manhattan's most expensive neighborhoods, including the most affluent Upper East Side. By the 1970s those who had entered Stuyvesant from private schools amounted to 40 percent of each class. The three special academic high schools were perceived by many as all that remained of the school system's excellence. In 1971 when Harvey Scribner threatened to change the entrance requirements, *The New York Times* quoted a middle-class parent as saying "our children would have no place else to go."[18] In 1977 when the Office of Civil Rights similarly challenged the elite schools, the president of the Parent-Teachers Association at Bronx Science was quoted in the *Times* as saying that the parents of the children in the elite schools "are what is left of the middle-class here in the city. They won't stay if their kids can't go to these schools."[19] New York City had more than one hundred other high schools. Of them, not more than half a dozen were still as good as high schools used to be, although not up to the standards of Stuyvesant and Bronx Science, which numbered several Nobel Prize winners among their alumni. During the 1960s, '70s, and '80s, an increasing percent of the graduating classes were accepted by the eight Ivy League colleges. The Stuyvesant Class of 1983, numbering 605, had 343 acceptances from Brown, Columbia, Cornell, Dartmouth, Harvard, Pennsylvania, Princeton, and Yale. In many instances, of course, students had applied to and been accepted by more than one. The 1983 class also had 277 acceptances from other prestigious universities—35 from M.I.T., 32 from Johns Hopkins, 27 from Duke, and 8 from faraway Stanford. In addition, members of the class had acceptances from fifty other colleges and universities. The *mean* SAT score of the 1983 class was 654 in math and 603 in verbal.

Yet, there was one group of Stuyvesant students in the 1970s and '80s that was much like the majority of working-class students who attended it in my day. Most members of it were either foreign born or first generation Americans.

When I did my research at Stuyvesant, I was impressed by the number of Asian students I saw. They appeared to be half of those in the library each time I worked in it. Initially, nevertheless, I had no intention of counting Asian as well as black faces. But I was unprepared for the degree of Asian achievement I recognized in the 1980s issues of *The Indicator*. Whole pages had none but Asian faces staring out from them. The class of 1980 had fifteen Chinese students all with the last name of Lee. I worked out the percentages of Asians for sixteen of the graduating classes and plotted them, along with the percent of Asians in the New York City population, on the following graph.

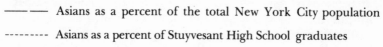

———— Asians as a percent of the total New York City population

-------- Asians as a percent of Stuyvesant High School graduates

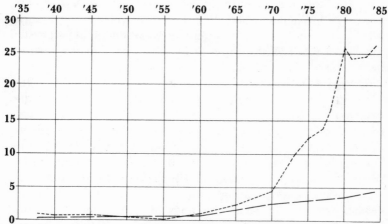

In my year, 1938, out of 850 graduates, only 7 were Asians, or 0.8 percent of the total. Even that was more than twice the city's Asian population at the time. It was 0.3 percent in 1940, rose slowly in the next two decades to 0.4 percent and 0.7 percent. Following passage of the Immigration Act of 1965 that did away with the preferential quotas for northern Europeans, New York City's Asian population jumped to 2.3 percent in 1970 and 3.7 percent in 1980. But the Asian percentage of Stuyvesant graduates zoomed from 4.4 percent in 1970 to 25.7 percent in 1980, and then to 26.1 percent in 1984, exceeding the city's percent of Asian population by six to seven times.

The rapidity of change in the ethnic composition of Stuyvesant's graduating classes indicates how absurd were the charges of cultural bias and racial discrimination entertained by Harvey Scribner and the United States Civil Rights Commission. The rapidity of ethnic change shows that the entrance examination to the three special schools was color-blind. (Exam papers had assigned numbers on them—no names or addresses—making it impossible for test scorers to be influenced by ethnicity, national origin, or gender. Only after the cutoff score was decided were the assigned numbers converted to the test-takers' names.)

The above graph raises, of course, the question of how such achievement by Asians is possible? How are they able to compete with middle-class and upper middle-class white students, many of them from the best private and parochial schools? (Graduates with Hispanic surnames in the yearbooks were so few as to be negligible.) When I raised such questions with Leonard Lurie, a former district superintendent in Manhattan, he suggested that I visit P.S. 124, the Yung Wing school in Chinatown, which he referred to as "Sam Cooper's school."

Samuel A. Cooper was the principal. He had spent, by 1984, all of his thirty-one years as a teacher, assistant principal, and principal in Chinatown, and had been born within walking distance of it in 1928. Chinatown was smaller then, consisting of about four square blocks bounded by Canal, Worth, and Baxter Streets, and the Bowery. It was in the southernmost portion of the Lower East Side. Chinatown had expanded and was continuing to spread into what was once Little Italy and the Jewish ghetto. The slum dwellings of immigrant Italian and Jewish families were now homes for Chinese families. Schools that had been attended by Italian and Jewish students, where many of them first learned English, are now attended by Chinese students. One is P.S. 42 at 71 Hester Street, which dates from 1897; another is P.S. 1 at number 8 Henry Street, built in 1896. In age of buildings, the section is the oldest in Manhattan. Many of its streets are so narrow that trucks can get through only with cars parked on one side of the street. Others are not much wider than the width of a single car. Walking about Chinatown on a Saturday or Sunday morning before the tourists arrive, one sees mostly Chinese adults and children and hears mostly Chinese spoken. Signs on all the shops and restaurants are in Chinese characters, and all the newspaper stands sell Chinese newspapers.

The Yung Wing elementary school occupies the three lowest floors of one of the two buildings in the only towering apartment complex in the area, forty-four stories high, and on a site shaped like an equilateral triangle. It was the former location of the once famous ladies' clothing store, Levine and Smith. The north side of the triangle abuts the foot of the Manhattan Bridge. Opposite, at the south apex of the triangle, is a large statue of Confucius, set in Confucius Plaza. The statue was presented to the city in 1976 by the Chinese Consolidated Benevolent Association in commemoration of the nation's Bicentennial Celebration. The Yung Wing school was paid for by Confucius Plaza Housing, and opened in 1976. In 1984 it had close to two thousand students. One bilingual class existed for each of the six grades and the kindergarten. Since most children remained in a bilingual class for less than a year, the classes existed chiefly to take in new arrivals of various grade-school ages from Hong Kong, Taiwan, mainland China, and ethnic Chinese from Viet Nam and other Asian countries.

Bilingual classes had been virtually mandated for foreign language speaking students by the federal Bilingual Education Act of 1968. Of the Yung Wing school's 54 teachers, close to 20 were Chinese speaking; of 6 paraprofessionals, 2 were Chinese speaking. But many parents asked to have their children removed from bilingual classes as soon as possible in order for their children to learn English faster. Cooper was sympathetic to this viewpoint. "In a bilingual class," he said, "instruction is given in English only about half the time. That's about two and a half hours a day." Something like ninety percent of Yung Wing students came from homes where English was not spoken, so school was the only place they could hear and speak English. Among their parents, moreover, there was no talk of having the school maintain their children's native language and customs. For that, the community had a Chinese school on Mott Street which some of the children attended after the regular school day.

This attitude toward English was very different from that of the Puerto Rican educationists I knew at the U. Mass School of Education, and which held sway in many predominantly Hispanic schools. They did not speak of bilingual *classes*. They spoke of *bilingual-bicultural programs* of several years' duration. If they had their way,

Hispanic students would remain in such programs from kindergarten through high school. I had heard and observed Puerto Rican's speaking unguardedly among themselves at a bilingual conference I attended on Cape Cod in 1974. They had openly talked of how to keep and create jobs for themselves, even to the point of excluding Spanish-speaking teachers who were not from "the island." I heard no discussion of what effects their venal goals might have on Hispanic children.

To Yung Wing parents, nothing was as important as having their children learn English. They recognized that this was the language in which their children would have to compete with others, and they wanted their children prepared to compete. Some parents with children in regular classes requested teachers who were non-Chinese speaking, reasoning that if their children could not use Chinese as a crutch, they would master English better.

When I asked Cooper about reading instruction and methods used, he replied: "*All* methods. I am not one of those who believes there is one method of teaching reading." He believed not so much in methods and materials as in teachers. He said that in his schools he had always had teachers of reading who were bright, knew that they were doing and understood children. It was his job to support them. "If a teacher finds that she needs a particular set of materials, supplemental books or other resources, my position is that I have to provide them." Cooper emphasized: "You can't supplant the teacher. A good reading teacher makes her own decisions." His views on reading instruction were much the same as Frank Smith's, quoted on page 97.

Exposure to written English was broadened by much encouragement to extracurricular reading, which Cooper said the students took to like ducks to water. He exclaimed, "These kids are *readers*!" I saw evidence of it during a tour of the school. Each classroom I entered or looked into had its own library, usually a rack or two of paperbacks. The school also had a separate library although Cooper complained that they could not get enough books for it. "But we have an excellent relationship with the Chatham Square public library," Cooper added. "We're constantly sending classes there. All the kids become members of the library and take out books. The librarian, Mrs. Swift, might as well be on my staff."

Cooper took such pride in the school and its students' ability to read that he was irritated each year when *The New York Times* published the annual results of the citywide reading tests, listing each school in rank order of its test scores. The Yung Wing school always stood high, well ahead of the majority of the city's six hundred other elementary schools. Although students in the bilingual classes did not take the test, they were averaged into its score. Then, too, many of the pupils had been hearing, speaking and reading English only for a year or two or three, and were not as fluent in it yet as they were on their way to becoming. To Cooper, the rank order insufficiently indicated how well they were doing. He published for his school's parents the ranking of Chinatown's six elementary schools, in which Yung Wing was in first place.

Cooper also showed exasperation that the school had lost its Title 1 status, although most of its families were among the city's poorest. Title 1 was for an economically disadvantaged category that provided extra federal funds. Part of the Board of Education's criteria for Title 1 status was the percent of a school's families on welfare. But for years the Yung Wing school had very few families on welfare. "Chinese people will do anything to avoid seeking public assistance even when they know they are entitled to it," said Cooper. "They'll take a third or fourth job first," meaning a third or fourth menial job a week like washing dishes in a restaurant. For many years, the Yung Wing and other Chinatown schools had been asking the central Board of Education to change its "percent on welfare" criteria. For years, the board refused but permitted Yung Wing and others to be exceptions to the criteria until Chancellor Frank Macchiarola ended the exception, and Yung Wing lost its Title 1 status beginning with the 1982–83 school year. Cooper had lost the funds for twelve teaching positions. He had to operate the school without an extra cent in city, state, or federal funds, as if it were a middle-class school.

That many of the school's students exceeded middle-class standards in achievement, was due largely to the standards of their parents—both parents. Very few Chinese families consisted of just a mother or a father. By any ordinary criteria, they worked excessively hard, most at menial jobs. Making great demands on themselves, the parents were as demanding of effort from their children whose work was their school work.

The demanded effort was reflected in the Yung Wing school's outstanding attendance record. For years it had been the best in the state. The school had, in fact, received national recognition for its attendance. Parents did not permit their children to miss school except for a real illness. Even then, Cooper said that it was not unusual for a teacher to discover a child in class who had come to school with a fever and have to send the child home.

Parents and children tended to want more homework than teachers assigned. Parents checked on it and cultivated the habit in their children of doing homework without fail. They took advantage of extra help. Some students who wrote well enough attended an after-school writing program three times a week even though it was intended for those who were in need of extra help. Their parents had a clear vision that the road to economic success in the United States was through education and they were making the most of what their new circumstances had to offer.

Chinatown had stability and continuity and was ever changing. Its restaurants and shops attracted tourists, diners, and shoppers, and were simultaneously a language and culture base. Each time I visited it, Chinese people got off the subway with me. I could only speculate about whether they lived in Chinatown and were returning from errands in other parts of the city, or lived elsewhere and were coming to work, shop, visit relatives, seek help from Chinatown's civic organizations, or do business there. The number living in Chinatown and the immediate area around it was estimated to be around 155,000 in 1984.[20]

Chinatown families, after becoming established economically, typically left to live dispersed in other sections of the city. The outward movement in recent years, Cooper said, was very large, and the influx from overseas was larger still. Some families who owned business and property remained in Chinatown for several generations. The Yung Wing school, being in Chinatown's geographical center, had more of these families than the other elementary schools. "If you stand outside in the morning," said Cooper, "you'll see some children brought to school by grandparents. The mothers and fathers are working. In some cases, the grandparent speaks no English and the grandchild knows little Chinese."

The enrollment of the Yung Wing school had been 100 percent Chinese when it opened in 1976. Although some non-Chinese children lived within its school zone, they attended parochial schools because their parents did not want their child to be "the only one." The school had an excess of classroom space at the time, having been built to a size that anticipated some of the future influx of Chinese from abroad, and Cooper wanted to make the school available to the non-Chinese residents. This was one of the reasons he started a program for gifted children for roughly the lower half of District 2, south of 14th Street, which took in Greenwich Village and Soho. The program was open to students who met the requirement of being in the top 1 percent of the population in intellectual ability, had IQ scores of 140 or better, following the guidelines of the Vincent Astor program. It brought into the school non-Chinese children from other schools, and then the local non-Chinese families began sending their children to Yung Wing. By 1984, it had become 85 percent Chinese, 8 percent white and 7 percent black and Hispanic.

Among many Chinese parents, however, the gifted children program was controversial. They liked the idea of the program but saw no reason why it could not have been 100 percent Chinese instead of somewhat more than half Chinese. Samuel Cooper's relationship with the Chinese community had always been excellent. In 1984 he was president of the Lions Club of Chinatown and was often introduced at Chinese gatherings as being three-quarters Chinese. Nevertheless, he lost some friends in the Chinese community because he had integrated the school. They could not understand why the gifted program could not have been for the top 5 percent of the student population in intellectual ability. Then, it could have been confined to Yung Wing and all the children in it could have been Chinese.

Chinese parents obviously believed in ability grouping, as did Cooper. "In heterogeneous grouping," he said, "teachers tend to teach to the middle of the class and the brightest and the slowest children do not get the work and attention they should have." The learning of all children, he firmly believed, was best promoted by grouping children by their abilities. And with respect to the gifted program, Cooper said: "The country desperately needs the gifts of these children."

For its 1170 students, the Yung Wing school had no special education classes. Several physically handicapped children in it attended regular classes; in the argot of educationists, they were "mainstreamed." Some fifty-eight children got extra help one hour a day for specific difficulties they were having. But in the nine years that Cooper had been principal of the school, he said that only six children had had to be transferred to other schools for special education classes. Yung Wing had the fewest number of special education referrals of any school in District 2 "by a long shot," said Cooper. "We take care of our own."

When I mentioned to him my findings of the extraordinarily high percent of Asian students at Stuyvesant, he said that many of them had started in the Yung Wing school. He also told me of another route up the ladder to a quality college education that I had been unaware of—Hunter High School. Unlike Stuyvesant, Bronx Science, and Brooklyn Tech, it was under the Board of *Higher* Education. It began in the seventh grade and had its own requirements for admission, which included two tests, one a written composition. Just to qualify to take the test, sixth graders had to be four years above grade level in reading and math. In 1983 the Yung Wing school had thirty-six such sixth graders, and nine of them were admitted to Hunter High School. In second place was P.S. 6 in the affluent Upper East Side with six admissions, and no other elementary school in the city came close.

During the several interviews with Samuel Cooper, he repeatedly gave the credit for the school's success to the Chinese students and their parents. Referring to himself and his teaching staff, he said: "We are blessed," indicating the degree of professional fulfillment felt in working with students totally committed to learning, who were well-behaved, respectful of parents, teachers and all adults. Keeping a stable teaching staff in the school was easy. Few teachers ever left to teach in other schools, and whenever a vacancy occurred, the telephones rang all day long with calls from teachers in other schools who wanted to transfer to it.

The parents of the Yung Wing children were also blessed, in my estimation, in having Samuel Cooper for a principal. I was impressed with how free his talk was of educationist cant. His school appeared equally free of educationist fads. It concentrated on basic, fundamental education, particularly speaking, reading, and writing English. True, Cooper was in harmony with what the Chinese parents understood education to be and he boasted freely of it. His Jewish heritage of respect for family, the law, effort, hard work, ambition, and learning, blended perfectly with Chinese respect for and adherence to the same qualities. Having been born in the Jewish ghetto of the Lower East Side and having lived the American dream of moving up to a better life through education, he saw the Chinese as living that same dream, and took delight that it was happening in his old neighborhood where he grew up.

What made possible his success as a principal, in my view, was his own excellent education. He was a product of the New York City public school system from the era when it was still first-rate. He had also gone to Stuyvesant for his first two years of high school, overlapping Thomas Sowell's attendance there, and then had transferred to Seward Park because that was where most of his friends went, including the girls. Like Sowell, he had been "oriented toward the intellectual life," and had graduated from CCNY. He had had some trouble in passing the Board of Examiners' tests for a teaching license the first time he took them. He failed the oral portion for pronouncing Long Island as if it were "Long Guyland." Teachers, then, were not expected to be ethnic models. They were expected to be many kinds of models, including the model of correct speech. No incorrect grammar or pronunciation was permitted in teachers or students. And one did not have to be Jewish to be corrected. My mispronunciations were corrected by my teachers.

The quality of Cooper's education informed all his decisions as principal. During my second interview, he mentioned that the day before a young Chinese woman had sat where I was sitting. She had been newly licensed to teach in New York City and was seeking a teaching position. When Cooper asked to see her license, she answered: "I didn't brung it." That was all Cooper needed to hear. "I will not hire a teacher for this school who cannot speak correct English," he said. "Unfortunately today, too many young teachers speak no better than that young woman." He added, "And she passed the Board of Examiners' tests!" Samuel Cooper was a school principal whom most professors of education would label old-fashioned, if not something more disparaging.

My next interviews were at I.S. 131, the Dr. Sun Yat Sen

school at 100 Hester Street, the street after which the very fine film *Hester Street* was named. Of the sixteen hundred students in this junior high, the largest in Manhattan, 82 percent were Chinese, 14 percent Hispanic, 2 percent black and 2 percent white. It, too, had one bilingual class for each grade to take in new arrivals from overseas until they could start to learn in English, usually anywhere from two months to a year. Students arriving from Hong Kong and Taiwan often had some English and had had good preparation in the academic subjects, particularly math. Their parents typically had a high school education. Recently, as in the Yung Wing school, more arrivals were from mainland China. The education of the parents of these students tended to be lower, disrupted in China's "cultural revolution" in the 1960s.

At the Dr. Sun Yat Sen school I had interviews with the principal and a guidance counselor, and also with a former member of the staff who did not wish to be identified. I was as unimpressed with the principal as I had been favorably impressed by Samuel Cooper. He was Archer Wah Dong, a Chinese American who neither spoke nor wrote Chinese. During my short interview, cut short by him, when I started to ask about students in his school gaining admission to the special high schools via the Discovery Program route, he asked: "What's the Discovery Program?" When I began to explain what it was, he interrupted me saying, quite defensively, that he had been principal in that school for only two and a half years, and I would have to ask one of the guidance counselors about the Discovery Program.

Every school has a tone, an atmosphere contributed to by everything and everybody in it, but particularly by the administration. The principal's office looked barren and unprincipal-like, especially the high bookcases that lined one wall, the shelves of which were empty. The school building was new, it was true, but had been occupied nine months before my visits, long enough to begin to reveal its character. The administrative staff outside the principal's office lacked the aura of a purposeful, pleasant cooperativeness that characterized the similar office at the Yung Wing school. I would learn that Archer Dong had previously been the principal of a vocational high school. When he took over the principalship of Dr. Sun Yat Sen, it had been a happy, well-functioning, high-achieving school with an excellent staff of highly experienced people. Very shortly, the staff perceived Dong as trying to operate the school as if it were a typical vocational school with typical problems of discipline, gangs, and drugs, problems which the Dr. Sun Yat Sen school did not have. More critically, teachers complained that he made high-handed decisions affecting them but without consulting them, and did not listen when they made suggestions. Morale had declined so that during the 1983–84 school year, a sizable portion of the staff was on leave of absence to get away from it and others were seeking to transfer to other schools. Dong had come to a happy, smooth-functioning school, and now there was much dissension in it.

The Dr. Sun Yat Sen school received most of the students from Chinatown's six elementary schools. Samuel Cooper had said that of the 140-or-so graduates of Yung Wing each year, about one hundred of them attended it. But District 2 gave all parents the option of sending their children to any junior high school in the district. Some of Chinatown's knowledgeable parents, aware of the situation at Dr. Sun Yat Sen, were sending their children to other junior highs as far away as the Upper East Side. Some of the best of Chinatown students were going elsewhere.

Nevertheless, in talking to Maria Ting, the guidance counselor interviewed, I got the impression that Dr. Sun Yat Sen students were as highly motivated as other Chinese students. She estimated that one-third of them had been in the United States for two or three years or less. Notwithstanding this enormous proportion of recent arrivals, 25 percent of the students gained admission to the special high schools, including Music and Art and Performing Arts, as well as Brooklyn Tech, Bronx Science and Stuyvesant. Long before school officials informed students about the special high schools, the Chinese students already knew about them. So did many of their parents. Such were parental and peer expectations about gaining admission that many Chinese students assumed that taking the entrance examination to the three special high schools was mandatory. Most also qualified as disadvantaged. Any who did not score sufficiently high to gain admission but had scores just below the cutoff points, could apply as "discovery" students. They were able to take disproportionate advantage of the Discovery Program, initiated originally with blacks and Puerto Ricans in mind.

By no means did the special high schools receive students just from the Dr. Sun Yat Sen junior high. Another junior high in adjacent District 1, although the majority there were Hispanic, had an enrollment of 30 percent Chinese. *The New York Times* in July 1984 reported a large and growing concentration of recently arrived Asians in Flushing, Queens—an estimated thirty thousand Chinese,[21] some of them quite affluent, from Hong Kong, having left in anticipation of that British Colony reverting to China's sovereignty in 1997. The same Flushing area had thirty thousand Koreans.[22] Chinese families also lived in other sections.

Stuyvesant's Asian students came from all over New York City. The overwhelming majority were Chinese and most of them either lived or had lived at one time in Chinatown. Other Asians included Koreans and a few Japanese. Harvard College announced in June 1984 that its entering freshman class in the fall would consist of more than 10 percent Asians, and a Stuyvesant guidance person told me that that percent included many from Stuyvesant.

In investigating the achievement of Asian students in Chinatown schools and Stuyvesant High School, I had uncovered specific information pertaining to New York City. The insight I gained was nevertheless generalizeable in explaining the high achievement of Asian students all over the United States.

With respect to black achievement at Stuyvesant, I was still puzzled by one aspect of my graph on page 164 showing the large and persistent gap between the city's black population and the percent of Stuyvesant's black graduates. What was the reason for the brief lessening of the gap from 1973–78? Why had the gap greatly widened thereafter? For possible insight I was going to show the graph to Murray Kahn, an assistant principal of Stuyvesant. But before I could, he was called away from his office. While I awaited his return, holding the graph in my hands together with the graph of Asian graduates, almost idly I held them up overlapped to the light. The result, omitting the black and Asian population lines, was this:

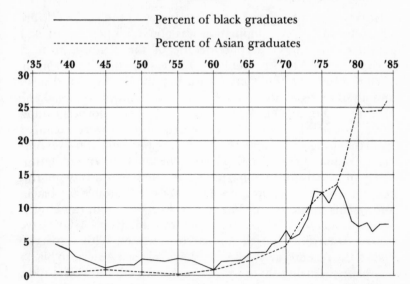

———————————— Percent of black graduates

------------------- Percent of Asian graduates

The decline in percent of black graduates after 1978 was directly due to the large increase in Asians. They had captured places at Stuyvesant that otherwise would have been won by members of other ethnic groups, including blacks.

As dismal as black scholastic achievement appears in this graph, the picture is much worse. Not all of the black graduates are American blacks—those whose ancestors arrived in colonial times. Many are of West Indian origin. The Immigration Act of 1965 not only increased the flow of Asians into the city. It also resulted in a large influx of immigrants from the West Indies—Jamaica, Barbados, Trinidad, etc. One of the Stuyvesant guidance counselors said he believed that were the records of the black students to be examined and parents' ancestry identified, probably half would prove to be West Indian. West Indians, relatively few in number compared to American blacks, have always achieved disproportionately higher than American blacks after arriving in the United States. Thomas Sowell has named some of them. "Prominent blacks of West Indian ancestry have included Marcus Garvey, James Weldon Johnson, Claude McKay, Shirley Chisholm, Malcolm X, Kenneth B. Clark, W. Arthur Lewis, Sidney Poitier, and Harry Belafonte."[23]

West Indian blacks probably accounted for most of the

relatively high percent of black graduates in my year of 1938, when the city's black population was about 5.5 percent. It had grown slowly in the second decade of the century, from 2 percent in 1910 to 3 percent in 1920, and then to 5 percent by 1930.[24] Much of the increase during the 1920s was due to immigration from the then British West Indies. In 1930, 17 percent of the city's black population was foreign born, meaning West Indian.[25] If blacks of West Indian ancestry were excluded from the foregoing graph, the line for the percent of Stuyvesant's black graduates from 1938–84 would be much lower and flatter.

All of the information specific to New York City in this chapter would be irrelevant were it not generalizable for blacks and Asians in the rest of the nation. Everywhere in the United States, no matter what part of Asia they came from, Asians have done extraordinarily well compared to whites. With respect to blacks, the recently arrived Asians have eclipsed American blacks completely, leaving them behind as if in an educational stupor.

Wherever there are large concentrations of American blacks in school systems in northern cities and throughout the South, the blacker the school system, numerically speaking, the lower the educational achievement. The blacker the teaching and administrative staff, numerically, the lower the educational achievement. Despite all the federal legislation in the name of improving schooling for blacks in the last three decades, a large mass of American blacks threatens to become a permanent educational underclass, a third world within the United States borders that is not developing and not emerging. I can say this so bluntly and pessimistically, more because of what I know about the field of education than what I know about blacks. I believe that blacks have the same capabilities as other groups, but are uniquely endangered. They will not realize their educational potentials without drastic changes, including their own habits of thought.

11

Inside the Heads of the Ten-Times Disadvantaged

Were a Gallup poll taken among New York City's Chinatown parents and black parents in Harlem, Brooklyn, or the Bronx, to elicit belief in the importance of education for their children, the tabulations for both groups would be identical. All would say that a good education is a prerequisite for their children's future success. Such a poll among Asian and black parents everywhere in the United States—city, suburb, or town—would yield the same results.

We can predict 100 percent belief in education's importance for Asian parents just from the disproportionately high scholastic attainment of their children. The prediction for black parents, on the other hand, must be based on other evidence. I offer the observations of Nathan Glazer and Daniel Patrick Moynihan:

> Negroes do place a high value on education. The educational attainments of young men and women are emphasized in news stories and announcements. Negro professionals stand at the top of the social ladder, and make the largest incomes. Parents continually emphasize to children the theme of the importance of education as a means of getting ahead; and this is true among the uneducated as well as the educated, the failures as well as the successful. And yet the outcome is a poor one.[1]

The above remains as true in the 1980s as when it was written in the early 1960s, including the poor outcome. The disproportionately low scholastic attainment of black students shows graphically in my chart of Stuyvesant's black graduates on page 164. They comprise a mere 7.9 percent of the class of 1984, including a significant number of West Indian ancestry. They underrepresent the city's black population of 25.2 percent by just under one-third. Asians, on the other hand, 26.1 percent of the 1984 class, overrepresent the city's Asian population of 4 percent by six to seven times. Proportionate to their respective populations, Asians exceed American blacks in the Stuyvesant student body by a minimum of ten times.

This ten-times Asian advantage holds true, I am sure, everywhere in the United States. After *The New York Times* reported that Harvard's 1984 entering freshman class was more than 10 percent Asian, I telephoned its admissions office to get an accurate figure and to find out the percent of black students. I was given the actual figures which worked out to be 11.1 percent for Asians and 6.5 percent for blacks. Like other Ivy league colleges, Harvard attempts to be, in large part, a national college. Of the nation's population, blacks make up 12 percent and Asians only 1.5 percent. The ten-times academic advantage of Asians over blacks holds true at Harvard.

How is this ten-times advantage possible? How can it be explained, particularly when most Asians are recent immigrants who are poor (like the overwhelming majority of the estimated 155,000 Chinese in New York City's Chinatown), and with the added disadvantages of speaking foreign languages and coming from different cultures? How do Asians so quickly, as well as disproportionately, utilize what is best in public schools so much better than American blacks? It should be obvious that *what is in the heads of the two groups is vastly different.*

I refer to nothing genetic. During my interviews at the Yung Wing elementary school, the Dr. Sun Yat Sen junior high, and Stuyvesant High School, I heard not a hint from anyone that he or she believed that Asians are innately superior. To the contrary, all attributed Asian superiority in academic achievement to other factors.

When I asked Samuel Cooper whether he and his fellow administrators in Chinatown schools found a lower incidence of mental slowness among Chinese students, he replied: "Speaking from my thirty-one years of experience, Chinese children are no different than the children of any other group. The proportions of those who are gifted, average, and those who have difficulties in learning, are the same."

Cooper had told me that out of 1,170 pupils in the school, 58 were IEP children. They had been evaluated by a psychologist, social worker, and educational evaluators, and an Individual Education Program devised for each child to overcome what were deemed learning disabilities. The IEP was carried out by special education teachers spending one hour, and in some cases two hours, a day in small groups of four and five, and by the children's regular classroom teachers during the rest of the time. When I asked Cooper how many of the fifty-eight IEP children were Chinese, he said that almost all were. Only four or five were non-Chinese. In other words, about 5 percent of the school's Chinese pupils had serious difficulty in learning, a proportion that Cooper said was the same for the children of all ethnic groups.

Since the ten-times advantage of Asians over black Americans cannot be attributed to anything genetic, it must be due to other factors. It must be due to the differences of what is typically inside the heads of the members of the two groups, keeping in mind that the brain is the seat of the emotions as well as the intellect, and that each affects the other. Most black parents and students do not believe the same things about schooling as Asian parents and students; do not feel as most Asians feel about curriculum, teachers, principals, and schools. Moreover, they share little in common of what it takes to achieve in school.

Take, for example, knowledge of and beliefs and feelings about mathematics. Children from Hong Kong and Taiwan who land in the upper grades of the Yung Wing elementary school and in the Dr. Sun Yat Sen junior high, are generally well prepared academically, particularly in math. Although Hong Kong's business economy has been booming for years, teachers with arithmetical and mathematical knowledge and skills have not been lured away from teaching. Despite Hong Kong's near full employment, no shortage of math teachers exists there as it has for decades in New York City where, in 1984, 930,000 people were on welfare. In the Crown Colony of

Hong Kong, the educational system is British—more traditionally British, probably, than schools are currently in Britain. Hong Kong's traditional educational system, moreover, is congruent with the educational systems in various Asian countries where the primary emphasis, too, is on academic subjects.

Asian parents, like others, acquire their views on schooling chiefly from their own school experiences and contacts with teachers. Since math was made important to them, they convey it to their children. The following is quoted from a *New York Times* report of a study to be published in 1985, directed by Harold W. Stevenson of the University of Michigan:

> "We observed one Chinese mother reading a story to her child about four mice who ran down a hole," Mr. Stevenson said. "She paused periodically and asked the child questions like: If only one mouse went down the hole, how many would there be left? We saw a lot of that kind of informal teaching that is fun but teaches the child elementary math concepts."[2]

The mother and child were observed in Taipei, the capital of Taiwan.

Observing and talking to parents and teachers was part of the crosscultural investigation of elementary schools in the three cities of Taipei in Taiwan, Sendai in Japan, and Minneapolis, Minnesota. The three cities and elementary schools in each were selected for being comparable, "judged to be representative of the mainstream of their cultures."[3] Minneapolis schools were also chosen for having few minority students, so as not to complicate the results. Standardized tests were administered in randomly selected schools to a sample of randomly selected first and fifth grade children, and compared for the three cities. One of the findings was that the Minneapolis pupils lagged behind the Japanese and Chinese pupils in academic achievement. Moreover, they lagged behind virtually from the day they entered the first grade.

As startling as this is, another finding is even more significant. The parents and teachers of the Minneapolis pupils had more years of formal schooling than the parents and teachers of the Chinese and Japanese children. For example, 58 percent of the mothers of the Minneapolis pupils had attended college, versus 22 percent of the mothers of Japanese pupils, and 13 percent of the mothers of Chinese pupils. Contrary to what one would expect, the greater college attendance of Minneapolis mothers was not reflected in their children's achievement.

Could it be that Minneapolis mothers learned little in college? Probably, according to another study that has been announced for publication in 1986 by Ernest L. Boyer, president of the Carnegie Foundation for the Advancement of Teaching. Boyer's study will examine the problem of many college degrees representing less learning than they once did. That Japanese and Chinese teachers are more effective in the classroom with less college attendance, comes as no surprise to me.

Schools of education have put into the heads of American teachers and consequently their students and parents, very different notions than are believed by the Chinese and Japanese. Ironically, Japan's educational system "was imposed by occupying American forces after World War II,"[4] an indication of how academically oriented we were then. The senior American policy makers who imposed the educational system along with a new constitution, we must remember, were mature men who started their schooling before World War I. That was when most schools of education were coming into being and had not yet affected the public schools. Educationists' anti-academic notions did not begin to be noticed in schools in our country until the 1950s, which coincided with the beginnings of the civil rights movement.

The movement was a gift of obfuscation to educationists, serving to divert the public's attention from its dissatisfactions with schooling, much the same dissatisfactions as in the 1980s. One of many books attacking educationists at the time, 1954, had a 1980s ring to its title: *The Diminished Mind: A Study of Planned Mediocrity in our Public Schools.*[5] The nonprofit Council for Basic Education was formed in 1956—a generation before the "back to basics" slogan of the late 1970s. Circumstances other than the civil rights movement also diverted public attention from the dissatisfactions with public schools. One was the Russians' surprise launch of their Sputnik satellite. The federal government reacted quickly, and the National Education Defense Act of 1958 was voted by Congress. The extra billions of dollars that the act provided over the years were intended to improve achievement in math and science, still unrealized in the 1980s. The 1950s and '60s were also decades of enormous expansion in higher education, a growth industry rapidly turning out people with doctorates to staff itself. All the while, until 1970, there was a teacher shortage. Teachers' colleges expanded, turning out more education majors than ever. But of everything that diverted attention from poor schooling, none was so permanent an instrument of obfuscation as the plight of blacks made poignantly visible by the civil rights movement.

Educationists used the movement for their own purposes, which were twofold. One was gain in money, power, and political clout. Beginning with the Great Society of the Johnson administration, the federal government provided funds for educational programs that also permitted education professors to increase their personal incomes, acquire all manner of perquisites, or "perks," and attain aggrandized status within universities. Two, the civil rights movement provided the rhetoric behind which to hide their lack of a body of pedagogical knowledge. Having failed to develop even effective means to teach reading and arithmetic, educationists adopted the rhetoric of the civil rights movement to move themselves onto a loftier plane. Now they were going to "change society," which to a considerable extent they had already done. By the 1950s, children in public schools were beginning to be noticeably less rigorously educated than their public-school educated parents. Thanks to the civil rights movement, educationists were going to "combat racism"; and with the women's movement, "combat sexism"; next, to "combat classism"; and finally to champion "sexual preference." Most especially, educationists are against "elitism," the term they use to combat academic excellence.

In getting grants from federal agencies, it helped enormously to have a dean whom the education establishment considered innovative, including the parts of the establishment employed in federal agencies in Washington, D.C. Dwight Allen, for a decade up to 1975, was regarded as one of the most innovative; and under his guidance $15 million in grants came into the school, over and above its budget from the university. When one of his assistants mentioned that I was submitting a proposal to the Bureau of Education of the Handicapped, he responded, "Oh, going in the front door. That's a switch!"

Included in each grant proposal of any size was a salary for the director of the program or "principal investigator." It was in addition to a professor's regular salary. Since the professors teach nine months of the year, the director's salary is often paid during the three summer months, hence Byrd Jones' reported $5,230 income from the COP Program for the summer of 1973. But probably the perks of a grant were as important as the extra income.

Professors normally do not have the backup or support services of executives in business. It was one of the first things I noticed when I joined the school. But with a grant of any size, the professor who directs a program suddenly has his own secretary, a telephone budget for calls beyond the local area, travel money, and one or more graduate assistants to whom routine work and errands can be delegated. Having funds for supporting graduate students on assistantships also expands the graduate program. With a large contract, such as the COP program described in the last chapter, the program director is suddenly the head of a small empire.

Ethnic politics made it easier for schools of education to get grants intended to improve the educations of black people if they had black people on their faculties as well as enrollments of black students. Education schools all over the nation recruited them. Some also created black faculty out of their own Ed.D. degree candidates, as did the U. Mass school beginning in 1968.

The gain in money, power and perks from grants was obvious to a group of black faculty and students in the school in the early 1970s who happened not to share in the gain. The group accused Dwight Allen of pecuniary self-interest and of running a "plantation of house blacks." It threw a picket line around the school in 1972 and kept it closed for several days in a vain attempt to gain a say in the spending of grant money. No one dared to try to break through the all-black picket line. One of the pickets was Rhody McCoy of Ocean Hill–Brownsville. He had gotten a quick Ed.D. degree in 1971 in less than a year while enrolled in one formal course, then was immediately made an associate professor.[6] Chairman of McCoy's dissertation committee was Robert L. Woodbury, possessor of the respectable Ph.D. in history from Yale. After the insurgent group failed in its purposes, Rhody McCoy and other black faculty in the group moved to other universities.

But although blacks recognized the gains to schools of education in acquiring black faculties and adopting black stances, blacks did not recognize that they also had been made stalking horses. The high-flown rhetoric of fighting in the cause of blacks was an excellent screen behind which educationists hid their lack of pedagogical knowledge and inability to help the education of *any* children, including those who were black. If blacks recognized that they had been made stalking horses, they did not let on that they knew. They concentrated on getting degrees, the credentials for jobs and better jobs in schools and colleges. During my twelve years at the school, at no time did I hear a black person complain about the poor quality of what the school offered in the way of learning.

I occasionally heard complaints from nonblacks. A Puerto Rican doctoral candidate was quoted in the local press, "The programs of the School of Education are the most efficient copout I have ever seen to cover up the incredibly low intellectual level of . . . courses."[7] Linda Best, from Trinity College, Dublin, said of a curriculum development course she had dropped, "I couldn't stomach it." One of my best graduate students complained of Mickey Mouse courses frequently. Asked why she had not chosen to work for a doctorate in an academic department, she replied, "An Ed.D. is easier." But never from blacks did I hear complaints about the quality of what was offered in the School. I knew of no black graduate students who took courses in academic departments, which they could have done.

Due to being seriously undereducated, they were unable to be critical of the quality of what they were getting. It was hardly their fault, of course. Almost all black Americans in the United States, except those from the West Indies, originate in the South where slightly more than half still reside. As in agrarian areas everywhere, education was less valued in the South than in industrially developed areas. Southern states underspent Northern states for educating whites as well as blacks, although the separate and unequal system of schools for blacks made them more seriously undereducated. The exceptions are so few as to prove the rule. Unfortunately for blacks who migrated to Northern cities after World War II, their children enrolled in school systems with a diminished ability to teach them, and the majority of blacks now living in the North and those still in the South remain undereducated.

But more serious than what blacks fail to know is what they believe that hinders their achievement. Early in the civil rights movement, most blacks were referred to as "disadvantaged," meaning no more than that they suffered the circumstances typical of any group that is poor. Then, that term was converted to other things:

> Some black educators and community-control activists charged that black children had been deprived of their own rich cultural heritage in feckless efforts to make them think and act like whites. To the standard analysis of the defects of ghetto education, they responded that black children needed to study their culture, to identify with black heroes, and to find classroom acceptance for the "black English" with which they were comfortable. As the number of black students on traditionally white campuses expanded rapidly in the late 1960s, similar demands were presented for black studies programs. Eager to cool racial tensions, colleges and universities [obliged].[8]

No college or university department obliged faster or more eagerly to accommodate to blacks than the education department, or went further in turning what had been seen as disadvantages into attributes of merit. Blacks were no longer "culturally deprived," they had a "rich culture" that made them different but equal. This was the atmosphere in which Peter Wagschal published his "Illiterates with Doctorates" article saying that the 3Rs had no future. Wagschal was not going against the educationist flow; he was going with the flow. He came embarrassingly close, of course, to describing existing circumstances within the field. Educationists were turning out semi-illiterates with doctorates, white and black. They had little further to go to reach outright illiteracy.

Academically deficient blacks, to be absolute screens for white educationists, had also to be set up in front offices as deans, associate deans, assistant deans, admissions officers, and program heads. Acting in accord with notions that blacks are just culturally different—and against the long-established educational norms of Western civilization—administrators of the U. Mass ed school could disregard GRE tests scores, no matter how low. The likes of Mary, described in Chapter 1, could be admitted with scores of 210 in computation and 240 in verbal. Such admissions were in keeping with the flow of educationists' rhetoric. So was the

National Education Association when it adopted black stances as its own, including favoring the abolition of standardized tests in public schools. Anyone who believes that the selection of Mary Futrell in 1983 as the president of the 1.7-million-member NEA had nothing to do with her being black, is naive.

Black educationists now have the same self-interests as white educationists, are now one with the field. The presence of blacks at all levels in it makes any criticism of the field, and any reforms that threaten jobs, easier to fend off with countercharges of racism or any of the many politer equivalents. Issues of poor teacher training, shortages of math and science teachers, the poor quality of education majors and low achievement in schools across the nation, are obscured, confused and hidden behind black issues.

Having become one with the field, black educationists contribute to the ten-times disadvantage of black students vis-à-vis Asian students. They have joined white educationists in putting dysfunctional notions into the heads of schoolteachers, administrators, and ultimately into the heads of black children—notions that make them less able to compete with members of all other groups in school and beyond.

Documentation is easy to find. All one has to do is look into the shut-off-from-the-public world of educationists. For example, see a book with the title of *Black Children*, published in 1982, written by black educationist Janice E. Hale.[9]

Before showing her order of priorities for teaching black children, we should know just how respectable Janice Hale is within the field. First of all, her book is published by a university press, and therefore presumably scholarly. Moreover, her credentials, taken at face value, are impressive. She is associate professor of education at Jackson State University in Mississippi; has a doctorate in education from Georgia State University; and has taught at Yale, the University of Connecticut and the University of California at San Diego. She acknowledges help and indebtedness to no less than forty-five people with doctorates at various other institutions of higher learning.

What priorities does Janice Hale establish for teaching black children in her book? She lists "academic rigor" *not in first place but in third and last place*.[10] It would be a mistake to dismiss such a low priority for academic subjects as just Mississippian or

Southern. Subordinating academic matters to other considerations is national; it is evident in New York City schools.

A glaring instance is in the city's predominantly black and Hispanic elementary and junior high schools. Since 1970, those in the lowest 45 percent in reading were permitted to hire teachers who have not taken or passed the New York City Board of Examiners licensing tests. They have been permitted to hire teachers who have passed, instead, the less rigorous National Teachers Examination.

One would expect local community school boards and parent school committees, concerned about their children's low achievement, to insist on hiring teachers from the same source as the high achieving schools. But, as with Janice Hale, they subordinate academic competence to other considerations, the prime one being ethnicity. Since black and Puerto Rican would-be teachers have a higher failure rate than whites in taking the Board of Examiners tests, they consider the tests to be culturally biased. Had the minority groups had their way, the state legislature would have abolished the Board of Examiners when it passed the decentralization law; the 45 percent rule was a compromise to allow local school boards composed of minority peoples to hire more minority teachers.

The stress on ethnicity reflects the educationist field as much as it does minority groups. It has stressed "pluralism" over "the melting pot," ethnicity over Americanism, and "role models" in lieu of traditional academic competence. Schools have lost sight of fundamentals, including the critical importance of the correct and clear use of American English, as the following sentence aptly illustrates: "How many pieces of the United States does America have?"

This question is attributed to a fifth grade teacher, Aida Infante, of P.S. 89 in Queens. Such a string of words would have been impossible for *The New York Times* reporter to invent.[11] For the answer the teacher wanted, she should have asked: How many states make up the United States?

Another of her questions was "If we go south, what country would [*sic*] we find?" Aside from the wrong tense of the second verb, thinking students might name any Central or South American country, but the answer the teacher wanted was Mexico.

The emphasis on ethnicity has also affected affluent suburban schools. Recently, too, in *The New York Times*, an Englishwoman married to a Bulgarian recounted some of the 1960s experiences of their American-born son in a school in Westchester County: ". . . he excitedly bore home shamrocks, menorahs, candy from piñantas, maps of Columbus' voyage and struggled to bring true African rhythm from his saxophone . . . celebrating the multi-faceted culture of his native land."[12]

Although his teachers made vague references to his "rich Slav heritage," there was little for his English half. While in the second grade, he plaintively asked his mother one night, "Mum, were there ever any English people who came and 'tributed to America?" "As he grew older, being half Bulgarian, he was invited to join various Bulgarian-American societies, to celebrate St. Cyril's Day, to crack Bulgarian Easter eggs and even to make a little presentation on Bulgarian Hour on cable TV."

Such stress on ethnicity at the expense of American history has a lesser effect in predominantly white suburbs than in cities where black and Hispanic students are concentrated. The stress is consistent with Janice Hales's priorities in her book *Black Children*. With academic rigor placed third and last in her curriculum for black children, in first place is "political/cultural (ideology)." Hale refers to all black people everywhere, including the United States, as being "in a colonial relationship with white people (Europeans)." She claims that "the labor power and resources of the colonized" are exploited, and states:

> Education for struggle has a consciousness-raising function for Black people, instructing them concerning the following realities:
> • who they are
> • who the enemy is
> • what the enemy is doing to them
> • what to struggle for
> • what form the struggle must take[13]

I would not quote from Hale's *Black Children* if her main ideas were not congruent with what I observed for twelve years at the U. Mass School of Education, read in the literature of the educationist field, and know of the workings of inner city schools. Other ideas exist among black educationists, to be sure, integrationist ideas as well as separatist notions, alternating frequently and confusingly from one moment to the next in the same people.

I do not know what portion of black people in the United States subscribe to Hale's ideas. But I do know that black people who are *educationists* subscribe to them. They do place ethnicity first and subject matter last. Most black educationists do speak of the white majority as "the enemy," if not always directly, then indirectly by innuendo and allusion. They seem to assume that the larger society must change before black children can enjoy equal educational opportunity. This is opposite to what is in the heads of Asians. They assume the opportunities exist in the schools to grasp.

Hale's *Black Children*, though published by a university press, is illogical and ill-written, though no more so than most books by white educationists. She takes readymade educationists' notions and adds to them notions of African culture in an effort to make black children different from white children. With the usual disparagement of "traditional" she says: "The emphasis of traditional education has been upon molding and shaping Black children so that they can be fit into an educational process designed for Anglo-Saxon middle-class children. We know that the system is not working."[14]

She fails to acknowledge that "the system," even as bad as it is, works extraordinarily well for Asian immigrant children. Nor does she acknowledge that it has and continues to work well for the offspring of West Indian blacks, about whom much has been written, a literature that Hale should be acquainted with. The following from *Beyond the Melting Pot* refers to British West Indians in Harlem during the 1920s and '30s:

> They were viewed from the beginning by native American Negroes as highly distinctive—in accent, dress, custom, religion (Anglican), and allegiances (they celebrated the King's birthday). Distinctive as they were, they were forced to live in the same quarters as other Negroes. Furious at the prejudice far greater than that among whites in their home islands, they were helpless to do much about it, Many, as a consequence, turned radical. Negro Communists and labor leaders, it has been said, were disproportionately West Indian.

But the West Indians' most striking difference from the

Southern Negroes was their greater application to business, education, buying homes, and in general advancing themselves. James Weldon Johnson (whose parents stemmed from British West Indies) described them in 1930: ". . . average high in intelligence and efficiency, there is practically no illiteracy among them, and many have sound English common school educations. They are characteristically sober-minded and have something of a genius for business, differing almost totally, in these from the average rural Negro of the South." They contributed disproportionately, all observers have agreed, to the number of Negro leaders and accomplished men.[15]

West Indian and American blacks have the same African origins, are of the same tribal mixture. The slavery practiced in the West Indies, moreover, was more harsh and exploitive than that practiced on the American mainland. Yet, in this century, West Indians and their descendants in the United States are a higher-achieving group, although probably never amounting to more than one percent of the total black population.[16]

Without going into the reasons that may account for the higher achievement, the differences between the two groups are the sum of the differences in their respective heads—what they know, believe, and feel. Each group has had a somewhat different culture to adapt to and borrow from since the time of their respective emancipations—1838 for West Indians and 1863 for American blacks. West Indians, however, have a higher acceptance of what they have borrowed from the dominant culture and made their own.

Take, for example, a group of them living in the metropolitan area of New York City who can be seen from May until September in Van Cortlandt Park on weekends and holidays, dressed in white from head to toe, playing cricket. They belong to the New York Cricket League of 15 clubs, comprised largely of Jamaicans, Trinidadians, Barbadians, Guyanese and others from the Leeward and Windward Islands. Founded in 1919, the league continues today. One of its members, in 1983, told a *New York Times* reporter, "Cricket is a gentleman's game," and explained that its code of conduct remains the strictest of any sport: "You cannot misbehave. You cannot question an umpire's decision or even look at him in a questionable way. Or else you can be thrown off the field and disciplined by the league".[17] He remembered the rare occurrence of a cricketer who, upset over a call, struck the umpire. He was banned from the league for life, and a report of his unseemly conduct was circulated to other leagues.

To anyone uninformed about West Indies history, it may appear that these black cricketers, dressed all in white, are trying to be white: British white, in this instance. Nothing could be further from the truth. A 1984 newspaper account from England, announcing that the West Indies cricket team was "creaming" the English team, emphasized the degree to which the game was "intertwined with statehood," independence from Britain.

> [West Indian] players and writers . . . got their ethos from the rules of cricket, learned to play it better than anybody else and then came to England to play cricket and drum up financial and political support for their cause.
>
> That fight [for independence], of course, is over. But the importance of cricket to the West Indies as a locus of national pride and achievement continues.[18]

In excelling at cricket, West Indians no more try to be white than American blacks are trying to be white in excelling at basketball. They have taken over the game and made it their own, even though it also remains the game of the whites who originated it.

It occurs to no one, of course, to disapprove of blacks who engage in sports that have no roots in Africa. Acceptance of first world sports appears to be total among blacks everywhere. But those blacks who have become acculturated to Western civilization's more intellectual aspects are often frowned upon and even ostracized by other blacks. One sees such reactions reported in the most unlikely places, such as an item on Paris, France, under Style in *The New York Times*. It reported on Paris' black society, its restaurants, discotheques, beauty salons, clubs, and so forth. A West Indian in one of the clubs was quoted: "Black Africans often don't like blacks from the Caribbean and vice versa." The reason? "Africans feel people from the Caribbean try to ignore that they were once African. They often say we have black skins and white minds."[19]

Blacks who dislike other blacks for having "white minds" show a deep-seated resentment of whites. The resentment pervades *Black Children* by educationist Janice Hale. But she goes further. She virtually denies that blacks can have "white minds." She denies that black children learn to think in the same way that white children learn and think. She bases her assertion on black children having a different "cognitive style."[20]

No medical or scientific evidence exists that black children have brains different from white children, which they would have to have in order to possess a different cognitive style. Cognitive psychologists have acquired a body of knowledge about learning, particularly how children learn their native language; and they take language-learning as the paradigm for *all* learning. They have found that children everywhere, regardless of geography or race, learn their native tongue in the same predictable way; and that all children are equally capable of learning any of the world's languages. Everywhere, children go through steps in learning to speak that are universally the same. In different parts of the world they learn different languages, to be sure, and much else that is different. But *the manner in which they learn, the cognitive steps they go through*, is universal. Strictly speaking, no different cognitive styles of learning are possible.

Nevertheless, educationists espouse the notion that different children learn in different ways, as when groups of black students score lower on tests than groups of white students. A black teacher on TV network news in 1983 said, "Black people don't think the way white people think." She said this in reaction to the news of differences in scores on the Florida state teachers' exam. It was passed by a much higher percentage of white candidates than black candidates. Schools of education promote the notion that black people do not think like white people think. It persists because of its utility as an excuse and defense. Janice Hale even refers to high-achieving college-bound black students as having "white" SAT scores. She complains that whites "seek the super-achieving blacks," instead of those from the lowest strata for schools and job-training programs,[21] as if the standards were different for Asians, whites, and other groups.

I said above that resentment of whites pervades Janice Hale's book. Her resentment may be more apparent than real. She has, after all, accommodated, done all that is necessary to acquire a university niche for herself and become part of the largely white educationist field. Within it, she has become a specialist like other blacks and whites. Her speciality is black children and how teachers should teach them. Were Hale to concede that black children learn no differently from other children, Hale would have no specialty.

I do not suggest that Hale is guilty of heartless self-interest. She could easily have arrived at her professorial rank and notions by following, unthinkingly, the dictates of the field and adopting its existing notions for her purposes. No cynical heartlessness was necessary for her to have done that, just a typical educationist mindset.

To be sure, she contradicts what most of the respected writers believe about black Americans—that they have lost all trace of African culture.[22] Hale professes to see persistent and significant Afro-characteristics in all blacks, including Americans. She speaks of "the culture, cosmology, history and perspective of Africans of the diaspora." One of her Afro-characteristics is: "Black children are motorically precocious. They are more active and have more physical energy to expend than white children. This physical precocity can be substantiated by the number of Black athletes who dominate major sports in numbers disproportionate to Black representation in the population."[23]

This supposed precocity also becomes one of the rationales for black children doing poorly in school. They enter school with "their high motoric activity," Hale says, and the school then proceeds to "crush their freedom and creativity." Additional Afro-characteristics, according to Hale, are energetic "body language," proficiency in "non-verbal communication," and preference for "oral-aural modalities." These Afro-characteristics, among others, are presented as virtues by Hale, which she complains that schools do not reward. Nowhere in Hale's *Black Children* does she stress the importance of becoming fluent in written language and arithmetic. Indeed, in Hale's view, black people "have been 'miseducated' into confusing their interests with those of the dominant society." This amounts to a rejection of American culture which, wherever acted upon, precludes black children from ever matching the educational attainments of white children, and dooms them to remaining at a ten-times disadvantage vis-à-vis Asian children. What Hale puts into the heads of future and present teachers leads only into a deadend.

If, on the other hand, we follow the lead of the most respected writers who say that all significant traces of African culture have disappeared among black Americans, then the only culture they have is that of the United States, bearing in mind that they have contributed to it. We must then ask what is the place of schooling in the United States? What are the typical attitudes toward it in the majority culture? What is the educational climate?

> In most high schools bright students stand outside the highly ranked peer groups, which are concerned mainly with popularity. Boys care mainly about cars and sports and athletic prowess; girls are concerned mainly with beauty and glamour and attractiveness. All of them regard dating and extracurricular activities as very important, and high-school elites confer the greatest weight to these aspects of student life. Brains and good grades bring few if any tangible rewards from adolescent peer groups.[24]

Daniel Bell's description is from the early 1960s but there is little reason to believe that peer groups have changed much in the meantime with respect to "brains and good grades." Recent surveys of students indicate that junior and senior high schools are valued chiefly as places to meet their friends.

Popularity and athletic prowess are also valued by most parents. Fathers encourage sons to engage early in organized sports. Instances have occurred of a son repeating the ninth grade so that an extra year's growth will increase the chances of becoming a high school star. The sports pages of newspapers got high readership long before television, which has greatly increased enthusiasm for sports. Unlike Olympic medal winners, people who work chiefly with their brains—research scientists, doctors, lawyers, engineers, computer scientists, novelists, historians, etc.—are not given ticker-tape parades to honor their accomplishments.

Stars of high school athletic teams are offered college scholarships despite low grades. Some universities take illiterate athletes who leave after four years of playing for them still illiterate.[25] Even with low SAT scores, star athletes gain admission to Ivy League colleges. "An outstanding basketball player with a 450 verbal score on the S.A.T. looks better to an admissions committee than an involved yearbook editor with a 600. In fact, three Ivy League colleges recently admitted athletes with S.A.T. verbal scores well under 400.[26] Even colleges with reputations for academic excellence sometimes overlook serious academic deficiencies in sports stars.

Young black students see that athletics is the road to college, without getting good grades, and beyond, to possible careers in professional sports. Each year's crop of new millionaires among professional athletes who are black fuels the dream. A perfectly adequate explanation for the disproportionately high representation of blacks among professional athletes and the disproportionately low representation among academic achievers is this: *They reflect the most obvious aspects of the American culture; they are exaggerations of it.*

Middle-class students, on the other hand, are more sophisticated in reflecting a greater range of the dominant culture. Though most of their energies, too, may be channeled into gaining popularity and athletic prowess, they are more often mindful of some need to achieve academically, especially if their elementary school preparation was adequate. Though they may not try to be "brains," they often try to meet some minimal standard, possibly with college or occupation in mind. There is, after all, an enormous difference between two outstanding basketball players, one with a 450 verbal score (just above average) on the SAT, and one with a 300 score (grossly below average). Middle-class peers at least permit averageness.

My daughter, Holly, had tremendous peer pressure to be more nearly average in the fifth and sixth grades, which my wife and I did not learn of until years later. Holly had been identified in the second grade as gifted in math. She was also a gifted reader. By the fourth grade she could fluently read aloud items on the front page of *The New York Times*. In the fifth and sixth grades, however, she had problems on examinations. She had to decide which and how many questions to answer incorrectly so as not to score higher than her best friend, the daughter of a professor in the engineering department. Any higher grade of Holly's so infuriated her best friend that she worked to turn the other girls against her. But although Holly was kept from showing her potential, her grades were nevertheless high. With working-class peers, they could have been quite low.

Typically in ghetto schools, the average is low, above which the group discourages anyone from rising, regardless of parental and teacher expectations. The potentially bright students seldom have a chance to shine.

When visiting the Dr. Sun Yat Sen junior high, I asked Maria Ting, the guidance counselor, if the high motivation of Chinese students rubbed off on the non-Chinese. She answered that black mothers had told her that they were glad their children were attending a school where motivation was high, but wished their children had Chinese friends. The black mothers complained that their children's black friends made fun of them when they attempted to study or go to the library.

Peer pressure among the Chinese students works in the opposite direction. Among them, the competition to achieve as high as possible is great. Sports and popularity are subordinated to academic achievement. This attitude, so different from what is typically in the heads of American white and black students, derives from their parents. Chinese and other Asian children are brought up to show deference and respect to parents, teachers, and all adults. Given parental scholastic goals, Chinese students work hard to achieve out of respect. This is why American teachers enjoy, find it enormously satisfying to teach Chinese children. Their obedience permits teachers to devote their time to teaching, uninterrupted by disruptive behavior.

Only one way exists in American schools to protect the more able child of any color from the venom of the less motivated or able peers. Separate them by ability, which is easy to do in city schools that have several classes per grade. Able black students, I am certain, desperately need such protection. Thomas Sowell says of his entering Stuyvesant High School: "It was gratifying to be with so many obviously bright and serious students, and not to feel that any attempt to use my own mind would be resented by slower classmates as 'showing off.' "[27]

Athletics is encouraged by the American school culture, but not intellectual prowess. The provisions for encouraging academic achievement, holdovers from an earlier age, are more resented today. Stuyvesant and other such selective high schools are called elitist but not the schools with athletic programs that recruit and produce athletic stars. Blacks do not complain of the tests that athletic coaches use to select and reject players for school teams. They accept the rules of athletics but not those of academics. They complain bitterly about inequality and cultural bias of tests of academic ability and charge that they are racially discriminatory. No one charges that the sport of basketball discrimates against people with short legs, or that the sport of gymnastics discriminates against people with long legs. The obvious physical advantages for particular sports and the hard work that goes into developing them are accepted by one and all. Intellectual prowess, on the other hand, is mysterious. Uneducated people, of whatever ethnicity, have no inkling of what it is and what is necessary to produce it. Thomas Sowell says of his parents:

> They understood—in the abstract—that Stuyvesant was a "better" high school, and they were proud that I had been accepted there, but its demands on my time and on their meager money seemed an incomprehensible burden. They even became suspicious of me, wondering if I was *really* at the public library as much as I said I was, or was off somewhere else getting into trouble. They found it inconceivable that anybody had to be at the library that often or that long. More than once I was asked, "What's really going on, Thomas? You can tell me, I'll try to understand." It would have been a good situation comedy, except that it was a tragedy that was tearing us apart.[28]

When he became ill and lost too much ground to make up quickly, Sowell decided to remain out of class for the rest of the semester, a decision opposed by all of his relatives. "Going to school was very important to all of them, though the substance of education or the prerequisities for its effectiveness were wholly unknown and a matter of no great concern to them."[29] Being recently from the South in the 1940s, with inadequate educations, they had no way of knowing what to be concerned about.

By the 1980s the majority of Northern black parents still had little idea of "the substance of education," while disproportionate numbers of West Indian blacks and Asian immigrants apparently did. They knew it had mainly to do with achieving academically. Moreover, we have evidence that Asians have a good idea of "the prerequisites for its effectiveness" that they bring with them from their native countries. It is one of the findings of the crosscultural study of the three elementary schools in Taiwan, Japan, and Minneapolis, previously cited: "The researchers also discovered cultural differences that could affect performance. Asked about the "most important factor in determining a child's performance in school," mothers in Japan and Taiwan were likely to give a high rating to 'effort,' while American parents were more likely to cite 'ability'."[30]

Asian parents provided time for their children to exert effort in studying. Far fewer of them, for instance, expected their children to do household chores—only 17 percent of parents in Taiwan and 28 percent in Japan, compared to 90 percent in Minneapolis. A Taiwan mother said it would "break her heart" to assign chores when her child might otherwise be studying. In keeping with the belief in effort, Asian children do much more homework. Among the 5th graders, the Japanese students spent 57 minutes a day doing homework and Taiwan students 114 minutes, compared to only 46 minutes for the Minneapolis students. The more time given to homework, moreover, is in the context of Japan and Taiwan having a school year of 240 days compared to the 180 days that is average in the United States. The school day in these two Asian countries is also longer.

Nevertheless, within the school day, Minneapolis students were found to spend much less time on academic subjects. The director of the project, Harold W. Stevenson, was quoted as saying that the American students spend:

> ". . . less than half as much time as the Chinese and less than two-thirds as much as the Japanese on academic activities."
>
> A principal reason, classroom observers found, is that American school children spend an enormous amount of time in such activities as talking to peers in class, asking questions unrelated to the lesson, wandering about the classroom or staring into space.
>
> "One of the most startling statistics was that, when we went to observe specific children, 13 percent of the first graders and 18 percent of the fifth graders could not be found in the classroom," Mr. Stevenson said. "This category did not even exist with the Chinese and was infinitesimal with the Japanese."[31]

The classroom and school practices of teachers and administrators in most American schools reflect the miseducations received in schools of education, their heads filled with hosts of dysfunctional notions that are passed on to students and parents.

This is especially true of blacks, whether students or adults. Nothing illustrates the sum of dysfunctional notions in their heads more than the unanimous response to a question asked of a group of black people brought together at the end of May 1984 by a public opinion research firm for *The Wall Street Journal*. The group, a representative sample of the black community in the Newark, New Jersey, area, had been assembled so that the *Journal* could report what they believed and felt about Jesse Jackson's candidacy in the Democratic presidential primary.

> When asked whether a black child has a fair chance in this society, the entire room breaks into laughter at what they consider to be a ridiculous question.
> "Society is not ready for that. They're not going to give you a fair chance. Why, I don't know. I think the majority of white people have a fetish against black people. They don't want to live next door to you and are not going to go to school with you."[32]

Had a similar group of Chinese people been asked the same question, they would not have laughed. They believe their children have a fair chance. They would have expressed no concern, moreover, about white people wanting or not wanting to live next door or go to school with them. As we saw in the last chapter, when the Yung Wing school's principal integrated it with 15 percent non-Chinese children, he lost friends in Chinatown who would have preferred it to remain 100 percent Chinese.

What adults believe about children's chances in school almost inevitably gets into their children's heads. Typically, Chinese children believe in their chances and succeed; black children disbelieve and disproportionately fail.

But the disbelief of black children and youths is selective, limited to scholastic achievement which, of course, affects almost everything else they may attempt or fail to attempt in life. Black children's disbelief also reflects what they learn from the other two major sources of beliefs in the predominantly white American culture—television and the schools.

Early in life, black children begin to see that the rewards for being crowd-pleasers are great—attention, applause, fame, money, becoming "somebody." In school, they observe that beauty and athletic prowess are admired and rewarded by peer groups, and can be the means of going to college or attempting modeling and acting careers. On television, they see a disproportionately large number of college and professional athletes, singers, musicians, comics, actors, and models who are black. Black youngsters notice their wealth, expensive clothes and cars, and acceptance by blacks and whites alike. Examples are Michael Jackson, Diana Ross, "Magic" Johnson, O.J. Simpson, and Bill Cosby. In the heads of black children and youths there seems to be little doubt that they have just as much chance as anybody else in becoming a crowd-pleaser.

Much of this book was written at a desk overlooking the south side of Manhattan's 14th Street, always crowded with shoppers. Long before I heard the term for it, I saw black youths giving daily sidewalk performances of breakdancing, music blaring from portable radios. Much of my research was done in the New York University library on Washington Square. Every time I walked through its park, various clumps of people were gathered around singers, musicians, or dancers. Most of them were black.

Though the odds are like the odds against winning the state lottery, black children and youths believe they have a chance to "make it" as professional athletes and entertainers. For each one who does, tens of thousands of hopefuls do not. In the last twenty years, nevertheless, they do not claim that they have been kept out of professional sports and show business by racism. They accept that part of the dominant white culture as being open to them.

But the mass of blacks—the millions on welfare and in low-paying jobs—often attribute their circumstances to racism. Many have no other explanation for being underrepresented in medicine, law, the sciences, engineering, corporate managements, and small businesses. Some blacks in business, making salaries of $40,000 a year, attribute not being advanced as fast as they would like to racism.[33] They disbelieve that white society is giving them a fair chance. Their disbelief is buttressed by there being some truth to it. Blacks are, indeed, kept out of some jobs, positions, and neighborhoods by pure prejudice, although to a far lesser extent than formerly.

It is understandably difficult for blacks to sort out what is due to racism and what to other causes. They are particularly chagrined and frustrated about their children not doing better in school. Seeing their children fall behind, blacks often hurl charges of cultural bias, racism, and discrimination, although this has become more difficult to do in inner city schools as black teachers and administrators have replaced those who are white.

Such charges have produced concessions in the past, but without the improvement expected. Colleges capitulated to demands for more black studies, more black students and faculty, separate but equal campus facilities. On the U. Mass campus, black students were given a separate section in the campus student newspaper where, in the 1970s, they often displayed writing that was incoherent. For inner city schools, blacks have demanded and gotten more black teachers, principals, and superintendents. Student achievement nevertheless continued low. No school system is blacker in the number of teachers and administrators than the Washington, D.C., system, which remains one of the least achieving in the nation. Black teacher and principal role models, miseducated in schools of education, have not produced the results blacks claimed they would.

Nothing tried in the last quarter of a century has helped. Educationally, blacks remain an underclass. The more than $60 billion (in 1980 dollars) in federal funds spent for the improvement of elementary and secondary education of the disadvantaged between 1965 and 1980 [34] made little difference. With the increased immigration from Asian countries, blacks have seen Asian students, equally poor and with the handicap of speaking a foreign language at first, leapfrog past them in achievement. This has created resentment. Black students in two Philadelphia high schools have shown Asians considerable animosity. A Laotian in the tenth grade of West Philadelphia High was hospitalized after being punched and shoved by a black student in a volleyball game in gym class. At University City, a Vietnamese student had his neck broken in an attack by a group of black students. In 1983, the Asian population in University City High School was 15 percent. A *New York Times* report stated: "Over the years, black students and parents have charged that preferential treatment is given to Asian students. Asians, many of them refugees, say they have been regularly victimized [by blacks] in the school and in the community.[35]"

Other such racial feelings and incidents have occurred across the country. In Dallas in 1983 a Cambodian sitting outside his apartment was beaten to death by a group of blacks. Subsequently, black youths threw stones at the Cambodian group he belonged to. At the funeral, one of the mourners said, "it's not good for us to live with black people here."[36]

Asian immigration to the United States is expected to continue in the years ahead. If blacks are unable to compete—if they remain at a ten-times disadvantage vis-à-vis Asians in academic achievement—a fear of Nathan Glazer's may come to pass—"A competition over who is more discriminated against, who more worthy of federal or other protection, may well develop, with nasty overtones."[37]

Such a competition may be underway in New York City. For years, its Chinatown schools have asked the central Board of Education to modify its guidelines for determining Title 1 schools so that they could be included. Title 1 provided extra federal funds for schools where students were "disadvantaged." The New York City Board of Education guidelines for determining such schools was a percent of families on welfare. Although the incomes of Chinatown parents were among the lowest in the city, although they were as poor as anyone else, few were on welfare. Chinatown school committees believed that the central Board's guidelines were unfair to their children. Acting on their behalf, the Community District 2 school board has retained a law firm to possibly bring suit against the central Board in federal court to force it to modify its guidelines. Such a suit would occur in the context of the school system being 70 percent black and Hispanic, with a Hispanic chancellor, and close to 20 percent of the top administrative posts in the school system held by blacks. It is a context rampant with ethnic politics.

But if blacks can consider taking some responsibility for being at a ten-times disadvantage vis-à-vis Asians, much can be learned and changed. Poverty, by itself, is not the cause of academic failure; neither is coming from a different culture; and nor is speaking a foreign tongue, or in accents unlike middle-class Americans. Having no role models can hardly be blamed for academic failure. Children of Chinese, Japanese, Koreans, Laotians, Cambodians, and Vietnamese immigrants have few teachers who look and talk like them. Many Chinese parents see advantages for their children in having American teachers. It helps them learn English faster. Being poor, culturally different, speaking a foreign language and having no role models, are obstacles that Asian students overcome by application and effort. Black students can do the same, providing they believe that they can.

As for oppression and discrimination, Chinese and Japanese people in the United States have been subjected to both, intensely. Until after World War II, the American image of a Chinese resident of the United States was the Chinese laundryman. Chinese were excluded from virtually all other occupations, and even from entering the country by the immigration laws. This is the origin of "Not a Chinaman's chance!" The Japanese Americans on the West Coast had their property confiscated and were shut up during World War II in concentration camps, unfairly and unjustly. Many of the Laotians, Cambodians, and Vietnamese very recently suffered unspeakable privations and horrors at the hands of others before gaining asylum in the United States. Yet, Asian peoples have not let past suffering, oppression, and discrimination keep them from taking advantage of the fair chance this society offers.

Asian immigrants appear to accept willingly the dominant white culture, while privately practicing their own customs. One hears no accusations from them that the schools are trying to give them "white minds." Asians accept the dominant culture while black Americans typically accept only that part which looms on television screens but provides relatively few jobs. They accept the crowd-pleasing opportunities and reject much of the rest.

Black Americans once accepted the dominant culture, including its most important part. Immediately after the civil war, the newly freed slaves begged to be taught to read and write, which the laws of most Southern states had denied them. Blacks sought education so eagerly that fifty years after emancipation, having started with nearly 100 percent illiteracy, they reached 75 percent literacy, an achievement that Thomas Sowell calls "remarkable."[38]

The first public high school for blacks, Dunbar, was established in 1870 in Washington, D.C. Its curriculum resembled that of the private secondary schools and came to include Latin, French, German, and Spanish; ancient, modern, European, and American history; mathematics, chemistry, physics, biology, as well as English, and economics. It was a traditional curriculum. To teach it, the school attracted black and white teachers with degrees from Northern colleges. Among the graduates of Dunbar High School were: "the first black general, the first black federal judge, the first black cabinet member, the discoverer of blood plasma, the first popularly elected black senator, the first black professor at a major university, and a long list of other 'firsts' in many fields."[39] Black Americans were accepting of society and its educational institutions, despite the obstacle of severe discrimination.

By the time of the civil rights movement, when hopes were raised that schooling for all black children would improve, public schools were in decline. In the North, they were unable to cope with the mass of newly arrived black students from the South as they had coped with the children of European immigrants early in the century. Retiring teachers who had resisted the fads and notions of educationists for decades were being replaced by young teachers who had less resistance to them.

Black Americans stopped being accepting of schools when their hopes of better educations for their children were dashed by continued disproportionate failure. In the 1960s they began demanding that the schools be turned over to them—community control and decentralization. In this they had the support and blessing of many educationists. But as Dr. Kenneth Clark pointed out, the "community," too, were victims of inadequate educations.

Black Americans were easy marks for the extravagant and unfounded claims of the early 1970s that children, especially black children, were going to learn from television—one more empty claim that makes evident that education professors did not know what they were doing. Had they known anything about instruction, learning, and how one medium differs from another, no part of television would have ever been called "educational." Television—and also film—is *the worst possible medium* for teaching most things, with the exception of what things look like. It excels at bringing vision from afar and little else, other than holding attention by introducing excessive visuals changes and movements, appealing to the most primitive portion of the human visual processing system.

It is of course mildly informative to see astronauts floating weightless in orbit around the earth. But nothing that made the space missions possible is visible. We cannot see the physics, the chemistry, the mathematics, the computer programs, the expertise in the heads of the astronauts, and the teams on the ground, that put them into space. Television is utterly useless in conveying bodies of knowledge, except as an aid in the sense that the blackboard is an aid. Language can be written on blackboards but it is from printed books that children must learn to read. The skills of a medium can only be learned within the medium.

Education professors, via their teaching of teachers, encouraged children to believe that television was educational. They encouraged the belief that *Sesame Street, The Electric Company,* and *Infinity Factory* were alternative ways to learn the beginnings of written language and mathematics. Publicity put out by the Children's Television Workshop, the U.S. Office of Education, and other agencies, indicated that these programs were primarily intended to help black children, and the publicity photographs showed them staring at TV screens. In the phrase of the early 1970s, the medium "turned them on," held their attention. The notion was destructive; in the 1980s it is apparent how little they learned, and it may have encouraged them not to learn.

In the 1960s and '70s the federal government was funding any scheme that seemed to promise betterment for blacks. All in positions to promise, promised. Professors of education put forward their schemes. The chief positive effect of them was to increase their personal incomes, power, and perks. They also used blacks as stalking horses. They adapted black stances and rhetoric, behind which to hide their lack of knowledge while appearing to be more high-minded and caring than anyone else, particularly other university departments. To their already long list of "educations"—driver education, vocational education, art education, etc.—they added urban education. They recruited black students and faculty, increased the number of black Ed.D. degree holders, made some education professors and administrators. The standards of schools of education were already low. It was a small step down to say that no reliable standards existed, and no attempt should be made to give blacks "white minds." White educationists hid behind the black rhetoric of "community control," black culture, black English, agreed that whites were inherently racists, and even appeared to identify with black Africa. It was all symbolized at the U. Mass School of Education by Dean Dwight Allen, dressed daily in a dashiki.

A black recruit to the school who, in himself, embodied typical contradictory attitudes toward the white society, who also advocated educational television programs, and who made an ideal stalking horse because he was famous, was Bill Cosby.

The young Bill Cosby starting out, while still a physical education major at Temple University, had to believe that society was not so racist that it would block him from becoming an entertainer. In order for him to drop out of college and try to gain a place in show business for himself, Cosby had to believe that white society offered him a chance. Otherwise, he could not have made the attempt to become an entertainer.

Bill Cosby's belief was well-founded. Having grown up a poor boy in a Philadelphia ghetto, whose mother worked in white people's homes as a domestic, Cosby became successful and wealthy. His mother came to be waited on and served by his white servants—at least those I saw in his home were white. At the head of his long and elegant table, his mother at his side, Cosby presided with great and justifiable pride.

But typical of other black people, and contradicting his own success, Bill Cosby also believed that white society was extremely racist. He repeatedly used this epithet in his dissertation.[40] In the first eleven pages of it, except for the first two, Cosby uses racism or a variant of it on every page:

> . . . a black child, because of inherent racism in American schools [,] will be ill prepared to meet the challenges of an adult future. [p. 3]

> . . . black children are trained to occupy those same positions held by their parents in a society economically dominated and maintained by a white status quo. [p. 4]

> . . . Teachers assume that urban [black] children are intellectually deficient. [p. 5]

... teachers—instilled with their own racist attitudes—are quick to make assumptions about the cognitive abilities of their [black] students: [p. 6]

... a lacksidasical [sic] attitude on the part of urban schools to change their process of education. [p. 7]

... the debilitating sense of worthlessness whites convey in a variety of ways and so feed the self-hatred produced by discrimination ... [p. 8]

... a first effort to combat institutional racism. [p. 9]

... the insidious nature of institutional racism ... [p. 10, l. 9]

Racism cuts deeply into the fabric of American society. [p. 10, l. 12]

The ferociousness with which racism is perpetuated ... [p. 11, l. 11]

... the depth and pervasiveness of racism within the white community. [p. 11, l. 15]

I do not know if Cosby recognized the contradictions in his views about how racist this society is. Though I was a member of his dissertation committee, I had no discussion with him on any portion of it. It can be argued that people in show business are less prejudiced than others. I believe they are less prejudiced. But entertainers usually make few of the business decisions about what is to be offered to the public. The mass audience is overwhelmingly white and everyone, at one time or another, has watched Cosby on television, seen his movies, attended his night club acts, and bought his records. Whites have bought the many products he has advertised in TV commercials. Were the mass audience racist to the degree of training black children "to occupy those same positions held by their parents," or perpetuating racism with "ferociousness," to quote Cosby, it is difficult to imagine how he and other black entertainers and professional athletes have come to be as popular as they are.

Cosby's assertions of racism in his dissertation, it should be remembered, was standard rhetoric of the school's administration and faculty, as well as much of the national black community. In my opinion, Bill Cosby repeated the standard rhetoric, unexamined.

The rest of his dissertation is just as standard. It repeats educationists' false notions and its research reflects the abysmally low standards of the field. Cosby mailed a questionnaire to teachers asking them to evaluate his *Fat Albert and the Cosby Kids* animated films for classroom use. His covering letter was on University of Massachusetts School of Education stationery, and signed by him. As anyone could have predicted, those teachers who mailed back the questionnaire gave favorable evaluations.

Cosby assumed that his films, along with *Sesame Street* and *The Electric Company*, were educational. He gives the standard justifications for believing so, based on false assumptions:

> The integration of the visual media into the urban classroom is of primary importance. Its utilization can help make certain problems much easier to deal with, for example, because of the difficulty urban children have of picking up a book and reading. If these youngsters cannot read due to whatever circumstances, and certainly it is proven that a certain percentage of our students coming out of high schools are still functionally illiterate, teachers must then try to educate in the next and easiest possible way. That is through the use of film. When used properly this medium can be just as important and just as fulfilling as reading a book.[41]

So usual is this statement of Cosby's in all its aspects that, quite literally, a thousand similar ones could be adduced. Let one suffice for all. It is by the chairman of the blue-ribbon panel convened by the College Entrance Examination Board to try to determine the causes of the long drop in SAT scores from 1963 to 1977: "I believe that a good teacher can make a course in radio, television, and film just as demanding and just as stimulating as a good teacher can make a course in basic English IV."[42] This statement, like Cosby's, assumes that all media are equal. With such an assumption, the blue-ribbon panel did not, of course, put its collective finger on the causes of the long decline in SAT scores, and in 1984 they were lower than in 1977.

The rhetoric and false notions that Bill Cosby repeats in his dissertation, he could have absorbed just from the polluted education atmosphere. He did not have to get them directly from any of the school's professors or educationists' writings.

He can hardly be blamed for repeating the notions of the field, of course. It was expected of him. He was meant to serve as a publicity shield, a blind, a stalking horse. His stalking-horse function was useful in 1983 as the wave of reports describing the low state of education began to crest. Dean Mario D. Fantini, in reaction, warned of the danger that the quality of education being called for by the reports could become elitist. And similtaneously, the school announced the 1983 William Cosby, Jr. Alumni Awards.

The awards are an example of obfuscation and resistance to the climate critical of education. The school did not announce why Cosby's name was attached to the awards. I doubt that Cosby selected the people to receive them. That was probably done by a committee of administrators and/or faculty. But the announcement did not say whether Cosby or the school established the awards.

Among those receiving them was Professor Peter H. Wagschal, the author of "Illiterates with Doctorates" and the enemy of reading, writing, and arithmetic. Another recipient was Shirley M. DeShields, director of the University Communication Skills Center who, in my day, had given teaching assistantships to Mary and another black graduate student I knew of who also could not read, write, and compute adequately enough to help college students.

Cosby as stalking horse was also useful in 1984. The University of Massachusetts made him one of four alumni to receive a distinguished service award. The announcement and Bill Cosby's photograph appeared in the university publication *The Alumnus*.

Of course, Cosby continued to derive commercial benefit from having a doctorate. In the fall of 1984 a new television commercial for Coke went on the air featuring him with Julius Erving, the professional basketball player. Both were called doctor, Julius Irving's sports nickname being Dr. J. The advertising theme was "two out of two doctors agree" on the merits of drinking Coke.

In recruiting Bill Cosby and awarding him an Ed.D. degree, the U. Mass School of Education made him also an educationist. In Cosby's educationist head, as evidenced by his dissertation, are dysfunctional notions common to the field, the same as those put into the heads of teachers and administrators in education courses. The teachers and administrators, in turn, convey the dysfunctional notions to black children, putting them at an enormous disadvantage vis-à-vis everybody else. The ten-times disadvantage they suffer with respect to Asian immigrants is primarily due to the Asian children having more appropriate and useful ideas about society and school from parents, traditional ideas untainted by the notions of American educationists.

Unfortunately for children, parents, and teachers, Bill Cosby has been made a symbol of educationists, a representative of them. Each time he is called doctor, or the letters Ed.D. appear after his name on television or in print, the public is reminded that he has a doctorate in education. He makes educationists look good. Cosby is as effective in what he does as they are ineffective in what they are supposed to be doing.

Cosby works wonderfully well with young children, as is apparent from the many TV commercials and programs he has appeared in with them. Had he become a school teacher, he probably would have been a great one. With his personality, intelligence, and liking for children, Cosby could have done more than entertain them. Armed with subject matter, he could have gotten them to learn it readily and thoroughly. Bill Cosby is all that he was before the U. Mass School of Education recruited him. His M.Ed. and Ed.D. degrees added nothing whatsoever to his potential for being a great teacher.

12

Education's Big Guns Asmoking

Numerous reports of studies of public schools were published in book form in 1983 and 1984 by some of the nation's leading educationists. The authors are the field's best and brightest. Their books reveal the deficiencies common to all 1,287 schools and departments of education in the nation, even as their authors do their best to hide them.

THEODORE R. SIZER
Former Dean of Harvard's Graduate School of Education
Chairman, Education Department of Brown University

Sizer is the author of *Horace's Compromise: The Dilemma of the American High School*, published in 1984. *Time* magazine called it a "major new report" of a five-year study by Sizer and a team of researchers who visited eighty high schools across the nation. Sizer's study was funded by the Carnegie Corporation, the Esther A. and Joseph Klingenstein Fund, and the Charles E. Culpeper, Gates, and Edward John Noble Foundations; the study cost $900,000. Sizer is undoubtedly one of the field's big guns.

His book shows him to be intelligent, sophisticated, knowledgeable, and a readable writer. The skill with which his book is written, however, is more clever than honest, hides more than it reveals, omits more than it includes, obfuscates more than it enlightens. Particularly obfuscating are his recommendations for schools. Some are senseless, others faddish, vague or general, and the rest politically and economically infeasible. His book amounts to a public relations ploy, throwing sand in the eyes of what two educationists have called "the swelling mob of 'ed school bashers.' "[1]

To be sure, Sizer finds much wrong with the schools. He finds so much fault that one education reporter called his book "grim."[2] Sizer wrote within the prevailing climate of public dissatisfaction with schools. But being critical of public schools is nothing new for professors of education. They have always been school critics. Damning what schools were doing has always been the means of getting them to adopt education professors' fads and notions. Like his peers, moreover, Sizer takes no responsibility, for himself or his field, for what he finds wanting "out there" in the schools. Sizer helps the reader forget that he is part of the monopoly that trained all of the teachers and administrators in all of the schools criticized. He writes as if schools of education do not exist.

For example, he gives several instances of good and bad teaching. Though he knows that each teacher observed took education courses in schools of education in order to become a teacher, he makes no mention of that fact. He does not show how their education courses affected their teaching. He lets us know that he favors the Socratic method but it predates schools of education by 2,500 years. To make the common observation that everybody recognizes good and bad teaching when they see it, is to beg the question of what schools of education contribute to it.

Several places in Sizer's book beg for enlightenment on teacher training. One such place is at the end of a series of recommendations to a principal who must supervise the teachers who will carry them out. Sizer has the principal respond, "A lot turns on those teachers. Are they good enough?" Sizer answers, "They've got to be."[3] No more than that; no enlightenment on how "good enough" teachers are to be prepared and by whom.

In omitting mention of ed schools, Sizer avoids any hint that they are responsible for what he finds wrong. At the same time, Sizer slyly makes claim to technical knowledge for himself and his field. He says that his book is intended for "the lay reader."[4] This use of "lay" would be appropriate for an engineer or a medical doctor; in Sizer's mouth, "lay" is unearned.

Although his book is described as a report of visits to eighty different high schools all over the country in a five-year study, it contains relatively few specifics for such an extensive study. Instead, Sizer engages in fiction—"composites," he says, "a blending of people and places," or "nonfiction fiction."[5] Sizer relies heavily on what he calls "word pictures," and they comprise about 25 percent of his book. Sizer's aim is not to give the "lay" reader an intellectual understanding. In educationist fashion, he aims to give "the essential 'feel' of schools."[6]

The very first "feel" Sizer gives is for the fictitious Horace, a dedicated high school English teacher who loves teaching and knows his subject. He would be the ideal teacher were it not for the "compromise" forced on him. Horace cannot give as much time to preparing for his classes, reading students' papers, and other attention to them as he knows he ideally should. He has to cut corners. His corner-cuttings are forced by his having to moonlight in another job, because the number of students in his classes is too large and the interest and motivation of many students too low. Nothing whatsoever is wrong with Horace as a teacher that a decent salary, a student load reduced by half, and more interested students would not rectify.

Sizer does not present fictitious Horace this bluntly. He takes thirteen pages to build favorable word pictures, giving sociological details such as where Horace lives, what time he goes to bed, gets up in the morning, arrives at school, starts his first class, leaves school in the afternoon, and gets home for dinner. Sizer's word pictures also include Horace in his classes, the teachers' room, and in his moonlighting job. Even Horace's thoughts are seen.[7]

By using this technique of fiction, Sizer depends on the willing suspension of disbelief with which the reader normally reads novels and mystery stories. With the skill of a public relations writer, Sizer created in Horace not a composite of all teachers but an idealized image of a high school teacher that can beguile the "lay" reader, and please his many constituencies. Among them are his sponsors—the National Association of Secondary School Principals and the National Association of Independent Schools. They did not pay for the $900,000 study but their names are attached to it. Sizer can admit to many of the conditions and circumstances that the school critics know exist but not to all of them, and not to their degree. Sizer's book had better not show high school personnel in too unfavorable a light. Beginning it with the fictious idealized Horace that dominates the book is sure to please all of Sizer's constituencies.

The most critical of them for Sizer is his immediate peer group, the others at the top of his field and in allied organizations, including the funding foundations, etc. They will have a yes-or-no say in Sizer's conducting future studies, and future appointments to prestigious positions. Education's other big guns will judge Sizer by how well his book holds off the "ed school bashers," how well it confuses those dissatisfied with schools until they become tired of the problem, or other problems take precedence.

Missing from Sizer's book is any substantive recommendations for the improvement of *teachers*—the aspect to which the few courageous state governors have paid most attention in proposing the elimination of education courses. Sizer avoids saying much about the quality of *teachers* by not reporting the large number of educationally impoverished teachers that he and his researchers must have come across in the 80 high schools visited.

To be sure, Sizer gives a few examples of bad teaching and lets us know a few of the mistakes observed. He reports that one teacher "kept calling the U.S. Cavary the U.S. Calvary." Another called Pikes Peak, "Pikers' Peak." But of all the educationally impoverished teachers that he and his researchers must have observed, Sizer offers only one example, and not until the last quarter of the book. It is from a social studies class doing a unit on the American West.

> We learned that the reason that Chinese were brought to the United States in the mid-nineteenth century was that it was cheaper to bring them here than to keep sending dirty laundry all the way across the Pacific.[8]

Sizer makes no comment on this teacher's gross ignorance of history, geography, and economics. He gives what I have quoted, no more. From my experience with teachers, plus what has been reported in newspapers and magazines, Sizer and his researchers must have collected from 80 high schools dozens more, similar examples of grossly ignorant teachers.

But Sizer avoids admitting that educationally impoverished teachers are a major school problem. Many high school classes are covered by "bodies"—teachers who are teaching out of license, particularly in math and science, and many others who are teaching "in license" took too few rigorous courses in the subjects they are supposed to be teaching. So acute is the shortage of math and science teachers that Georgia state education officials in 1984 imported eight West Germans to teach those subjects in Georgia high schools.[9]

For math and science, nevertheless, Sizer recommends that they be merged into one department, one area of study, and taught together. He suggests, in effect, that a severe shortage of math teachers be joined to a severe shortage of science teachers to form a new kind of Gargantuan shortage—a close to 100 percent shortage of teachers who know enough math and chemistry, math and biology, math and physics, to teach them simultaneously.

Sizer is against teachers teaching by telling, although humans alone can learn from being told. Lower animals are limited to learning from experience, or doing, although some can learn from watching something being done. Sizer advocates "coaching" and offers the athletic coach as the model of teaching. The student first attempts something, such as throwing a javelin or writing an outline for a paper. Then, to improve the student's performance, he or she is informed of what was good and/or bad about the performance. The student is of course informed with speech that is, of course, "telling." But Sizer calls it "coaching." Being against "telling" but for "coaching" diverts attention from speech, language, and substance to the simpler and vaguer; from content to method. It is the sort of reduction to absurdity that educationists dote on, and may lead to "coaching education" being added to all of their other educations.

Sizer says, "Telling is cost effective. . . . That's why it is so popular in schools."[10] He avoids the historical perspective that it is much less cost-effective than it used to be. As cost-per-pupil rose everywhere in schools, student achievement declined. Teachers in general are typically less able to say what they mean when they "tell," and students less able to comprehend what they hear, even when the "telling" by first-rate teachers is precise and clear.

Sizer is sophisticated in being all things to all constituencies, including "lay" readers, without being obvious. As a bone tossed to the field's severest critics, he uses the term educationists, in the phrase, "the monstrous pretentious language of some educationists."[11] This term is hateful to professors of education. It signifies a critic who distinguishes them from "educators," professors in other departments. But Sizer uses the term only once, for which his peers are sure to forgive him. They will recognize it as part of his obfuscating in defense of their field. Sizer is simultaneously mindful of the divisions among professors of education. Most are probably behaviorists, or Skinnerians, while others lean toward cognitive psychology, as represented by Jerome Bruner. With both groups in mind, Sizer quotes both Skinner and Bruner, in one instance on facing pages.[12]

For the "lay" reader to object to anything in Sizer's book is difficult. Whatever he or she may object to, there is a contradictory sentence or so elsewhere in the book. Though true that he has written as if schools of education do not exist, for example, he nevertheless makes a passing reference to "moonlighting education professors."[13] Sizer avoids any precise recommendation for upgrading teachers. Nevertheless, he says that they need "rigorous preparation"[14], which can be interpreted as needing more ed school courses. But then again, three pages later, he says, "after teacher candidates have gained a solid mastery of their subjects, *their training must be almost wholly school-based,*" (Sizer's italics),[15] which sounds as if he were advocating fewer education courses. The reader takes his pick from unelaborated fragments.

While Sizer makes no overt claim to any body of knowledge and expertise, he does so covertly. He slyly implies it with "lay" reader, and also with the words "Further scientific" in his sentence, "Further scientific examination would uncover students' different learning styles."[16] His cleverness in this sentence exposes something quite serious. He inadvertently admits that there is no basis for "different learning styles," which he uses elsewhere in the book, and educationists have been using as if bona fide fact for decades. Although Sizer favors all students becoming literate and numerate, he also stresses the importance of "nonverbal communication." He does not use the term, possibly with the educated "lay" reader in mind who may consider it trivial, but he accomplishes the same thing with a description.[17] Sizer says schools must concentrate on the intellect yet also on the "humanistic."

Nowhere is Sizer more corrupting of understanding than his confusing the humanities and the very different term "humanistic," as he does in the following from his introduction: ". . . the humanities' place deserves fresh emphasis. We deal with adolescents' hearts as well as brains. . . . If I err, I hope that it is toward the humanistic side."[18]

I believe Sizer created the confusion deliberately. As a former high school English teacher with a doctorate in education *and history* (Harvard 1961), Sizer knows that the humanities consist of art, history, philosophy, and literature. He should know that they are among the noblest achievements of the human race, that they stir the imagination, arouse the sensibilities and expand the individual's intellectual horizons. "Humanistic education," on the other hand, means something utterly different. Sizer should know because he has been a leading promoter of it, under the guise of "moral education."

> In 1970 Theodore Sizer, then dean of the Harvard School of Education, co-edited with his wife Nancy a book entitled *Moral Education.* The preface set the tone by condemning the morality of "the Christian gentleman," "the American prairie," the McGuffey *Reader,* and the hypocrisy of teachers who tolerate a grading system that is "the terror of the young." According to the Sizers, all of the authors in the anthology agree that "the 'old morality' can and should be scrapped."[19]

Little did the American public know that the ethics and morals of the Judeo-Christian tradition, fully represented in the humanities, were being scrapped by humanistic education professors, led by those in the Harvard and U. Mass ed schools. The leading exponent at U. Mass was, and still is, Sidney Simon, known for "values clarification." Simon preaches that nobody, including parents and teachers, has any set of right values to pass on to children.

> The student has values; the values clarification teacher is merely "facilitating" the student's access to them. Thus, no values are taught. The emphasis is on *learning how,* not on

learning that. The student does not learn *that* acts of stealing are wrong; he learns how to respond to such acts.

The values clarification course is, in this sense, contentless.[20]

One does not have to be a fundamentalist Protestant, Roman Catholic, or Orthodox Jew to be outraged by this ethical nihilism. One can be chiefly concerned about the threat to the liberty-preserving institutions of the United States and of Western civilization.

> The success of the values clarification movement has been phenomenal. In 1975 a study from the Hoover Institute referred to "hundreds perhaps thousands of school programs that employ the clarification methodology" and reported that ten states have officially adopted values clarification as a model for their moral education programs. Proponents of values clarification consider it inappropriate for a teacher to encourage students, however subtly or indirectly, to adopt the values of the teacher or the community.[21]

The other leading underminer of traditional morality, represented in Theodore Sizer's 1970 anthology, is Harvard's Lawrence Kohlberg. He, too, is against "the old bag of virtues." He, like Sizer, sees high school students as "serving time, like prisoners" in schools where teachers act as agents of the unjust social system. His aim has been to turn schools into "just communities." To put his ideas into effect, he founded the Cluster School in Cambridge, Massachusetts, in 1974, about which many articles and doctoral theses were written. Six years later:

> . . . the school was in a shambles and just about to close. The school was racially divided; drugs, sex, and theft were rampant; and Kohlberg was fighting bitterly with the teachers. Here was a school—with thirty students and six exceptionally trained dedicated teachers—that by any objective standard must be counted a failure. Yet in American professional education nothing succeeds like failure. Having scored their failure in the Cluster School, the Kohlbergians have put their ideas to work in more established schools. For example, they now exercise a significant influence in such diverse public school systems as Pittsburgh, Pennsylvania; Salt Lake City, Utah; Scarsdale, New York; and Brookline, Massachusetts.[22]

Even school systems that have not adopted values clarification programs, or have not tried to establish "just communities," have been greatly affected. Teachers in general are reluctant to indoctrinate in any way. Students deprived of, and ignorant of, the Western moral tradition are left with moral relativism. They tend to see individuals as not responsible for anything, ascribing all instead to society. A professor of government at Harvard who gave an undergraduate course on the Holocaust was disturbed to find that of the one hundred enrolled: "a majority of students adopted the view that the rise of Hitler and the Nazis was inevitable, that no one could have resisted it, and that in the end no one was responsible for what happened."[23] The professor came to the conclusion that if some of the students in the course had been judges at the Nuremberg trials, they would probably have acquitted or pardoned most of the Nazi defendants.

This information, including the quotations above, are from an essay in *The American Scholar* by Christina Hoff Sommers. Although I have firsthand experience of Sidney Simon at the U. Mass ed school, Sommers' essay lays out the harm done by Simon, Sizer, Kohlberg, and their followers so clearly that I prefer to quote from it. A paragraph of Sommers' indicates how what is taught in ed schools shows up a few years later in college freshmen:

> Students who have received the new moral instruction [in secondary schools] have been turning up in freshmen college classes in increasing numbers. While giving college ethics courses during the past six years, I have become convinced that the need for a critical appraisal of the claims and assumptions of the movement is urgent. My experience is that the students who received the new teaching have been ill served by their mentors.[24]

This is the background of much of what Theodore Sizer has promoted and stands for. It accounts for things in *Horace's Compromise* that the "lay" reader cannot understand and was not meant to understand. Sizer does not explain, for instance, what he can mean by "Finding the right way to elicit each students' self-esteem."[25] But as Sizer said, he intended to give a "feel" rather than a thoughtful understanding. His "feel" is nonetheless an attempt to indoctrinate, and comes from one who professes to disbelieve in indoctrination.

Horace's Compromise is a thoroughly vapid book. Sizer could have written 80 percent of it, particularly his nonfiction-fiction portions, without visiting any of the eighty high schools included in the $900,000 study. To call it a report is a sheer conceit.

SARA LAWRENCE LIGHTFOOT
Professor, Harvard's Graduate School of Education

Lightfoot is the author of *The Good High School: Portraits of Character and Culture*, published in 1983. Part of her study was funded by the Carnegie Foundation for the Advancement of Teaching. Beginning in 1979, the same year that Sizer's study started, Lightfoot visited six secondary schools—public high schools in two cities and two suburbs, and two New England prep schools. So detailed is her book that it is longer than Sizer's study of eighty high schools by 176 pages. Particularly significant, in light of the low academic achievement of black students everywhere, is that Professor Lightfoot is black.

Like Sizer, she wrote her book in reaction to the growing dissatisfaction with the public schools. Lightfoot's reaction, however, is less guileful and subtle. She is overtly defensive. In the face of all the public criticism of schools, she examines them for "goodness." This attitude, together with personal details she gives of herself, show her to be smug and complacent.

Lightfoot is surely aware that the masses of black students have disproportionately high failure rates at every level of schooling. Black graduates of public schools have higher rates of failure in taking examinations for college entrance, corporate employment, admission to the armed forces, to police and firemen's academies, and other civil services, including exams for promotion. Black college graduates disproportionately fail exams for teachers' licenses. Despite the enormity of the problem of low academic achievement among blacks, Professor Lightfoot pays scant attention to achievement. Instead, she examines high schools for goodness, in which academic achievement is secondary. Typical of educationists, Lightfoot prefers the intangible to the tangible. As ed school professors have been doing for decades, while Rome burns Lightfoot fiddles. She says:

> I do not see goodness as a reducible quality that is simply
> reflected in achievement scores, numbers of graduates attend-

ing college, literacy rates, or attendance records. . . . "Goodness" is a much more complicated notion that refers to what some social scientists describe as the school's "ethos" . . . [it] encompasses less tangible, more elusive qualities that can only be discerned through close, vivid description, through subtle nuances. . . .[26]

Sizer said that his method in writing was to present "word pictures"; Lightfoot says hers is "portraiture." She begins by giving the details of sitting for her own painted portrait. She tells what she wore, the problems of holding a pose, what people thought of her portrait when finished. She attempts, moreover, to connect these details to what she calls her "portraits" of high schools: ". . . my experience with the medium and the process influenced my work as a social observer and recorder of human encounter and experience. As a social scientist I wanted to develop a form of inquiry that would embrace many of the descriptive, aesthetic, and experimental dimensions that I had known as the artist's subject."[27]

This sort of stuff takes up chunks of her book—most of her twenty-six-page introduction and, at the end of her book, a ten-page afterword she calls "The Passion of Portraiture," in which she calls it "a highly interactive research form."[28] It is not the stuff to help black children achieve what they are capable of achieving or, for that matter, any other children.

Lightfoot's interest is in surfaces, camera shots reversed 180 degrees from herself. She gives endless detail that is irrelevant to instruction and pedagogy, which remain largely hidden. She gives long descriptions of school settings, often the sociology of the setting, school physical plants, and the people in them, especially the headmasters and principals. For instance, she says of the principal of John F. Kennedy High School in the Bronx:

> A man in his fifties, Mastruzzi stands about five feet seven inches tall but appears to be much taller. He has a youthful, muscular look underneath a balding head and quick energy that keeps him on the move. Impeccably dressed, Mastruzzi appears at school each day in carefully matched color combinations. His ties are wide and lively, his short sleeve shirts are rolled up twice at his upper arm, and he wears a subtle gold chain bracelet. Although his individual features do not strike

me as classically attractive, several women describe him as "very handsome."[29]

This is a portion of one of nineteen paragraphs that Lightfoot devotes to chiefly describing this principal.

But there is more method in this than meets the eye. Like Sizer, Lightfoot is mindful of the many constituencies of schools of education. Among the chief of them is high school personnel. It is from this pool that schools of education fill many of their graduate courses, and get many of their M.Ed. and Ed.D. degree candidates. Faced with mounting public criticism, moreover, ed schools need their political support to maintain the status quo. Sizer appealed to this constituency by creating his idealized, fictitious Horace. Lightfoot appeals to it by going the "reality-based" route. She names schools and their personnel, which she acknowledges is "a significant departure from the classic traditions of social science."[30] In elaborately describing the schools and personnel named, she accomplishes the same purpose as Sizer. She keeps them as friends.

Even when Lightfoot makes them look silly in the eyes of the "lay" reader, she does so inadvertently because she is an educationist, thinks and writes like one. One of the schools she visited is Milton Academy, a private prep school outside of Boston. Of its headmaster, who is also an alumnus of the Harvard School of Education, Lightfoot writes:

> On this glorious fall day, Pieh has awakened and run several miles in the early morning air. In his early forties, tall and lean, he seems to combine the elements of mind, body, and spirit—believing the expression of one enlivens the others. I imagine that he must run in order to think. There is a balance and composure in his presence, a gentle and benign leadership. Everything is understated and said with a slight hesitation as if he is still thinking about it.[31]

Elsewhere, Lightfoot says that Jerome Pieh has a "tentative listening style,"[32] whatever that is. Perhaps Pieh's tentativeness in talking and listening was learned at the Harvard ed school while a disciple of Ted Sizer, where he undoubtedly picked up "the 'humanistic' approach to education"[33] that Lightfoot ascribes to him. Of Alonzo Crim, the superintendent of schools in Atlanta, and also an alumnus of the Harvard School of

Education, she writes, "He exudes thoughtfulness, [and] focus. . . ."[34]

Although Lightfoot takes pains to flatter each member of school staffs that she mentions, in many places in her book she fails to find "goodness." She shows particular resentment of achievement, both social and academic, and the groups who have achieved. She does this particularly in describing Highland Park, a well-to-do suburb of Chicago and its high school with its 65 percent Jewish enrollment. Lightfoot characterizes the town as one of "rich pushy Jews." The following is a sample of that characterization:

> During my visit to Highland Park, the supermarket was the place where I witnessed heightened aggressiveness. Some residents joke that you "risk your life" when you go shopping in Highland Park. Perfectly coiffeured and manicured ladies, in Adidas tennis outfits, race for position at the check-out counter, pushing carts into each other and barking directions to the salesperson. Outside the store, the parking lot is a chaotic scene with lots of impatient honking and stealing of parking places. Occasionally shouting battles erupt as a silver Mercedes 450SEL outmaneuvers a burgundy Cadillac Seville.[35]

Lightfoot maintains her "supermarket jungle" image in describing the high school. "Every teacher I spoke with . . . complained of the intense competition among students and the extreme pressure from parents that their children achieve in school."[36] She cited the vice-principal in charge of discipline as saying that he "never ceased to be amazed by the arrogance and elitism of some students and is turned off by their overly protective and entitled parents. . . ."[37]

Lightfoot's attitude toward achieving Jewish students is much the same, though milder, in her descriptions in the other high schools. At Brookline in Massachusetts, where they constituted 45 percent of the school population, Lightfoot says that the Jewish population "is declining as parents grow worried about the increasing [ethnic] diversity and what they perceive to be a lowering of standards."[38] Jewish parents could believe standards were being lowered after the arrival of the new principal, Robert McCarthy, in 1980. He shortly set up a school governance structure "to approximate Lawrence Kohlberg's notion of a 'just community,' "[39] and combat the unjust social system. The new principal also brought into Brookline a disciple of Kohlberg's from the Harvard School of Education to work on the "just community" under a federal grant. This is an instance of the federal government financing the spread of ethical nihilism.

Lightfoot is against ability grouping, as are most other educationists. She favors a shift in "the ideal of excellence" from academic rigor to some form of absolute leveling, absolute class equality. Wherever Jews can be used as the example of class inequality, she uses them. Of Brookline High School in Massachusetts, she says: ". . . divisions among racial and social class groups are reinforced by the school's grouping practices. The working class Black students who travel from Boston are disproportionately represented in the lowest rungs and the upper middle-class Jewish students dominate the Honors and Advanced Placement courses."[40]

Of Highland Park High School outside of Chicago, Lightfoot says that the honors courses are filled with bright Jewish students, and that Italian parents complain that those courses are taught by the best teachers, that their children rarely get them and are seldom encouraged academically.[41] Of John F. Kennedy High School in the Bronx, which is a disadvantaged Title 1 school, Lightfoot wrote:

> Only one teacher I spoke to claimed that the three levels (Remedial, Average, and Honors) are actually "tracks" mirroring social class designations in the wider society. "The Riverdale kids from the hill [Jewish] are in the Honors courses, the Kingsbridge kids are in the 'on level' courses, and the Black and Brown kids from Harlem are stuck at the bottom."[42]

The two secondary schools that Lightfoot visited that have virtually no Jewish students, are the two at the opposite ends of the social scale—George Washington Carver High School in Atlanta, and St. Paul's Episcopal prep school in New Hampshire. Comparing them, Lightfoot said:

> The inequalities are dramatic, the societal injustices flagrant. One has feelings of moral outrage as one makes the transition from the lush, green 1,700 acres of St. Paul's to the dusty streets of the Carver Homes where the median income is less than $4,000 a year.[43] [and where 80 percent of the families

are headed by single parents, and a higher percentage are on welfare.[44]]

Lightfoot keeps speaking of "persistent inequalities," as if there were ever a time and place in the universe where everyone was equal. She gives no credit to inequalities being much less in the United States than in any other country in the world—including Russia and its satellites, China, and every black African nation. The only possible exceptions are the Scandinavian countries.

Nothing in Lightfoot's book offers hope or guidance in reforming education for millions of academically low achieving black children and youths. Lightfoot merely repeats the standard rhetoric of educationists. She says of Milton Academy that its one black teacher "can only be interpreted as tokenism." She quotes this teacher as saying, "Without more role models, they [Milton's black students] feel terribly lost." Lightfoot comments that "the majority faculty rarely are sensitive to the special needs of black students."[45] But at Carver High in Atlanta the principal and almost all of the teachers are black. Presumably, they are sensitive to the special needs of their black charges, yet even Lightfoot recognizes that academically they are doing abysmally. Lightfoot parrots the standard role-model rhetoric, unexamined.

At St. Paul's, a more exclusive prep school than Milton Academy, Lightfoot quotes a black female student as complaining, "We have to do all of the stretching and changing. They will always remain the same whether we're here or not."[46] This quote is in the context of Lightfoot's saying that St. Paul's transforms the student. "It is expected that the unusual [minority] students, not the curriculum or pedagogy will have to be transformed." Lightfoot misses the point that *that is what education is*. The student is transformed. Without the transformation there is no education. To make schools over into the likenesses of children, *whoever the children are*, is to destroy education.

The disadvantaged student, of course, pays a price in becoming transformed. He or she becomes different from parents, relatives, and former peers, and is sometimes alienated from them. That is a high price to pay but it is not nearly so high a price as remaining ignorant and uneducated for a lifetime.

In her secondary school portraits, Lightfoot ignores an already established pattern that is connected to another that she merely alludes to: "In the last several years, the Black applicant pool at St. Paul's has yielded fewer and fewer qualified students. Increasingly, prospective students have been turned off and intimidated by approaches and images that have worked well with their more privileged and white counterparts."[47]

She seems to justify black students being "turned off and intimidated," because the school has failed to accommodate to them. Black enrollment has also declined at Milton Academy, as it has at all of the most competitive colleges. Sufficient financial aid for college is available, at least for poor disadvantaged students. The guidance counselor at Stuyvesant assured me that such students who are academically able, have no trouble attending the most expensive colleges in the nation. But it is chiefly disadvantaged Asians who are taking advantage of the existing opportunities. Black college enrollments decline as Asian enrollments climb.

This established pattern should have been obvious to Professor Lightfoot, but she makes no mention of it. She shows no recognition that all students, including those who are black, face an ever growing competition from Asians. In the year 1983, alone, 48,668 immigrants entered the United States from Hong Kong, Taiwan, and China. When those from the Philippines, Vietnam, Korea, India, and Laos are added, the total number of Asian immigrants in 1983 came to 213,116, plus an unknown number of illegal immigrants.[48] With each passing year, Asians will make up a larger portion of the population. With each passing year, chiefly blacks will lose ground to them unless something profound and drastic happens to aid blacks to achieve academically.

Professor Lightfoot, however, in her efforts to maintain the status quo of schools of education, is complacent. She is most obviously so in the last chapter of *The Good High School*, where she goes out of her way to attack critics of the public schools. She calls school critics muckrakers,[49] forgetting that the muckrakers of the turn of the century have a respected place in American history: "The task which they set themselves, consciously or unconsciously, was that of saving political and economic democracy, and realizing what one of them called the

Promise of American Life. In so far as the progressive movement achieved this end, the credit belongs largely to the muckrakers."[50]

In defending schools, Professor Lightfoot makes her biggest error in attributing much of the public's disappointment and disenchantment to nostalgia and romanticism. She says: "Perception of today's high schools . . . are plagued by romanticized remembrances of 'the old days' and anxiety about the menacing stage of adolescence. Both of these responses tend to distort society's view of high schools and support the general tendency to view them as other than good."[51]

Her view of their goodness is disputed by Claude Brown, the author of *Manchild in the Promised Land.* In 1984 he published an article comparing his life growing up in Harlem in the 1940s and 1950s and what it is like growing up there today. The article points out a critical difference in degree of literacy:

> Today's manchild has fewer choices than my generation, and those choices are more depressing. As a final desperate recourse, we could always resort to enlisting in the armed services. Manchild 1984, [is] unable to pass the written exams for the services . . .[52]

Would Lightfoot accuse Claude Brown of "romanticized remembrances of 'the old days' "? Would she dispute with him whether schools in Harlem—and in all the other Harlems in the big cities—are just as good today as they were in the 1940s and '50s?

Brown recognizes a numb, inarticulate yearning in the nation's ghettoes for direction, something to hang on to and give hope. He says: "Admittedly, a significant percentage of this country's young black men are too bitter, too cynical or, for various other reasons, too intractable. And some are definitely incorrigible. Yet most of them possess a hunger for guidance and advice so profound it would be too humiliating to express it even if they could."[53]

As she reveals herself in *The Good High School*, Professor Sara Lawrence Lightfoot of the Harvard School of Education exemplifies why black people with a "hunger for guidance," will not get it from educationists, including those who are black.

JOHN I. GOODLAD

Professor and former Dean, Graduate School of Education,
University of California at Los Angeles

Goodlad is the author of *A Place Called School: Prospects for the Future*, published in 1983. In announcing its publication, *The New York Times* quoted Patricia Albjerg Graham, the current dean of Harvard's School of Education, as calling it "probably the most comprehensive study ever made of American schools."[54] Goodlad begins his book: "American schools are in trouble. In fact, the problems of schooling are of such crippling proportions that many schools may not survive. It is possible that our entire public education system is nearing collapse."[55] From this clarion of alarm, the reader might think that Goodlad is in sympathy with the prevailing climate of public dissatisfaction with schools. Nothing could be more untrue.

The climate in which he did his study and wrote his book was created not by the likes of him—not by deans of schools of education and their professors. Frequent news reports of low and declining achievement in schools together with innumerable instances of ignorant, uneducated teachers created the critical climate. A cartoon in *Harper's* magazine in 1979 showed striking schoolteachers carrying picket signs on which the words were misspelled. *Time* magazine in 1980 did a cover story entitled, "HELP! Teacher Can't Teach." Full-page newspaper ads for that issue of *Time* quoted an English teacher as saying, "I teaches English." *U.S. News & World Report* in 1983 did a cover story, "What's Wrong With Our Teachers?", illustrated by a teacher wearing a dunce cap. *Newsweek* in 1984 also showed a dunce-capped teacher to illustrate its cover story "Why Teachers Fail." Such examples are endless. All three of television's commercial networks did special programs that were similarly critical. One showed an insurance company in Boston teaching simple arithmetic and basic English to a group of its clerical workers.

The truth of all such criticism is denied in Goodlad's book. He does not say that the news media lied, but the effect is the same. One would think that the reporters and writers for *Time, Newsweek, Reader's Digest, Harper's, The New York Times*, and the television network news departments of ABC, CBS, and NBC, and all other news agencies live in a different world than Goodlad. They do.

Goodlad's world is schools of education. That is his day-to-day milieu, as well as his daily bread, a fact he omits from his book. Although he and his staff asked teachers a set of 120 questions about their work, no questions were asked about the usefulness of their education courses. Like Sizer and Lightfoot, Goodlad examines public schools as if they are unaffected by schools of education.

Goodlad does not paint word pictures and portraits. His study was designed to produce numbers. Goodlad uses the numbers to counteract what, in an interview with Edward Fiske of *The New York Times*, he called the "negative forces" criticizing the schools. From his vantage point of forty-three years in education, Goodlad said that calls for school reform were cyclical. "We need to see what we can accomplish in about a decade before the negative forces begin again." He also told Fiske that just the day before (in July 1983), he was presenting his ideas to a group of teachers when one responded, "Look, we made a lot of progress with some of these ideas [Goodlad's] in the 1960s, and now they are gone." Goodlad said the time would come again "to inject them into the system."[56] His primary ideas date from the 1960s, when educationists seized on the civil rights movement and hid their lack of knowledge behind social relevance. As Thomas Sowell describes it:

> "Relevant" and "irrelevant" became magic words that superseded logic and empiricism. "Social" was another incantation that put various schemes ("innovations") above discussion and made objections or questions about them seem petty, mean, or dirty.
>
> "Socially relevant" was a double whammy. One would as soon stand in the path of an express train as oppose something that was "socially relevant"—whether or not there was *any* evidence that it did any good, or considerable evidence that it did harm or violated basic principles of logic. Questions of fact became questions of intent. Even the most devastating facts could be countered by asking where you were coming from.[57]

Goodlad's nostalgia for the 1960s is not as recognizable in his book as in Fiske's interview. It is there all the same, buried under a plethora of "data" and an aura of scientism.

Goodlad's seven-year study from 1975 to 1983 was carried out in thirteen representative communities in seven areas of the country, from inner city to rural areas. In each he studied a "triple"—the elementary, junior high, and high school. Like Sizer and Lightfoot, Goodlad studied schools not by achievement—test scores, percents going to college, dropout rates, and so forth. He avoids these indices by which the public usually judges schools. Unlike Sizer and Lightfoot, however, he collected data to quantify. Questionnaires were distributed to and interviews conducted with 17,163 students, 1,350 teachers, and 8,624 parents. The results are arranged in tables of percentages, bar graphs, pie charts, lists of mean scores, as well as Goodlad's words about them. Over one thousand classrooms were also observed and conclusions reached about them. Goodlad had a staff of forty-three full- and parttime researchers—doctoral students from his school of education—plus site coordinators and a secretarial and clerical staff.

The cost of the study was not given but must have amounted to millions of dollars. Funding was provided by fourteen different agencies and philanthropic organizations—the U.S. Office of Education plus various funds, corporations, and foundations, including the Ford and Rockefeller foundations.

Much of *A Place Called School* can hardly be understood without recognizing that, like most educationists, Goodlad is a behaviorist. He was chairman of the blue-ribbon committee formed to investigate the U. Mass School of Education after its scandal in 1975. One of the findings of the resulting Goodlad report, as it is called in the school, was that too few of the faculty were behaviorists.

Throughout his book, Goodlad talks of student and teacher "behaviors," rather than what they know. He calls the typical teaching that teachers do, for instance, "frontal teaching."[58] The phrase diverts attention from what teachers *say* in the classroom to where they are located in it. In other words, he empties teachers of content. But behaviorism is anything but a conceptual whole. In talking of mentation, not a behavior, Goodlad uses the field's empty-of-content clichés. One is that students have different "learning styles."[59] Goodlad says that students learn "how to learn"[60] in school, although their acquisition of spoken language indicates that they knew how as infants. Another cliché is "listening skills,"[61] used also by Lightfoot. A student paying attention may or may not comprehend what is heard. But comprehension is not part of the educationist working vocabulary. What educationists mean by listening skills, none has ever divulged.

The most incriminating fault of Goodlad's study is its failure to address why public schools continue to turn out young people hardly able to write their full address, read the mail deposited in their mailboxes, or fill out an application for employment. The U.S. Census Bureau has found that 99.5 percent of Americans have completed the fifth grade and so it reports that 99.5 percent of the population is literate. The Census Bureau assumed, quite reasonably, that all who have completed the fifth grade should be able to read. But numerous studies indicate that about one in five Americans reads below the fourth grade level. They are the nation's functional illiterates. In the District of Columbia alone, functional illiterates number one hundred thousand and half of them are parents.[62]

But Goodlad's study, called by the dean of Harvard's ed school "probably the most comprehensive study ever made," is grossly incomplete. It fails to examine why the public schools keep producing functional illiterates. In vain will the reader of *A Place Called School* seek acknowledgment of the problem between its covers. But if the reader should look for "illiteracy" under "I" in his index, he or she will find instead, "Information, need for." This item is not subsumed under another; it stands alone. In Goodlad's mind, even information can be contentless.

For Goodlad to attempt to address the horrors of inadequate literacy, he would also have had to talk of his other momentous omission—schools of education. It was not until education professors began to undermine reading instruction in the 1920s that children's failing to learn to read became a singular problem. Within ten years, in the 1930s, remedial reading was introduced, first in the elementary schools and subsequently in junior high and senior high schools, culminating in the late 1960s in college "bonehead English." In the 1970s professors of English began to complain that some graduate students in their departments could not write coherently.

But Goodlad's study was not designed to address any aspect of literacy and its effects on all subsequent learning of academic subjects. Goodlad looks past academic subjects as if they are invisible. A chapter heading of his is "Beyond Academics." His eyes are on social equity, derived from what has been called "the trash decade" of the 1960s.

This is most obvious as Goodlad attacks the widespread practice of ability grouping in schools' early grades and tracking in the upper grades. He says that the thirty-eight schools he studied indicate that "schools receive children differentially ready for learning," that they educate them "differentially in the classrooms," and graduate them "differentially prepared for further education, employment . . . and social mobility." Goodlad is not talking about *individual* differences but *group* differences, which he would have schools wipe out. He claims for schools the power and the right to "counter-vail the sociological realities of the surrounding culture." Goodlad goes beyond equal opportunity to "equal outcomes."[63]

Equal outcomes in schools is the last refuge of educationists who have no body of pedagogical knowledge. Goodlad does not consider himself a scoundrel, of course. Educationists do not admit to being a special-interest group. As Thomas Sowell has so aptly put it:

> The academic world is one of the most effective special-interest groups precisely because it does not think of itself in those terms. Its words have the ring of sincerity when it turns every form of social malaise into a reason why its members should receive more money and power. Racial strife becomes a reason for academics to conduct a thousand social experiments leading to a million articles, reports, Ph.D. [and Ed.D.] theses, and so forth—costing billions of tax dollars. Poverty in general is a gold mine. . . . Crime and violence provide another ready market for "expertise" (the quotes because nothing has actually worked). Academe has even mass-produced and mass-marketed its own parochial viewpoint, which looks for "solutions" to social "problems"—like answers in the back of a textbook. *Have notebook, will travel.* Academics will research anything—except the effectiveness of their own schemes growing out of previous research.[64]

Sowell wrote this in 1975, the same year that John Goodlad began his seven years of "research," financed by fourteen different funding agencies, including the U.S. Office of Education. The reader will look in vain in his book for any admission of culpability of schools of education for the "trouble" that public schools are in. To the contrary, he or she will find the expectation that education professors will acquire more power and opportunities to make money in the future, an expectation that can be termed "rational" because that is what each failure has led to in the past.

Each of Goodlad's recommendations for schools would increase, directly and indirectly, the influence and power of the ed schools. He proposes layers of teachers with a head teacher at the top who would be required to have a doctorate—enormously expanding the number of graduate student applicants for the ed schools. "Head teachers would be recruited in a nationwide search," says Goodlad. This would lead to more "head hunting" by education professors, similar to the head-hunting they currently do for school superintendents. Education professors moonlighting as head-hunters—often favoring those who took courses with them—get paid for their services, of course, by boards of education. (One of the most successful of these, in amount of employment, has been Harold Hunt of Harvard's School of Education.) Goodlad recommends that schooling begin for children at the age of four, creating a whole new teaching specialty, and hence new education courses for teachers of four- and five-year-olds. Goodlad would abolish all ability grouping and tracking, thereby creating new problems for principals and teachers, for which education professors would offer new solutions.

Goodlad's seven-year study exemplifies the irresponsibility of education professors, reflects them perfectly as an unconfessed special-interest group intent on its own survival and, if possible, further expansion and aggrandizement.

ERNEST L. BOYER
Former United States Commissioner of Education
President, The Carnegie Foundation for
the Advancement of Teaching

Boyer is the author of *High School: A Report on Secondary Education*, published in 1983. Boyer is not an educationist. His original specialty was speech pathology, of which he was a professor. Early in his career he switched to college and university administration, eventually getting the top jobs at the federal office of education and the Carnegie Foundation for the Advancement of Teaching. His book jacket reports that in 1983, he was selected by his peers as "the nation's leading educator." This peer approbation reflects the high visibility of his lofty positions and few stands, if any, that have offended any group.

In reporting the publication of Boyer's *High School, The New York Times* said it was "a somewhat more upbeat appraisal of American education than other recent studies." It quoted Boyer as saying, "The tide of mediocrity started to ebb in the latter part of the 1970s"[65]—four or five years before 1983, when the U.S. Commission on Excellence in Education first described that tide. In telling how his study was initiated, Boyer wrote:

> In the spring of 1980, the Board of Trustees of The Carnegie Foundation for the Advancement of Teaching met to consider a proposed study of American secondary education.
>
> The trustees quickly acknowledged . . . the first years of formal schooling are crucial, that each level of learning depends upon the other, and that if students make a poor beginning, prospects for future academic progress are diminished. . . .
>
> Still, the trustees agreed that the upper years of schooling are strategically important, too.[66]

This rationale points to studying the crucial first years of elementary school, not high schools. Within three short paragraphs Boyer changes direction twice, as if afraid of where his logic will take him.

The chief beneficiaries of Boyer's frequent reversals are educationists. Being primarily responsible for putting the nation at risk, it is this large guilty group that Boyer takes pains not to expose and offend. The risk of doing so would have been great had he studied the first years of elementary school, taught by former education majors. This is where too many pupils of all social classes make inadequate beginnings in reading and arithmetic and become academically handicapped through the rest of their schooling. The most handicapped, particularly poor whites and minority children, are the ones who will later become the high school dropouts. The somewhat lesser handicapped will become the inadequately literate high school students, some of whom will nevertheless go on to college. But even to mention elementary school reading instruction is to touch a sore spot for educationists because the ability to read over the decades has drastically declined. Political rather than educational reasons dictated Boyer's decision not to study elementary schools.

In *High School* he also takes pains to curry favor with educationists. He points out, for instance, "Non-education professors often forget that three-fourths of a prospective [high school] teacher's time is spent, not in education, but in the school of arts and science."[67] Boyer avoids mentioning the term "schools of education" throughout his book. Teacher education is nevertheless so notoriously bad that Boyer must admit to some of it. He points out that six out of ten high school teachers have master's degrees or better. That they are almost all in education Boyer fails to mention. He quotes the typical teacher as saying that teacher preparation is mostly a waste a time, that learning to teach is done in the classroom. Then, reversing himself, Boyer says, "While many speak disparagingly of teacher preparation courses, we conclude there is important information uniquely relevant to teachers."[68] He goes on to make four recommendations for improving teacher preparation, each one more dubious.[69]

He recommends that teachers know the history of schooling in the United States. To what end he does not say. Much more crucial to high school teachers of math, chemistry, physics, biology, English, history, and languages would be the history of civilization, inclusive of literature, art, and science. It is more germane to teaching their subjects than the history of schooling. Part of Boyer's recommendation is that future high school teachers be informed about "current issues confronting public education." Boyer seems unaware that schools of education reek with such courses. They are the favorites of education professors and their students. They permit "rapping," and indoctrination without anyone knowing anything about what they are talking about. Such ed school courses are the reason why so many issue courses have trickled down into high schools—nuclear war, toxic wastes, poverty, the environment, death and dying, etc., unloading onto adolescent shoulders the unresolved difficulties of adults.

Boyer's next recommendation is that future high school

teachers "study theories of learning." But this is precisely what schools of education lack. The typical Ed Psych course is a survey of various theories—behaviorism, psychoanalysis, gestalt, cognitive, developmental—usually condensed in one ill-written textbook. Although the course is most often given in the psychology department, it accurately reflects education professors, among whom there is *no agreement on any learning theory*. There is early childhood education, in which the Swiss psychologist Piaget is often followed. But education professors have a limitless ability to misinterpret and misapply any theory. Fads abound. One U. Mass education professor was an ardent believer in educating the right brain, though he never made clear how this was to be done. No agreement exists among educationists on how to apply any of the numerous psychological theories.

Boyer's third recommendation concerns writing. He says, "The skills involved in the teaching of writing should be well understood by all teachers." Can writing be taught? If Boyer knows how, the world is waiting to receive his knowledge. At the present time, no one can teach writing any more than anyone can teach how to ride a bicycle. Writing can be *learned* and a teacher can aid the learning by setting standards and holding students to them. To do this, of course, the teacher must be able to write. Boyer's apparent lack of this understanding may explain why his book is full of non sequiturs, sudden reversals in direction.

Boyer's last recommendation is most destructive. "A course in technology and education—including the use of computers—should be required of every prospective teacher." Since he couples technology and education, he apparently does not mean a computer course in the computer science department. He means the typical educational technology course featured in schools of education since the 1950s, but with computers added. It will be a hardware course empty of content, as are most education courses. The hardware will be demonstrated but how it applies to the classroom and the subjects teachers teach will only be talked about with enthusiastic rhetoric.

This recommendation is based on Boyer's sixteen-page chapter on technology, which is a disaster of misconception. William James wrote, "The intelligence of man consists almost wholly in his substitution of a conceptual order for the perceptual order in which his experiences originally came."[70] If Boyer understood James he would not tout media appealing primarily to the senses, such as television. Boyer complains of obsolete equipment in schools, because in 1979, 61 percent of the television sets in classroom use were black and white, not color. He complains, too, of "little or no training among teaching staffs in the use of television,"[71] that of the nation's teachers only 17 percent have had any such training. In a book on high schools, he is enraptured of *Sesame Street* for preschoolers. Boyer's enthusiasm is because it "so captured" their "eyes and ears."[72] Boyer fails to understand that television is a medium that calls attention to surfaces. It captures the eyes, to be sure, but rarely the mind. If Boyer understood this he could not have said that "Cable television is also well suited to in-service programs for teachers and administrators."[73] Viewers pay attention to the looks of things rather than the substance of what is seen and heard. Concepts come almost exclusively in words or math and science formulas, and are best studied in print.

Many of Boyer's recommendations for technology sound like the educationists' rhetoric of the 1950s and '60s, which I reported in Chapter 5. The undermining of literacy is television's chief effect on education professors, the teachers they train, and children. But Boyer says: "We conclude that television offers a rich resource for the nation's public schools. And we recommend that school districts with access to a cable channel use the facility for school instruction and that a districtwide plan for such use be developed."[74]

Boyer also recommends the establishment of a National Film Library with federal support and that the films be available for scholars and students: "If we could tap the great music, the great literature, the great science, the illuminating history now on film to enrich great teaching in the schools, we could, we believe, within a decade have the best and most broadly educated generation in history."[75]

Typical of Boyer, these recommendations for teaching with technology are an about-face from enumerating, as he does at the beginning of his technology chapter, the educational failures with it in earlier decades—the teaching machines, educational television, language laboratories, talking typewriters, and other equipment, some of it gathering dust in school storerooms.

Much of Boyer's book is written without reference to the fifteen high schools that are the subjects of his study, in which educationists played leading roles as observers. The team of twenty-three observers was headed by a dean of a school of education. Fifteen on his team were education professors, each from a different ed school, and included Sara Lawrence Lightfoot from Harvard. Most of the few remaining observers were educationist-trained. Among them were no professors of English, math, history, or other academic departments. Although Boyer is not an educationist, in writing *High School* he might just as well have been.

Sizer, Lightfoot, Goodlad, and Boyer All Told

What is chiefly remarkable about their books is what they omit. All are silent about schools of education. No pride is taken in them; no blame accepted for or ascribed to them. That teacher preparation should be improved is said in the abstract without specific reference to schools of education. No criticisms of them are acknowledged and no defenses made. They are as silent on where teachers come from as proper Victorians were about where babies come from.

They are equally silent on the horrendous failure of schooling for the nation's mass of black children, and the fantastic success of Asian immigrant children. The ten-times difference between their academic achievement is ignored by ignoring the nation's special elite public high schools. These elite schools have enormous *educational*, rather than *sociological*, implications for the reform of schooling to benefit *all children regardless of class and ethnic group membership*.

The intent of the many silences common to all four authors is to maintain the status quo by keeping hidden from the public all that can turn its influential members into "ed school bashers," demanding their abolition.

GREGORY ANRIG
Former State Commissioner of Education for Massachusetts
President, Educational Testing Service (ETS)

Gregory Anrig has an Ed.D. degree from the Harvard School of Education (1963). He has been president, since September

1981, of the Educational Testing Service, best-known for its Scholastic Aptitude Tests (SATs). ETS has had only three presidents since it was founded in 1948. The first and second had academic backgrounds, but with Anrig ETS switched to an educationist.

In addition to being the former state commissioner of education of Massachusetts, he is among those from whom Sizer sought advice, before publication, on drafts or portions of drafts of his book *Horace's Compromise*. Anrig was also on Goodlad's advisory committee for his study, *A Place Called School*. Gregory Anrig has had a hand in hiding the culpability of schools of education from the public.

Before he became president of ETS in 1981, its SAT tests had been intensely criticized. Some criticisms were rational and well-founded, Others were calls for beheading the messenger that brought the bad news of academic decline. Most vociferous were the spokespeople for black organizations, joined by education professors hiding behind black stances. Among other charges, they claimed that the tests were racist and intended to keep blacks down. The 1.7-million member National Education Association (NEA) had also adopted black stances behind which to hide teacher's inadequacies. The NEA had called for the abolition of all standardized testing. In selecting one of the educationists' own for its president, ETS hoped to allay the criticisms of its tests and survive and prosper.

Gregory Anrig was selected despite considerations pointing to the hiring of a businessman. ETS's existing market for its tests was expected to shrink in the years ahead due to the decline in the number of high school graduates, and other declines. Despite being a nonprofit institution, ETS is big business. Its revenues in 1982 amounted to $123.6 million.[76] ETS has a college-campus-like headquarters in Princeton, New Jersey, and a staff of two thousand employees. To maintain itself, ETS needed new customers for its tests, probably in the private sector. Nevertheless, keeping the business it had in schools and universities was the first consideration; and it selected Gregory Anrig as president.

The wisdom of choosing an educationist, from ETS's standpoint, seemingly was confirmed in 1983 when Anrig publicly tried to help teachers and the NEA maintain their status quo in Houston, Texas, and Arkansas. At issue was the use of ETS's National Teacher Examination. Normally, it was used to test prospective teachers. But Houston used it and Arkansas planned to use it to test teachers already employed in their school systems.

The Houston school district did some preliminary testing, using the pre-professional skills portion. More than three-quarters of the teachers tested failed the reading section. Teachers' groups in Houston filed formal complaints with ETS. At the same time, the Arkansas affiliate of the NEA was up in arms because: "the Arkansas Legislature approved a sweeping set of curriculum and other reforms that included a provision for the testing of all current teachers in reading, writing, and mathematics. Teachers who fail the test must return to college for further training and will lose their jobs if they cannot pass the test by 1987".[77]

Gregory Anrig reacted like an educationist in letters to Superintendent Reagan of the Houston schools and Governor Bill Clinton of Arkansas. Anrig told them that ETS was against the use of its National Teacher Examination to test on-the-job teachers and that ETS would not permit its use for that purpose. Among the several reasons Anrig gave to a reporter was ". . . it has not been shown to be relevant to the knowledge of those already on the job."[78] He was willing to forego test fees in order to side with the teachers and the NEA. This act of public partisanship casts some doubt on the reported increases in SAT scores.

In 1984 a one-point gain in verbal and a three-point gain in math scores were reported. The president of the College Board, which sponsors the SAT tests administered by ETS, called the gains "significant and encouraging." He said, "We seem to have turned the corner in seeking to improve American education."

Is such optimism justified in the light of Anrig's partisanship? SAT scores reflect the performance of teachers as well as students. At a time of intense criticism of teachers, might not a desire for a rise in test scores produce a rise? I do not suggest a doctoring of test scores, just that they can become inflated as they have in the past, according to one of the College Board's own reports.

I refer to *On Further Examination* issued in 1977, the report of the advisory panel convened by the College Board to determine the cause of, at that time, the fourteen-year decline in SAT scores. One of the technical psychometric analyses showed that an "upward drift" had occurred in scoring, and "the declines in ability the SAT measures have been 8 to 12 points larger than the recorded and reported scores indicate. The panel considered casting its report in terms of figures adjusted to reflect this difference, but decided against this because of the impossibility of identifying the year or years in which the drift occurred."[79]

The total drop in verbal and mathematical scores between 1963 and 1977 was reported as a total of 80 points when the actual drop was 88 to 92 points. In subsequent years, too, the reported scores were never adjusted downward to reflect the full drop. The upward drift in scoring SATs, having occurred once, could occur again.

Other factors also tend to increase the scores artificially. In 1983, Fred M. Hechinger of *The New York Times* raised the question of how secure SAT tests are and the responsibility of ETS to enforce security. He reported that large holes exist in the security system, and that student cheating in a variety of ways was rampant in the high schools during test-taking. He reported that teachers who did not wish to be named "blamed pressures not only on students [to score high] but on school administrators to raise test scores. But when it appears that cheating is condoned, several teachers said, the effect is devastating."[80]

Possibly a majority of students do not cheat and the majority of teachers and administrators do not condone cheating. But an enormous portion of the education establishment, particularly at the top, has shown that it will do anything to hide the field's shortcomings and preserve the status quo. Preserving the status quo includes supporting all portions of the establishment, among them teachers in danger of losing jobs, and the NEA.

LAWRENCE A. CREMIN
Professor and President from 1974 to 1984
of Teachers College, Columbia

Cremin has been described by former education editor of *Newsweek*, Gilbert Sewall, as "this country's acknowledged master of educational scholarship."[81] One of his education histories won him a Pulitzer Prize and he serves with Barbara Tuchman, among others, on the editorial board of the well-edited and written *American Scholar*. Cremin is one of the few educationists respected by outsiders, but still a typical educationist in some pernicious ways. Though Sewall is an admirer of Cremin, he quotes him as admitting that some schools were in terrible shape. "But society gets what it deserves."[82]

This notion of Cremin's permeates the educationist field. I gave an example of it at the beginning of Chapter 9. A graduate student, in response to my question of why schools do a poor job of teaching math, said that "the culture doesn't support it." Boyer in *High School*, in the context of saying that the schools should not be blamed for the rising tide of mediocrity, uses the notion this way. "Schools can rise no higher than the communities that support them."[83] Had Boyer said instead, "Math can be taught no higher than the knowledge of math in their communities," he might have recognized how irresponsible the notion is.

So should Lawrence Cremin. He knows that ed schools claim the same professional status as engineering, law, and medical schools. But what would one think of engineering schools if, confronted with collapsing bridges and tunnels caving in, they collectively shrugged their shoulders and said, "Society gets the engineering it deserves"? Or if medical schools, confronted with a spate of patients dying on operating tables, responded, "Society gets the surgery it deserves?"

While Cremin shirks his field's responsibility for schools by blaming all on society, in an interview with Edward Fiske of *The New York Times* he also claims the opposite. He grandly claims for schools, and by implication schools of education, the ability to change society. In response to a question about the wave of recent reports critical of schools, part of Cremin's answer was, "They've . . . given very little attention to what I would call the unfinished equity agenda of the 1960s and early 1970s."[84]

Typical of his field, Cremin has it both ways. Schools are handcuffed by society yet, Houdini-like, they can change society with an "equity agenda."

HARVARD GRADUATE SCHOOL OF EDUCATION
Patricia Alberg Graham, Dean

For decades Harvard has been the biggest gun among the ed schools. Its many Ed.D. degree graduates, like Anrig of ETS and Mario Fantini of the U. Mass ed school, hold influential positions all over the nation. What the Harvard ed school brings up, proposes, makes new, soon has adopters elsewhere.

In August 1984 it sponsored a four-day international conference on "critical thinking," "reasoning," or "thinking skills." Three years before, in 1981, the National Assessment of Educational Progress had announced new and disturbing evidence of further decline in the mental abilities of the nation's youth. Its reading tests indicated drops in the "inferential comprehension" of teenagers. For example, 58 percent of seventeen-year-olds were unable to figure the area of a square, given the length of one side. This latest evidence of decline had touched off a new movement among educationists—to teach thinking skills as a discrete subject.

The establishment of this new barony aptly illustrates how educationists turn an old failure into a new success. Having diminished ability to read with reading skills, they introduced remedial reading. Having undermined ability to compute with math skills, they introduced remedial math. Having diminished the ability to write, they introduced writing skills. For students no longer able to follow verbal instructions, they introduced listening skills. Having diminished all that contributes to thinking, educationists would now try to teach thinking skills.

As catastrophic as this sequence is, it has been very obvious to some people for decades. Twenty-five years before the Harvard ed school conference, in 1959, Jacques Barzun had summed up the results of educationists' skills until then. ". . . when skills came in," he wrote, "skill went out."[85] He summed it up in *The House of Intellect*. Educationists despise intellect and hate Jacques Barzun. I once heard a media colleague pronounce, "Barzun is an elitist," the last syllable hissed through clenched teeth.

Though the Harvard ed school has contributed mightily to the fact that "Johnny can't read," write, compute, comprehend, and think, its international conference was a huge success. Its

252/

conferees numbered over 700 and came from 30 states and 20 countries. Hundreds more would-be conferees were turned away because there was no more space. Part of the excitement about the field of thinking, some said, was its sheer newness.

> One of the conference's organizers, Prof. David N. Perkins of Harvard's Education School, said he worried sometimes that "thinking" had become a buzz word, particularly in his own field of devising ways to teach thinking to children. But he added, "I don't mind if the teaching of thinking becomes a fad as long as it becomes part of the national consciousness."[86]

Over one hundred papers were presented—one of them by the director of the Center for Critical Thinking and Moral Critique at Sonoma State University in California. Two University of Virginia researchers insisted that they had found one of the major problems that plagued education—"teachers love knowledge."[87]

New terms were introduced. One was "sigfluence" standing for "positive, long-term, significant, impactful, interpersonal influence."[88] The conference organizers of the Harvard School of Education undoubtedly hoped that "thinking skills" would have "sigfluence."

THE NATIONAL EDUCATION ASSOCIATION (NEA)
Mary Hatwood Futrell, President

The NEA is education's Big Bertha, numerically speaking. It has 1.7 million members, or 71 percent of the nation's public school teachers. Each member pays $261 in union dues, providing the NEA with a war chest of approximately $375 million a year. Much of it is spent to elect politicians considered friendly to it and defeat those it considers its enemies. Aggressive campaigns are carried on via lobbying, TV commercials, direct mail, and with a force of 1,172 fulltime political field workers.[89] Its annual meetings resemble political conventions. *The New York Times* reported in 1984, "The 7,000 teachers from around the country sat with their state delegations as if attending a political convention and the huge Minneapolis Auditorium was festooned with placards and banners proclaiming support for . . . [political candidates]"[90]

But doubts are plentiful about how democratic the union is,

how representative the NEA union leaders are: "Since the early '70s, the NEA has undergone an ideological transformation. It is now one of the nation's most ardent organized advocates of Great Society-style mandates, adhering to New Left and 'revisionist' theories of American history, culture and education."[91]

One writer has characterized the NEA as encouraging "citizens in general and children in particular to despise the rules and customs that make their society a functional democracy."[92] The NEA has gone out of its way to take sides on issues having nothing to do with schooling—ERA, nuclear disarmament, gun control, abortion rights, and affirmative action.

The radical nature of the NEA's leadership reflects much of what has gone on in schools of education, including using blacks as stalking horses. The NEA even has its own extreme definition of racism: "All white individuals in our society are racists. Even if whites are totally free from all conscious racial prejudices, they remain racists, for they receive benefits distributed by a white racist society through its institutions".[93]

To oppose proposed school reforms, the NEA uses blacks and Hispanics as spokespeople, including its president, Mary Futrell. Utterances are chiefly political, but when couched in educational terms, the nonsensical educationist training shines through. The following was written by Mary Futrell to object to recent legislation in some states that permits liberal arts college graduates to become teachers without having taken ed school courses first: "Laws that allow prospective teachers to sidestep instruction in the techniques of learning to teach actually harm, not help . . ."[94] The only thing clear in this statement is that Futrell wants to retain the schools of education.

ALBERT SHANKER
President, American Federation of Teachers (AFT)

Shanker's union of about 580,000 members is similar in most ways to the NEA, particularly at the bargaining table negotiating union contracts with school systems. The major difference between the two unions is in responding to the public's criticism of schools. While the NEA adamantly and shrilly opposes all proposed reforms, the leaders of the AFT are more rational and willing to discuss them. The reason for the difference, in my opinion, is that the AFT leadership is a product of the New

York City public school system when it was still good and superior to most others. Albert Shanker and his staff are better educated and show more intelligence than their counterparts in the NEA.

Known for his "Where We Stand" advertisements in *The New York Times* and other publications, Albert Shanker usually makes more sense than education professors. For many years he has called for old-fashioned academic standards and particularly emphasized the need for school and classroom discipline, the lack of which is a major obstacle to instruction and learning across the nation.

Shanker has acknowledged the correctness of criticisms of schools of educaiton, though still defending them. In December 1983 he headed a column of his, "Abandon Schools of Ed? Not So Fast." His acknowledgment of the possibility must have chilled education professors. But nothing damned educationists more completely than the following utterance of Shanker's at the AFT's convention in 1984: ". . . there are two million teachers, most of whom have negative things to say about whether the education they got was helpful. A doctor might criticize medical education, but he would not say he would be better off without his professional training, as a teacher would."[95] This statement of Shanker's is what almost all teachers say when they are being candid.

Of course, Shanker is first and foremost a union leader. Like all union leaders he will do what he thinks best for himself and his union. He will not abandon schools of education for the ever-so-faint aura of professionalism that their existence gives teachers and administrators, and the pay increases most school systems give for taking additional ed school courses while on the job. Shanker will not abandon them unless he can persuade his membership that to do so will lead to increased salaries on the one hand, and the making of teaching into a respected profession on the other, and without weakening AFT power. Shanker can be considered a potential supporter for major school reforms that can accomplish these things.

THE FOUNDATIONS

Danforth; Carnegie, for the Advancement of Teaching; Carnegie, of New York; Commonwealth Fund; Charles E. Culpeper; Ford; Gates; JDR 3rd Fund; Martha Jennings; Charles F. Kettering; Esther A. and Joseph Klingenstein Fund; Lilly Endowment, Inc.; Charles Stewart Mott; Edward John Noble; Needmore Fund; International Paper Company; Peramorphosis, Inc.; Atlantic Richfield; Rockefeller; and Spencer.

There are 21,967 foundations in the United States.[96] Recapitulated above are just those that funded the studies of Sizer, Lightfoot, Goodlad, and Boyer. Their assets of untold billions give foundations immeasurable influence over others. As funders of studies they are among education's big guns.

Their influence on education is varied. Some of it is productive and benign. No foundation money was ever better spent than that of the Spencer Foundation in support of the work of Bruno Bettelheim that is incorporated in *On Learning to Read*. On the other hand, much foundation influence on education has been destructive. In funding the studies of members of the education establishment primarily responsible for the low state of education, the above foundations acted irresponsibly, in my opinion, though conventionally.

A prominent philanthropist, J. Irwin Miller, speaking at the 1984 annual conference of the Council of Foundations, suggested:

> As the world around us becomes more confusing and in many ways more terrifying, foundations appear to be impelled to play it safer and safer. Increasingly we fund conferences and studies, whose proceedings immediately begin their long accumulation of dust on some library shelf, but also cause no criticism and are good for some nice lunches.[97]

But before studies in book form begin to gather dust, they are reported by the news media through which their noxious notions are chiefly spread. So many studies and reports had appeared by September 1983 that Edward Fiske of *The New York Times* referred to their "babel of recommendations."[98] His colleague Fred Hechinger reported on the "Rush of Contradictory Ideas on School Reform,"[99] and in another article asked in the headline, "But Will Anything Come of All Those Reports?"[100]

In considering the proposals they funded, how critically did the above foundations weigh them? With education's body in need of major surgery, did they get second and third opinions?

Before deciding to fund proposals, did the foundations have them reviewed by critical thinkers, such as Jacques Barzun, Thomas Sowell, or Richard Mitchell, the underground grammarian, to name just three. Any could have pointed out that no study of public schools would have much value if it omitted the effects of schools of education. Taking their effects into account could have been made a condition of funding Sizer's, Lightfoot's, Goodlad's, and Boyer's studies.

In addressing the Council of Foundations, J. Irwin Miller also told the foundation officers: "Arrogance is our occupational virus." Boyer in his *High School* is infected with that virus. Although his acknowledgments suggest that most of it is based on the findings of others, *High School* is his book. Throughout he uses the editorial "we," presumably as president of the Carnegie Foundation for the Advancement of Teaching. His tone is pontifical as if the pope of education, repeatedly saying "We recommend, we propose, we conclude, etc." Although he is political in trying to cover all bases and being all things to all people, his ignorance stands out unequivocally in the four regressive recommendations he makes to improve teacher preparation. And Boyer promises yet another education study to come in 1986, this one of colleges.

CHESTER E. FINN, JR.
Professor of Education and Public Policy,
Vanderbilt University

Finn is that rare educationist who does not sound like one. He is an excellent, intelligent writer and has the courage to criticize his fellow educationists, including some at the Harvard Graduate School of Education from which he has a doctorate. He is a refreshing break in educationists' otherwise stolid ranks.

I include him among education's big guns asmoking because he recently has become a major voice for reform. Yet he fails to go the distance to where his intelligence should take him. He continues to defend schools of education. He said, with a coauthor, in 1984, "We do not propose . . . to join the swelling mob of 'ed school bashers.' "[101] Finn has a secure position in his field, has made a name for himself in it.

In 1980 he published an article in which he identified the origins of what he called the "liberal consensus" that contributed mightily to the devastation in public education. Finn says that the liberal consensus grew out of the:

> Ford and Carnegie Foundations and four or five smaller ones; the elite graduate schools of education such as those at Stanford, Harvard, Chicago and Columbia; the major national organizations of teachers and educational institutions, such as the National Education Association, the American Association of School Administrators, the National School Boards Association, and the American Council on Education; the various groups represented in the Leadership Conference on Civil Rights; the big labor unions; the political appointees in the education-related agencies of the federal executive branch . . . and the writers of education editorials for major metropolitan newspapers including *The New York Times* and *The Washington Post.*[102]

I believe that Finn is correct in naming these institutions and others as the origin of the liberal consensus that has transformed equal opportunity in education into equal outcomes, so dear to the hearts of black and Hispanic organizations. But Finn neglects to ask why the liberal consensus was so terribly successful in contributing to the educational devastation.

In the early 1980s we saw among Protestant fundamentalists a conservative consensus to attack the teaching of evolution in the schools. Their attacks largely failed. Evolutionists were able to beat them off because they had a unified body of evidence for evolution from the fields of biology, physiology, geology, genetics, etc. Without their knowledge they might have lost to the creative evolutionists and thus have had to stop teaching evolution.

Had the elite schools of education had a comparable body of knowledge for their field, they would never have contributed to the liberal consensus. Had it arisen in other institutions, the ed schools would have been able to resist it. But precisely because they had no body of knowledge, a coherent theory of pedagogy and learning, the elite ed schools added to and eagerly embraced the liberal consensus. It enabled them to hide their deficiencies behind blacks, use them as stalking horses.

DIANE RAVITCH
Adjunct Professor of History and Education
Teachers College, Columbia University

Without a doctorate in anything, Diane Ravitch has become the field's best and most honest writer of education history. She belongs, in my opinion, on the other side of 120th Street, the widest in in the world, that separates Teachers College from the rest of Columbia. Were she a member of the history department, she could permit herself to reach the conclusions that her admirable work points to. That she holds back was apparent to Christopher Lehmann-Haupt when he reviewed her book *The Troubled Crusade: American Education 1945–1980*. In a short review he called attention twice to her holding back:

> One expects . . . a blast by the author of the liberal do-gooders and proponents of federal intervention in local affairs who might be construed to have been indirectly responsible for a sorry state of educational affairs.
>
> But Mrs. Ravitch fails to conclude . . . with a fulmination. Instead, she trails off into slightly platitudinous expressions of hope for the future.
>
> . . . at times her narrative assumes the aspect of a very dark comedy, and one fully expects her to pronounce some dire moral at the end.
>
> But she never does.[103]

Neither Ravitch nor Finn, with whom she is aligned, is able to bite the hand that feeds them. Rather, each denies what must have come to mind. Together with a third author, they wrote that they had looked for no single "smoking gun" to blame for the low state of education. They said, "there is plenty of culpability to go around."[104] In this they were of course correct. The rest of the academic world is also implicated.

College and University Professors

Professors—not deans and other administrators—are generally in charge of everything pertaining to instruction. One of the obligations of professors is approving all courses and programs. At U. Mass, for example, professors can offer an "experimental course" for two or three semesters, then must submit it to a University committee for approval. (This would not hold true for Teachers College, Columbia, which is a legal entity separate from the rest of the University.)

The proposed course is reviewed by a committee of professors from various departments under the guise of quality control. In effect, the procedure permits ignoring quality. The committee accepts course descriptions at face value, and so encourages falsifications. If an education professor submits a three-credit weekend workshop on racism for committee approval, for example, the description of it may have all the earmarks of a rigorous semester-long course. It may include a number of books to be read prior to the weekend and call for prior and post consultations with the instructor. The description may even claim to teach theory or theories. If so, the committee will not ask what it is or even if any agreed-on theory exists. It might reject the course, in fact, if it did not claim to teach theory. After approval, neither the committee nor any other university body monitors the course to see if it is taught as approved; no check is made to see if anyone in the course reads any of the books or confers with the instructor. In most university departments, courses are taught in their approved forms, especially in the rigorous disciplines. But an education course usually becomes whatever the instructor makes it. Not once in my twelve years at U. Mass did anyone inquire about or look into what I was actually teaching.

Faculty responsibility for instruction also includes all personnel recommendations for hiring, reappointment, granting of tenure, and promotion. But legalistic procedures make each department autonomous. Universities, in practice, impose few restrictions on their ed schools that they cannot circumvent. On most campuses, the professors in the academic departments have permitted the school of education to be a perpetual intellectual slum.

Quite apart from educationists, however, the professors in most colleges and universities have deteriorated along with their students. In 1977, a professor of English at Glassboro State in New Jersey was so appalled by the constant misuse of the English language by administrators and fellow professors that he self-published a campus journal in which he exposed their errors and corrected them. He called the journal *The Underground Grammarian*. He is Richard Mitchell and his method was to take memos, reports, and newsletters of the college president, deans, department heads, and professors, and expose the meaningless jargon, tortured syntax, and excess verbiage in them. To the embarrassment of the authors of the bad English, Mitchell named them. Among those whose language he ridiculed was the head of the communications department. A memo of a campus planner was exposed for its misplaced modifiers, syntax errors, and pretentious language, with Mitchell adding, "This is the work of a vice-president . . . [who] is paid $28,359 a year." Mitchell of course offended many people on his campus, but said in his own defense: "Bad English is a form of malpractice in an academic professional."[105]

But Mitchell is a rare exception among English professors. Most will not risk offending for what they believe in. Too many, moreover, have betrayed the humanness of the humanities in pursuing ponderous analysis and pretentious jargon: "One does not talk about novels or stories, poems or plays any more; one 'decodes' or 'deconstructs texts.' One does not explore and evaluate an author's thoughts and perceptions for the purpose of strengthening mind and illuminating life; one seeks clues to 'performative linguistic acts' for the purpose of achieving 'critical enablement'."[106] Such jargon has been called the "higher illiteracy."

Other English professors encourage the more common kind, as members of the National Council of Teachers of English. It was this group that in 1974 endorsed the proposition that students have "a right to their own language." This right was proclaimed in a special issue of *College Composition and Communication*. The group holds annual conventions and John Simon attended its sixty-seventh in New York City. He found presentations on "visual literacy," "The Future Appreciation of Television Reading," and "Being Open and Creative with Gayness in High-School Classes." Still another was "Teaching Reading to College Students."[107]

Professors are supposed to be intellectuals. Being intellectual is what they are paid to do. In exercising their intellects they are expected to run the risk of offending others, as Mitchell did in his *Underground Grammarian*. They are given the academic freedom to do so, are protected by tenure, the virtual guarantee of a lifetime job. But in recent decades this protection has generally not produced the desired results:

. . . the very people whose work is based on the relationship between ideas and reality are exempted from having to demonstrate such a relationship—while merchants, athletes, policemen, and others looked down on by academics are regularly forced to demonstrate such a relationship and to pay heavily for discrepancies. For academics, the only test is whether what they say sounds plausible to enough people, or to the right people.

Tenure, "academic freedom," and other insulations are intended to free the intellectual process from political and quasi-political pressures, but they end up freeing the intellectual from a need to respect the intellectual process or to recognize any objective reality beyond his fancies or the fashions of his fellow academicians.[108]

These are the words of Thomas Sowell, who has been labeled by liberals as an arch-conservative. Let me therefore quote a well-known liberal, shortly after his retirement as a Harvard professor of economics. He refers to academics as a "priestly class," distrustful of outsiders, and therefore deliberately obtuse. John Kenneth Galbraith has written:

Complexity and obscurity have professional value; they are the academic equivalent of apprenticeship rules in the building trades. They exclude outsiders, keep down competition, preserve the image of a privileged or priestly class. The man who makes things clear . . . is a recusant or a scab. He is criticized not only for his clarity but for his treachery.[109]

Excepting Galbraith, Sowell, Mitchell, and other academicians, most college professors are intent on their own privileges and comforts. They cannot be expected to fight for public school or university reforms. Reforms will have to be imposed from outside of their ranks.

13

"The Near Nihilism of the Present"

The above is quoted from United States Senator Daniel Patrick Moynihan's speech about education to a 1984 convocation of a school of education.[1] It accurately indicates the degree of education's low estate. The phrase less accurately describes the ed schools. In them, nihilism is total.

The totality is illustrated by the U. Mass ed school's reaction to my last act as media program director. The name media program and my title of director were both misleading. I directed nothing educative and the four media faculty and their courses added up to nothing programmatic. Each media professor did his or her own thing. Professor Liane Brandon taught film production, but refused to accept my course in the planning of educational films on storyboards as a prerequisite for her course. She would not discuss it even when students, every so often, pointed out that our two courses were a logical sequence and should be offered as such. Brandon lived in Boston, came to Amherst on Tuesdays and departed again on Thursdays. The media faculty could not meet together on a Monday or Friday, and Brandon never acceded to an occasional request to make an exception in her schedule. Professor Ray Wyman was an internationally known hardware specialist who recently had spent time in Saudi Arabia as a consultant to that country, advising on what media equipment to install in the new schools it was building with petrodollars. Wyman taught media equipment operation in his courses, which was anathema to me. Professor Patrick Sullivan's basic course was educational photography. With his Ph.D. in English, he should have known better than to elevate pictures above words. The media program had no more coherence and educative justification than others in the school, except possibly the reading program. But the reading program had only two professors, and its teaching was undermined by the spurious notions of the other programs, including media. My title of director meant chiefly that I did the paperwork—answering inquiries from potential graduate students and memos from school administrators and committees.

My last act as director was my answer to a memo requesting a long-range plan for the media program. At the time, 1981, the university was engaged in long-range planning. Each department and school was to submit a plan for itself to the central planning committee. Although budget-cut talk was in the air, the university administration and each department would strive for the fiscal status quo.

I knew what the school administrators wanted—a memorandum justifying the program's future with the kind of rhetoric Ernest Boyer uses about technology in his book *High School*. But for a couple of years I had been quietly discouraging potential graduate students. To those typically ignorant, I pointed out the poor job prospects; to the occasional bright student, the field's intellectual and practical dead end.

I failed to discourage all applicants. Some admitted as Ed.D. degree candidates held positions "in media" in other state education agencies, and were sophisticated in getting their way. Sometimes, they avoided me and my courses, and acquired doctoral committee chairpersons whose specialties were other than media. But no specialty in education has a body of knowledge and, in practice, professors regarded each other as authorities in nothing. Virtually all professors in the school of education, in fact, held most colleagues in contempt.

A symptom of the contempt was a series of anonymous satirical takeoffs on the school's weekly newsletter, the *Beacon*. The satire was called Bacon, and was similarly distributed in faculty mailboxes. The following samples of its derision are from its April 1983 issue:

Summer Film Series:	"Rocky Horror Picture Show" (a stirring portrayal of the School's Faculty Assembly)
	"Personal Best" (a film that has absolutely nothing to do with the School of Education)

Pop Quiz:	For all of you who have read *The One Minute Manager* by Ken Blanchard [a professor in the school], the Bacon staff challenges your recall of its contents:
	(1) *The One Minute Manager* is:
	    (a) small
	    (b) expensive
	    (c) piffle
	    (d) all of the above

Special Masters Program:	The School of Education is taking applications for its new (??) M.A.B. (Masters of Administrative Bungling) Degree. This special program will involve an extensive weekend seminar, with pay, led by the School's very own BAB's (Best Administrative Bunglers). Qualifications: distaste for teaching, inability to work well with others, no integrity.

Bacon was first suspected to be the work of some disaffected graduate student. As more appeared, a couple of issues a semester, it became apparent that its author knew too much about the school and the university to be other than a faculty member. Speculation about which professor it might be also typified faculty members' poor self-images. The only names mentioned were the few graduates of liberal arts colleges, in apparent recognition that holders of education degrees were not inventive enough, nor able to write other than educationese. I was a suspect. Only after I had left the school and Bacon continued to appear did suspicion of me cease.

The speculation that I was behind it was stimulated, no doubt, by my memo about the future of the media program, sent to the school's long-range planning committee. In it I recommended that the program be abolished and its faculty used in other ways. My memo avoided any tone of derision or snideness. It was straightforward and scholarly in that I made my case on rational grounds, citing authority. One citation read: "At present, educational technology is not a pure science, an art, or an academic discipline. It can be called a 'field' only as a term of convenience. It still lacks a central body of theory and a corpus of recognized knowledge. It still lacks well-developed techniques of investigation."[2]

These words described the field of education itself. Senator Moynihan, in his "near nihilism of the present" speech, also referred to "the absence of any adequate theory regarding the nature and machinery of human learning."

I sent copies of my memo recommending the abolition of the media program to my media colleagues, and to the university's central long-range planning committee, knowing that the school would not pass on my recommendation to it. I did not expect to influence the university committee. I knew better than that. The year before, I had sent copies of the school's *Alumni Newsletter* containing Wagschal's article "Illiterates with Doctorates" to half a dozen professors in academic departments, including two in the English department. I had called their attention to the Wagschal article in the expectation of outcries against the school's undermining the university's reason for being, but I heard none.

I wrote my memo recommending the abolition of the media program chiefly because I could not do otherwise. From past experience I knew it would elicit nothing but silence. Even so, it gave the school one last chance to open, if only by a crack, the door of doubt that it was not totally irrational and irresponsible. As I waited, I scanned faces of memo recipients when I spoke to them or passed them in the halls. I did not get so much as a non-verbal acknowledgment.

Never in the business world had I written a memo that went unacknowledged. Had I recommended to the head of any advertising agency I was with that a portion of it be abolished, I might have been fired or promoted, but not ignored.

Finally, my media colleague Patrick Sullivan made one faint

allusion to my recommending the abolition of the program. His office was a few doors down the hall from mine. Opportunities to speak of my memo were plentiful. But Sullivan waited for an occasion when discussion of it would be impossible. He waited for a doctoral committee meeting in which the candidate and a professor from the sociology department were also present. For my benefit, Sullivan said that what he was doing as a professor was important and he would not give it up "for a million dollars," a trite phrase for a Ph.D. in English. His was the one small squeak of denial in the otherwise solid silence.

My experience with silence in the U. Mass ed school prepared me to recognize the same silence in other educationists. What Sizer, Lightfoot, Goodlad, and Boyer omitted from their books spoke louder than their hundreds of thousands of words. Their omission of schools of education and effects on public schools was thunderous to my ears. They concentrated on sociology— elaborate descriptions, real and fictitious, of students, teachers, principals, and schools; compilations of answers to questions of opinion; well-known facts and figures rehashed; and the false notions and clichés of the field endlessly repeated.

Had I been with any other ed school in the nation, I am sure that my experiences would have been much the same as in the U. Mass School of Education. Its talk was of everything but education. Not only were ideas about learning and teaching not discussed in faculty meetings, faculty retreats, etc., such ideas were impossible to broach with individuals. Whenever I started to approach some aspect of learning I was cut off by a denial or a change of subject. I had more conversation about education with the maintenance man who cleaned my office than I ever had with my fellow professors.

My conversations with the maintenance man occurred during a period when I was doing my writing evenings in the office. An attraction of a university position in 1970 had been more time for writing. Within my first five years I had four published articles in educational journals, in addition to my unpublished, misconceived book-length manuscript on Harvey Scribner. Getting published in educational journals was easy for me until I grew critical and substantive. My three articles, "Beware of the 'literacy' for which there is no language," the second on how television holds attention, and the third on the misuse of pictures in instructional materials, were all turned down by numbers of the field's journals. They would publish nothing fundamentally critical of any portion of the field, or contrary to prevailing notions. They enforced the same silence as the school, the same silence about ed schools maintained in the studies of Sizer, Lightfoot, Goodlad, and Boyer.

There was no such restraint in chatting with the maintenance man who cleaned my office. He told me that since he had to be a "janitor," his word, he thought it would be pleasant to be one in "a community of scholars," his voice inflecting the quotes around the phrase. We both laughed at its hollowness. Much of what he said indicated that he knew the nonsense in the school and its spillover into the public schools.

He was a man about my age but what we had in common had less to do with how long we had lived than when we had gone to school. He was Irish, grew up in Boston; I in New York City. But public schools everywhere then provided a common basic education, stressed a common heritage. Although I was a graduate of an Ivy League college and he was not, we could discuss ideas together as I and my fellow education professors could not.

With respect to age and education, my sharpest image is of my father-in-law reading a novel, his huge thick-fingered hands dwarfing the paperback they held. He had toiled with his workman's hands most of his seventy-six years. He was Norwegian, had left school and gone to sea at the age of fourteen. Yet he was more literate with eight years of schooling than many young people are today with sixteen years of schooling and college degrees. Moreover, he had learned to speak, read, and write English without further schooling. He said that he had just picked it up. My father, who was English, had also left school at the age of fourteen. One of my most affectionate memories of him is his reading to me as a small boy. My father and father-in-law read newspapers, magazines, and occasionally books. They were informed about what was going on in the world, inferred much from what they read, and could discuss it.

Public or common schools early in the century were able to turn out boys of fourteen sufficiently literate and numerate to be lifelong readers for pleasure, users of math, and able to continue learning on their own. What had happened since then in the United States was schools of education. The kindest word to be said for them is that they are failed experiments. The presidents of Columbia, Harvard, John Hopkins, and other scholars who initiated them, expecting them to develop a body of pedagogical knowledge, expected what was probably impossible. Classroom teaching involves too many variables to be categorized or described with any completeness. Classroom teaching therefore remains more art than science, relies more on intrinsic than conscious knowledge.

But schools of education, once having been brought into being, had a vested interest in surviving and expanding. They justified themselves by belittling all past teaching in substance and method. They attacked, out of self-interest, everything traditional. Some education professors aggressively attacked literacy, and all other education professors, by their silence, countenanced the attacks. Certain education professors aggressively attacked traditional Judeo-Christian ethics and morals, overwhelmingly subscribed to by Americans affiliated and unaffiliated with religious organizations. All other professors of education, by their silence, condoned these attacks. The attacks were clandestine, carried on out-of-sight of the public, where the studies of Sizer, Lightfoot, Goodlad and Boyer have kept them. Schools of education have operated without checks, without effective restraints, and without the public's knowledge.

The report of the National Commission on Excellence in Education, appropriately titled *A Nation At Risk*, said, "If an unfriendly foreign power had attempted to impose on America the mediocre educational performance that exists today, we might well have viewed it as an act of war." Schools of education constitute that "unfriendly power," which has remained hidden and "foreign" to the general public. Schools of education subversively increased their hold on public education decade by decade for almost a hundred years to bring us to "the near nihilism of the present." Because they are dangerous to the social fabric of the nation, schools of education must be destroyed, must be abolished. The enormous sums of money spent to maintain them should be redistributed to local school systems so that they can begin the repair of nearly a hundred years of damage to them.

The Making of a Teacher, published in 1984, gives figures useful in arriving at a rough idea of how much money would be available for redistribution by the states. The number of colleges and universities turning out teachers in the United States amounted to two-thirds of all four-year institutions of higher learning, or 1,287.[3] Broken down by states, the number in New York, for example, is 96, in Pennsylvanis, 87, California, 79, Texas, 64, Illinois, 58, and Massachusetts, 49. Schools and departments of education in the United States employed, in 1983, 27,432 fulltime and 10,927 parttime faculty.[4]

An accurate figure of what they are paid is difficult to arrive at. The average salary of full professors in various education specialties ranged in 1983 from $31,419 to $34,348 in private institutions; and from $27,440 to $39,064 in public institutions. These figures are from the *Chronicle of Higher Education* (February 29, 1984), which also gave average salaries for all ranks of education faculty (full, associate, assistant professors, etc.). The range in private institutions for all ranks was $27,091 to $28,344; and in public institutions, from $22,336 to $30,292. Since there is no way to average such figures, I arbitrarily take $27,000 to represent the average for all ranks for both public and private institutions and add 11 percent for fringe benefits—life and health insurance, pension contributions, etc. The cost to the nation of fulltime education faculty is $822 million. For parttime faculty, teaching one course per semester, for example, and getting one-third of what is average for all ranks of fulltime faculty, this cost would come to $110 million. The total of faculty salaries during the regular academic year would be $932 million.

Typically, however, the annual salaries of college and university faculty are for only nine months of the year, September through May. When they teach during summer sessions, which most schools of education have, the professors are paid extra for these courses. If just one-quarter of the education faculty work part of the summer, six weeks, for one-sixteenth of the annual average salary for all ranks ($1,688), that brings the total for instructional salaries for the full year to $1.12 billion.

To this figure must be added the salaries of deans, associate or assistant deans (U. Mass has 3 associate deans) or department heads, administrative staffs, secretaries, technicians, copying machine operators, and maintenance men. Also to be added is the cost of building maintenance and repair; cost of equipment maintenance, and replacement—typewriters, computers, copying machines, media equipment, vehicle operation (the U. Mass ed school had two vans and faculty checked out cars from the university car pool); costs of utilities—telephone, electricity, air conditioning, and heating.

Depending on the institution, there are also costs of debt retirement, incurred in the case of state institutions by the state; the costs of pensions of retired faculty and pension obligations building up for future retirees; and the loss in local real estate taxes due to tax exemption for being an educational institution.

I would put the cost to the nation of operating all schools and departments of education at $1.5 billion at a minimum. What share of this is for public, state operated institutions I would estimate at 80 percent, judging by the fact that "Eighty percent of teacher education students go to public institutions even though well over half of the colleges and universities training teachers are privately controlled."[5] That puts the total expenditure that the fifty states could reallocate to local public school systems at $1.2 billion, a considerable sum with which to help start lifting public education out of "the near nihilism of the present."

To eliminate schools and departments of education from colleges and universities, each state legislature must change state requirements—eliminate all education courses for teachers and every rank of administrator from assistant principal to state education commissioner. The state legislature can set new requirements, such as a B.A. degree in the liberal arts with a concentration in English and history, particularly American history. Secondary teachers should be required to have an adequate number of courses in the subjects they teach.

The state legislature, too, should prohibit local school systems from giving automatic pay raises to teachers and administrators for taking education courses. New requirements for employment in all other county and state education departments would also have to be established. Deprived of customers, schools of education would have to close down. To close them quickly, however, state legislatures will probably have to take a hand.

College administrators are reluctant to do what is necessary. For example, while enrollments in education courses dropped precipitously in recent years, the number of education faculty dropped hardly at all. Between 1973 and 1983, course enrollments declined by 35 percent, new teacher graduates declined 53 percent, and newly admitted teacher education students declined 44 percent. But during the same period, fulltime faculty declined only 2 percent, and parttime faculty declined only one percent.[6]

Would eliminating schools and departments of education cause disruptions? None whatsoever. The general public, unaware of schools of education and what they were doing all along, will not miss them for an instant. Local school systems should feel an enormous sense of relief, and for many reasons. The principal one should be the relief of a whole layer of supposed experts being removed from above them. The removal would place more responsibility on the shoulders of administrators and teachers. From then on, they would be expected to be the chief experts in schooling, not college professors who, as a rule, are more resented than respected by school personnel. As one principal of an elementary school in New York City recently expressed it: "If I hear another School of Education dean lecture us about what we should be doing, I'll strangle the hypocrite. "[7]

14

To Make Teaching Professional

I once had an elementary-school teacher in one of my courses whose personality was so different from her appearance that I wondered if she was an instance of a split personality. Her body was mature and adult but what she did and said was childlike in the extreme. Her handwriting was like that used to introduce first-grade writing in script form. Her voice was abnormally high-pitched, weak, and tentative. She asked questions about the obvious. When I wondered aloud about this teacher's childlike qualities to a graduate student of mine, Joan Schell, who had been an elementary-school teacher, she responded with a knowing smile, "It's an occupational hazard."

Since then, I have seen charges that elementary-school teachers have been "infantized." They complain that they are not treated as mature enough to make decisions. Others in the many-layered hierarchy above them prescribe the programs in reading, math, and other subjects—the textbooks they must use, the teachers' guides they must follow, the worksheets they must hand out to pupils, and the standardized tests for which they must prepare their charges to score at grade level. They also complain of being isolated, of having little or no conversation with other teachers, and, in many schools, of being treated like children by principals.

Classroom teachers will remain low in status for as long as schools of education exist, will never be considered experts in what they do. Professors of education reserve that status for themselves, although most have spent little or no time as classroom teachers. Enjoying the trappings of professorial ranks, and the privileges of higher education, education professors have led comfortable, charmed lives for generations. Whatever aura of scholarship their universities may have has rubbed off on them—Harvard's ed school being the perfect example. Even though they are considered intellectual inferiors by most professors in academic departments, the university organization accords them equal status in all the ways that matter to educationists. They are called doctor, the same as those in the rigorous disciplines. They are paid equal or comparable salaries, sit in the faculty senate, have a voice in university-wide committees, fill important university and administrative posts, and even become university and college presidents. Education professors can put up with disrespect and snide remarks behind their backs for the professorial comforts they enjoy, and for the power they wield.

They turn out more people with doctorates than any other university department, and in some instances and times more doctorates than all other departments combined. Their graduates fill all the key posts in all the public school systems, and almost all in the federal education department and its many bureaus, and the education departments of the fifty states. Most United States commissioners of education and most state commissioners of education have been educationists. They also hold positions in other state agencies—state hospitals and correctional facilities, for example, and the United States Department of State's Agency for International Development (AID). Some of them direct training programs in business corporations. Their influence and effects are without end. The sales success of *The One Minute Manager* is but one example.

As members of a powerful yet intellectually inferior group, professors of education prevent those with good minds from entering their field. This is not difficult. Educationists merely act themselves. In the fall of 1941, as a Columbia College undergraduate, I took Education Seminar for Juniors at Teachers College. I dropped it after one semester because it was the only course I had that had no substance. It killed any inclination I might have had to become a teacher. Millions of other college students have avoided becoming teachers for the same reason. In 1980 when my eldest daughter, Karen, graduated with honors in English from U. Mass, some of her English major friends were inclined to become teachers. But they said that they could not stomach the idea of taking courses in "that ed school" to become certified.

"Weak students gravitate to weak faculties," said James D. Koerner in his *The Miseducation of American Teachers* in 1963.[1] That education students are academically inferior to those in most other fields has been shown by all comparisons made since 1932.[2]

Educationists also have made conscious efforts to keep the more able from entering the field. In the early 1970s when hordes of students were clamoring to be admitted to graduate study in the U. Mass School of Education, Dean Dwight Allen boasted that many who were rejected had better academic records than those admitted. It was no idle boast. *The Hampshire Gazette*, in 1975, quoted the former Dean of the Graduate School as saying:

> Some 52 per cent of the graduate students admitted to the School of Education had grade point averages below the minimal requirement of the university. In addition, students who were rejected by the school had as a group a higher grade point average than those who were accepted into the graduate programs.[3]

Educationists have derided the teachers they have produced. In the 1950s, they coined the most belittling term imaginable— "teacher-proof"—to describe "materials and programs that couldn't be wrecked by teachers, no matter how incompetent they were," to use Albert Shanker's words of protest against the term,[4] which is still in use.

Sympathy can be felt for teachers—for the way they are treated by the layer on layer of "experts" above them, for being on the receiving end of innumerable policies, directives, and programs that they have no hand in making. They also receive most of the blame for what is wrong with the public schools. Nevertheless, teachers are the products of their ed schools, and have all the weaknesses of them. In claiming that they have been "infantized," made powerless, they fail to do so on educational grounds.

Unlike education professors, teachers have few publications of their own—put out and written by teachers. What few exist have tiny circulations. One is a magazine published three times a year, *Radical Teacher*. Although it describes itself as "a socialist and feminist journal on the theory and practice of teaching," I hunted in vain through its issue devoted to elementary school teachers for ideas different from those of education professors. The teachers quoted show themselves to be as alike as peas in a pod in regurgitating the field's clichés. The issue even contains the latest cliche, "critical thinking,"[5] and a new pseudo literacy— "critical literacy."[6] The teachers blame their dissatisfactions not on ed schools but entirely on their school systems, the hierarchy and structure of them. They want more freedom but most are too undereducated and miseducated to be able to use the freedom productively for students. The radical part of *Radical Teacher* is the socialist-feminist outlook, and even in this they are reminiscent of many professors of education. They, too, want to rid the world of sexism, racism, and classism.[7]

The unforgiveable weakness of the vast majority of elementary-school teachers in this nation is their inability to turn children into readers. This inability hurts all children without exception. It most grievously hurts the children of the poor of all ethnic groups. Indeed, the ways in which elementary-school teachers try to teach, acting on the spurious notions acquired in ed schools, actually discourage and turn many children away from learning to read. In some children, teachers can destroy the insights necessary to learn to read that they acquired at home.

We should recall from Chapter 7 on the damage educationists have done to reading instruction, that Bruno Bettelheim and his coauthor observed reading instruction in the best schools of predominantly middle-class school systems, and "only in what each school considered its best classrooms, taught by its best teachers." Many of "the best" teachers defended using reading materials that made little or no sense to their charges, and which they themselves considered boring and vacuous. Even they have been discouraged by their training from thinking for themselves. They consequently give rote teaching performances, adhering slavishly to ill-conceived materials, teachers' guides, and methods.

Failure to read well is the root cause of most of the horrendous academic problems that students have in the upper grades of elementary school, junior high, high school, and even college. Students who do not become good readers are unable to learn in history, science, math, and English courses, and cannot extract information from computer manuals and computer screens. Yet none of the recently published studies by educationists have addressed what happens educationally in the early grades of elementary schools. Bettelheim's study of reading instruction is recent, but he is not from the ranks of educationists, and is largely ignored by them.

It may be inconceivable to the reader still that the educationist field is as incompetent and destructive as I have shown it. How is it possible that 1,287 university and college departments and schools of education, employing 27,432 fulltime and 10,927 parttime faculty, work against the public interest? If inconceivable, I can sympathize with the reader's doubt. It took me years of direct experience at the U. Mass School of Education, and much private study and writing to come to the conclusion that ed schools should be abolished, and that a whole new breed of teachers should be developed by other means, beginning with those for the first elementary grades.

To help the reader resolve doubt, I propose a final piece of evidence, a difficulty to stimulate the reader to make up his or her mind anew. It is a difficulty that has everything to do with instruction and learning and nothing to do with sociology—not ethnicity, class, or gender. How does the reader interpret the following experiment carried out with the following apparatus?

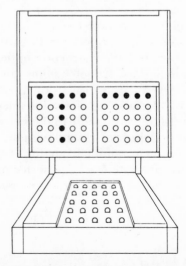

This is a bulb-board.[8] Attached vertically to the back of it is a stand to hold patterns to be copied. When bulbs are pressed corresponding to the patterns shown, such as the T on the left and the single top row on the right, the bulbs light up. A bright five-year old boy easily copied these patterns, and also more complex patterns of a square formed by the outside rows, and that of an E and an H. But when shown a diagonal, the boy inexplicably pressed the bulbs at random. He was told to look at the pattern again, run his finger over it, and try again, which he did. He continued to press the bulbs at random. Then the boy was shown which five bulbs to press to form the diagnoal. Delighted, he quickly began pressing each of the correct five bulbs in sequence. After about fifteen seconds, however, apparently having lost the memory of the visual configuration, he was back to pressing the bulbs at random again.

The difficulty I pose for the reader is how to explain why the boy is unable to copy the diagonal, even after being shown. Does the reader's explanation, moreover, permit instructing the boy so that he will know how forever after?

While the reader ponders, we can review how educationists might typically attack the problem of the bright five-year old. As I have repeatedly said, they have no agreed-on views or practices of learning and instruction, only various notions. Taking one at a time, here is how educationists might apply some of them:

1. "Readiness" is one notion, as they use it in "reading readiness." I believe it is based on little more than if the child learns, he is ready; if he does not learn, he is not ready. Since all eight-year-olds have the ability to copy diagonals, just wait until the five-year-old becomes eight.
2. Educationists who are behaviorists might address the boy's problem as not being motivated, that some reward should be offered him, ignoring that he successfully copied the other patterns without rewards. Behaviorists would also attempt to condition the boy with their typical method of breaking down the diagnonal into its smallest parts. First, they would have the boy press over and over again the first and second bulbs that begin the diagnoal, in the repetitive manner of "See, Jane, see!" in reading primers. Then, they would have him

endlessly practice pressing the second and third bulbs, and so forth. After this hyperrationalized, tedious instruction, they would expect the boy to be able to replicate the complete diagonal. He might be able to replicate it to pass an immediate test, but he will not retain the ability indefinitely because it will still not make sense to him.

3. Another group of educationists might attempt to say something about his "learning style." But this notion is applied in most instances to those who do not learn by reading. Typically, users of the learning-styles notion would recommend that he be taught with pictures; or possibly that he is auditory and should be taught by speech or audio tape recordings, which could hardly help the five-year-old in this instance.

4. Despite the success of the five-year-old boy's having followed directions well in copying all patterns except the diagonal, some educationists may suggest that he has a listening problem. They might prescribe exercises that would supposedly sharpen his listening skills.

5. There are educationists who concern themselves with teaching "life skills." They might decide that being able to copy a diagonal is not one of them and dismiss the five-year-old's inability as irrelevant.

6. Others might say that the boy must have a poor self-image, be culturally deprived, or even emotionally disturbed, none of which is helpful in teaching him how to copy the diagonal.

7. Still other educationists might ascribe the boy's inability to a learning disability, one of numerous supposed neurological disorders. They would say that the five-year-old is unable to copy the diagonal for the same reasons that many children appear unable to copy words, reversing letters, and so forth. Learning disability is currently the most popular diagnosis. In 1976, the year after Congress passed the Education of All Handicapped Children Act requiring public schools to provide services for handicapped youngsters, including the learning disabled, the number of students served under the Act was 800,000. Eight years later, that figure had more than doubled to 1.8 million children.[9] A graduate student of mine who was an elementary school principal told me that the temptation to label students L.D. was great. Schools get additional federal funds for each student so labeled. But

even though learning disabilities is a favorite notion of educationists, there is little agreement among them on how to treat the disabilities.[10]

To get back to the difficulty posed for the reader. Would he or she choose any of the educationists' explanations above?

The people who conducted the experiment with the bright five-year-old, one of many experimental subjects, were *not* educationists. They were internationally respected Jerome S. Bruner et al, as described by David R. Olson. They are cognitive psychologists who, unlike educationists, respect mind and language. They know that our ability to see what is in front of our eyes depends on what knowledge we possess *behind the eyes*, and that such knowledge is most readily conveyed to another person by language; that language is the prime means of instruction.

They taught the five-year-old boy who first pressed the bulbs at random in his efforts to copy the diagonal by giving him the concept of it. Their instruction ". . . consisted of telling the child of what the diagonal consists." "See, the criss-cross starts in the corner." "It goes straight across the middle." "It ends in the other corner." "This kind of training produced 100 percent success."[11]

In the series of controlled experiments from which this is taken, just as effective as telling the children, was asking them where the crisscross started, where it went and ended.

This is an example of children acquiring knowledge—not a skill. The coaching that Theodore Sizer attempts to make into a fad, cannot apply here. One can only coach when a student performs something imperfectly. With respect to the diagonal, the five-year old could not perform it at all. He needed *knowledge*, not skill.

The example also exemplifies the limitations of trying to learn from visuals. As David Olson points out: ". . . even simple geometrical concepts are invented and then imposed on the world as ways of representing that world; they do not arise simply from looking at the world."[12]

There are educationists who know the work of Bruner, Olson, and other cognitive psychologists without being influenced by it. Others try to implement it, but without disputing the rest of the field's incompatible notions. Those as political as Theodore

Sizer in *Horace's Compromise* can quote both cognitivist Jerome S. Bruner and behaviorist B.F. Skinner, though their theories are as opposite as night and day.

What the foregoing example of the five-year-old boy before the bulb-board illustrates most of all is that educationists fail to credit children with having minds. It is utterly inconceivable to most of them that children like mental challenges—as long as they make sense. The example also exemplifies that rigorous investigation of learning is conducted not by education professors but by cognitive psychologists.

This brings us to what is the best undergraduate preparation for future teachers. The best is a rigorous liberal arts education. The humanities are the most likely to produce a literate person, a critical person, a person who can think for him or herself, and can act accordingly. We have a well-known example of such a person in Marva Collins.

In the early 1960s Marva Collins became a second-grade teacher in the Delano school on the west side of Chicago, located in a neighborhood that would soon become a black ghetto. Collins had no elementary school certification, had taken no elementary education courses, and hence had no practice teaching. She had a B.A. degree from Clark College in Atlanta, Georgia. Because of the shortage of certified teachers at the time, she was hired as a second-grade substitute teacher. At first she followed the prescribed curriculum. But she soon recognized how bored her pupils were with their readers filled with pictures and "Run, Pepper, run!"

I interviewed Marva Collins in the spring of 1984 for this book, and I would estimate that she is more literate than the vast majority of the nation's public school elementary teachers. She also is a strong personality of decided views, and is controversial within the black community. Professors of education and public school teachers who are black particularly do not like her for her criticism of the public schools since she left Delano and opened her own private school.

Marva Collins stopped using the Delano school's reading programs not long after she started teaching the second grade. Instead, she brought into the classroom books from the library and bookstores—*Aesop's Fables, Grimm's Fairy Tales*, Hans Christian Andersen, La Fontaine's *Fables*, and Tolstoy's *Fables and*

Fairy Tales. The stories allowed her to introduce discussions about the universal human qualities of greed, malice, happiness, and joy. She wanted her students to be excited about reading, to understand that it is not an exercise in memorizing isolated words and phrases but full of meaning. As the world found out from *60 Minutes* broadcasts, the TV documentary drama about her, and her book coauthored with Civia Tamarkin,[13] Marva Collins succeeded admirably in turning her pupils into readers.

American schools need to be rebuilt from kindergarten up, using as their chief building blocks, a new breed of teachers. This does not mean that all prospective teachers must be recent college graduates. "New" means meeting a higher standard than previously. People changing careers who could do so would be more than welcome. The same applies to current classroom teachers.

Qualifications of the New Breed of Teachers

High qualifications attract the highly qualified. With the basic requirement of a liberal arts degree, the undergraduate major of each candidate need not be specified other than that it be in an academic subject—not physical ed, home economics, or communication studies. A required number of courses can be specified in English, math, history, and cognitive psychology.

English majors should be looked upon with favor, particularly from the better four-year colleges. But a major in English these days is no guarantee of an adequately literate person. The key is ensuring that a candidate has an active concern for language, can speak "written English" well, with clarity and precision. To ensure it, prospective new-breed teachers should pass a writing test. They need not be budding novelists, essayists, playwrights, or poets. The ability to write simple, straightforward, idiomatic English is what the test should reveal. I would recommend that the writing test consist of a series of questions requiring answers that are specific and factual, of less than a hundred words. The kinds of questions I have in mind are these:

1. Explain, as simply as possible, what a sentence is.
2. Explain the difference between the verbs "imply" and "infer."

3. Describe what a diagonal in a rectangle is, without using drawings.
4. Explain the practical advantage to hearers and readers of using "few" when referring to number, and "less" when referring to quantity.
5. Explain what a fraction is, and give the three common ways of expressing fractions.
6. State all that can be inferred from the sentence: "Go down to the teachers' room and bring me the brown mug with the chipped handle."

Question 4 probably requires some knowledge of information theory to answer correctly, learned in courses in cognitive psychology.

Such a written test probably should consist of at least thirty questions, with a high percentage set for passing. It need not become another standardized test originated by such as the Educational Testing Service, and need not be statewide. It can be a test devised locally by a school system.

Teachers learn to teach by teaching, and there is no substitute for it. Nevertheless, a prospect can be eased into teaching by spending a semester working as a teacher's helper. Preferably, the teacher should be a good one. But if a poor one, the new breed of teacher, being especially literate, may learn much by silently noticing what the teacher does poorly.

The new breed of teachers must be allowed to be professional. Being professional means assuming full responsibility for turning pupils into readers, writers, and users of math. The teacher must be free to make decisions, preferably along with colleagues, on what instructional materials to use, and how to use them. He or she must not be expected to slavishly follow programs and teachers' guides dictated by "experts" from above. Nor should they be expected to get pupils ready for yearly standardized tests. These indicate little worth knowing. Currently, of the fourth graders who score at grade level, it is impossible to tell *from their scores* which ones are on their way to becoming good readers and which will fall further and further below grade level as they move through the upper grades. With sole responsibility for their progress, intelligent, literate teachers should be able to tell how their pupils are doing, and modify instruction accordingly.

Being professional means having the opportunity to meet with fellow teachers, and having time to study and investigate. It means not having to take a summer job, except in one's own field, such as summer-school teaching, or camp counseling. With the money saved by abolishing schools of education it should be possible to increase starting and subsequent salaries of teachers in the first three or four grades of elementary school by thirty percent.

It should be possible, too, to develop merit awards. Merit pay appears to have worked in some places and failed in others. Much apparently depends on local circumstances. Perhaps across-the-board merit increases could be given within a school showing marked improvement over previous years. Much has been made of establishing "career ladders" for teachers. At the present time, the ladder into administration is through schools of education, taking certification courses for administrators. With such certification removed, it should be possible for teachers to move directly into assistant principal and principal positions based on past performance.

Freedom to be professional does not mean freedom for teachers to "do their own thing." They must be held accountable by the principal for teaching the agreed-upon curriculum.

The first step toward making elementary school teachers professional is to abolish schools of education. Only then can we have a new breed of teachers with an active concern for language, the prime teaching tool. Only then will the aura of "expert" be transferred from remote education professors to local classroom teachers. Only then can funds become available to substantially increase teachers' salaries.

I am aware of the enormous roadblocks in the way of implementation. Good proposals to offset the destructiveness of education professors have been argued for generations. In *The Diminished Mind*, a book published in 1959, the author wrote:

> Over twenty years ago [before 1939] Albert Jay Nock ended a series of lectures on American education with the pessimistic observation that we have gone so far in the wrong direction that when we realize the need to change we will no longer have it in our power to effect the change. There are equally pessimistic prophets with us today [1959], many of whom feel that the public schools, at least, are sunk so deep . . . that they must be written off as a casualty.[14]

In 1983 a significant number of parents in the United States had their children in private schools. Most may have written off the public schools. The percentages of students in private schools in the 1983–84 school year were: Boston 24, Cincinnati 27, Cleveland 25, Grand Rapids 25, Milwaukee 27, New York City 24, Orleans Parish 32, Philadelphia 32, Pittsburgh 26, Rochester, NY 25, San Francisco 29, South Bend 24, Yonkers, NY 26, and those in a number of other cities and areas were only slightly lower.[15]

Nevertheless, there are substantial reasons for believing that my proposals can be implemented. First of all, never before in the history of the United States has so much attention been given to reforming education. Never before have so many state governors played active roles in educational reform—Governors Clinton of Arkansas, Castle of Delaware, Harris of Georgia, Orr of Indiana, Ashcroft of Missouri, Kean of New Jersey, Nigh of Oklahoma, Alexander of Tennessee, White of Texas, and Bangerter of Utah.

Another healthy sign comes from a 1984 survey of teachers, in which 38 percent favored permitting school districts to hire talented people who do not have teacher certification.[16] The 38 percent represents three-quarters of a million teachers.

Influential private citizens are actively working for school reforms, notably H. Ross Perot, Chairman of Electronic Data Systems Corporation. *Time* quoted him as saying, "It is very important that we don't turn out technological robots who confuse data with wisdom."[17] Perot showed his courage in Texas by sharply criticizing the schools' obsession with football, marching bands, and baton twirling.

In our fifty states, all it will take to get the ball rolling for the rebuilding of American education is for the first state to remove all educationist courses from all certification requirements, and close down departments and schools of education in its state colleges and universities. Given the courage of example, other states will follow, paving the way for turning teaching into a profession.

Conclusion

Until now, the American public has had little inkling of how destructive schools of education are. So unexpected and shocking is it that even intelligent people may react at first with disbelief. Some may try to deny my evidence by rationalizing that it pertains to the U. Mass School of Education, and none other. Although much of this book is autobiographical, all of its evidence pertains nationwide. Schools and departments of education across the country are not identical. But in promoting false notions, fads, and trivia—in lieu of a body of knowledge—they are all alike, and have been since their inception.

For example, the nominalistic fallacy, visual literacy, dealt with in Chapter 4. I first heard the term in the U. Mass School of Education, but it was in use everywhere else. It was promoted and referenced, without challenge, in the field's national journals—*Audiovisual Instruction, Change, The English Journal, Language Arts*, as well as in the advertising of Eastman Kodak. Allied organizations promoted it—the National Council of Teachers of English, the National Education Association, and the education departments of many of the 50 states. The education professors who attended the 8th annual conference of the International Visual Literacy Association in Nashville with me were all from other schools of education. The chief ed school promoting the fallacy at the time was that of the University of Iowa.

I give a brief history of educational technology in Chapter 5. The specialty came into being not at the U. Mass ed school but in others, notably those of Ohio State and the University of Southern California. One of the largest media programs is offered by the ed school of the University of Indiana. The drawings that fail to teach the words "clean," "big," "dull" and "sharp," on pages 53 and 54 are from a set distributed nationally to schools of the deaf by the Bureau of Education of the Handicapped of the U.S. Office of Education. The bureau personnel responsible for the distribution had degrees from ed schools other than that of U. Mass. The mindless rhetoric of the media technology specialty pollutes our education atmosphere. The president of the Carnegie Foundation for the

Advancement of Teaching, Ernest Boyer, repeats the rhetoric in his book *High School*.

All schools of education fail to distinguish between the looks of things, information that is solely visual and information that is incidentally visual—languages that communicate across the senses of sight, hearing, and touch. Instead, they promote the opposite—that all media communicate equally. The notion, inherent in Wagschal's "Illiterates with Doctorates," is common to the entire field of thirty-nine thousand ed school instructors, thousands of their graduates in federal and state education agencies, and millions of school teachers and administrators. Not all of them subscribe to the notion, it is true. Few of the non-subscribers, nevertheless, recognize that language is the teacher's prime teaching tool. Not even professors who are specialists in reading instruction object in any effective way to the field's false notions that undermine literacy. Besides, a relatively small number of education professors are engaged in teaching reading instruction and other aspects of language. The net effect of the field—not just single schools of education—is to depress drastically the development of literacy. Schools of education have operated as one enormous illiteracy machine.

Like other university departments, schools of education are closely related to their counterparts in other universities. Peer review is internal by immediate colleagues, and external by peers elsewhere. Tenure and promotion depends in large part on *outside* peer review. The system works reasonably well in the rigorous disciplines. But the education field, having no body of knowledge, has no intrinsic yardstick by which to measure its candidates. Education professors tend much more than others to judge by political considerations: the "right" attitudes toward minorities, for example, or whether or not the candidate is a member of a minority group. Just as political, is evaluation by what new fad or notion a candidate is identified with. The field has a constant need for new notions, no matter how false, to cover up the failures of past notions. The highest accolades are accorded to education professors deemed "innovators." They are most readily hired from other ed schools, and given tenure and promotion.

Dean Dwight Allen came to the U. Mass ed school from the Stanford School of Education with a reputation for advocating "flexible modular scheduling," called "gimmickry," in *Crisis in the Classroom*.[18] Dean Mario Fantini came to the U. Mass ed school identified with "community control," in Ocean Hill-Brownsville which was a disaster for the New York City public school system. The education professors who organized and attended Harvard's 4-day international conference in 1984 on "critical thinking" or "thinking skills," were excited by the "sheer newness" of it. What excited them was not thinking in itself but a brand new fad that blurred the past failures of notions about reading, writing, and computation. The most prestigious schools of education are the prime generators of new fads and notions. The latest fashions and the word "new" are as important to them as they are to advertising copywriters.

I am by no means the first to advocate the abolition of schools of education. Their elimination has been urged, directly and indirectly, by many others before me. A professor of education at the University of North Carolina at Chapel Hill, in 1984, lamented in *The Chronicle of Higher Education*, "THESE ARE THE WORST OF TIMES for schools of education. The quality of our educational system is under renewed attack, and schools of education are receiving . . . criticism." He went on to say that the legitimacy of ed schools and their survival was "being debated in the universities."[19] A political science professor at the University of Massachusetts, Jean Bethke Elshtain, wrote in *The Nation* in 1982, "Schools of education must be phased out." She called them what many others have called them before her, "intellectual wastelands."[20] A professor of English at the California State University at Fresno, Kenneth Seib, recommended in January, 1984, in *The Chronicle of Higher Education*: "Phase out schools of education and place teacher training in appropriate academic disciplines. Richard Mitchell, of the *Underground Grammarian*, and others have made clear the drain on education that educationists have become.'[21]

An extensive body of literature exists that is damning to educationists. A few books and articles from it are listed in chronological order on page 291. Three of the last four on the list are by professors of education.

Of all the heavily financed studies and reports that were published in recent years, it should be noted that none were of schools of education, the very hub of the education establishment. Sizer, Lightfoot, Goodlad, and Boyer took pains in their books not to talk about schools of education and their effects on the public schools. What they kept hidden I have revealed, breaking their code of silence.

That I held professorial rank in the U. Mass School of Education during all but the first year and a half of my twelve-year stay there without getting tenure, is unusual. The how and why of it is contained in the remark of a friend in the school. "You're a remarkable man," he said. "You want tenure but only on your own terms." I had turned down the chance to acquire an Ed.D. degree, though warned that it was a virtual necessity for tenure. Instead of continuing to write publishable articles as I did at first, I became critical. When I could not get my critical articles published, I put them into a book manuscript, thinking to make an end-run around the educationist journals that had rejected them. At the time, 1976–1977, I was reviewed for tenure and received a positive recommendation from the school's Personnel Committee and Dean Mario Fantini. The university adminstration, however, rejected the recommendation on the grounds that I was insufficiently published. It nevertheless permitted me to go on two-thirds time for three years to get my book into print. Basic Books showed interest for a time, then declined to publish it. I wrote other versions with similar results. Finding no way to become effective by my own standards, I gave up wanting tenure—on February 5, 1979, to be exact, the day I lowered the Dean's wife's grade. My sense of relief was enormous, although the oppressive atmosphere of the school was not dispelled completely until my appointment ended in 1982 and I returned to New York City.

What I have written in this book may alienate some readers—other than those who are educationists. They may feel that I have singled out blacks unduly for adverse disclosures and criticisms. A few may call me racist. I know that my views and attitudes remain unchanged since I wrote about the success of school integration efforts in Teaneck as a triumph, helped elect Teaneck's first black councilman, and worked for Bergen County Fair Housing as a tester, enabling black families to buy homes which otherwise would have been denied to them. I am no less a friend in this book than when given my Human Relations

Award by the Urban League of Bergen County in 1968. I still believe in school integration where feasible, and that all people regardless of ethnicity, religion, or national origin should have a free choice in buying any home they can afford. I still believe in equal opportunity for all in obtaining jobs.

It is because I remain a friend that the pseudo-benign attitudes of educationists toward black students were and remain loathesome to me, an abomination because of the disastrous educational effects on black school children. Educationists, in operating their illiteracy machine, have used blacks to hide their educational incompetence. But out of ignorance and for the sake of jobs, black educationists have become a willing part of the illiteracy machine. Too willingly have they and other black groups cooperated in turning employment in large city public schools into what amounts to jobs programs.

I am not against the principle of jobs programs. Nathan Glazer in his *Ethnic Dilemmas* reported that Daniel Patrick Moynihan once proposed, for social reasons, to restore two mail deliveries a day by hiring fifty thousand additional postal workers. Such a jobs program would be in the public interest, a social and economic benefit for all.[22] But putting credentialled "bodies" into classrooms is a social, economic, and educational disaster. It creates an immobile underclass of the illiterate and semi-literate, a danger to themselves and the rest of society.

In using Stuyvesant High School to compare the achievement of black and Asian students, I was aware that my comparison might be labelled invidious. Coming in the context that it does, the comparison can be viewed that way only by those who prefer the usual political stances over the truth. My saying that black students are at a ten-times disadvantage vis-à-vis Asian students makes stark how polluted is the education atmosphere in this country. Recently arrived Asian immigrants and their sons and daughters are fortunate. They retain their traditional values and ideas about education, untainted as yet by the notions of American educationists. Moreover, they see the United States as the land of opportunity and from the beginning make the most of it with strenuous efforts in school.

Black Americans can do the same. It is true that their difficulties to some degree are due to the white majority, but far less than formerly. They are held back chiefly by their own beliefs about the larger society, schooling and language, destructive beliefs that are nevertheless encouraged by many of their political leaders and abetted by educationists. All groups stand to gain from putting my recomendations into effect, and none more than black Americans.

Forty Years of Apt Criticism

1945   *Teacher in America* by Jacques Barzun

1953   *Educational Wastelands* by Arthur E. Bestor

1954   *The Diminished Mind: A Study of Planned Mediocrity in Our Public Schools* by Mortimer Smith

1959   *The House of Intellect* by Jacques Barzun

1962   *Anti-Intellectualism in American Life* by Richard Hofstadter

1963   *The Miseducation of American Teachers* by James D. Koerner

1970   *Crisis in the Classroom* by Charles E. Silberman

1972   *Black Education: Myths and Tragedies* by Thomas Sowell

1980   *Paradigms Lost: Reflections on Literacy and Its Decline* by John Simon

1981   *The Graves of Academe* by Richard Mitchell

1982   *On Learning to Read: The Child's Fascination With Meaning* by Bruno Bettelheim & Karen Zelan

1983   *The Troubled Crusade: American Education 1945–1980* by Diane Ravitch

1984   "The Continuing Crisis: Fashions in Education" by Diane Ravitch, in *The American Scholar*, Spring 1984

1984   "Ethics Without Virtue: Moral Education in America" by Christina Hoff Sommers, in *The American Scholar*, Summer 1984

1984   "The Excellence Backlash: Sources of Resistance to Educational Reform" by Chester E. Finn, Jr., in *The American Spectator*, September 1984.

Books to Enlighten On Reading and Learning

Reading Without Nonsense by Frank Smith

On Learning to Read: The Child's Fascination with Meaning by Bruno Bettelheim & Karen Zelan

Understanding Reading (Third Edition) by Frank Smith

Comprehension and Learning by Frank Smith

Notes

Chapter 2: No Body of Knowledge
1. Thomas Sowell, *Black Education: Myths and Tragedies* (New York: David McKay, 1972), p. 221.
2. Whitney M. Young, Jr., "Guidebook for a Workable Revolution," *New York Times Book Review*, February 18, 1968, p. 6.

Chapter 3: Then and Now
1. John Dewey, "Pedagogy as a University Discipline," *University Record* (University of Chicago Press), September 18, 1896. Quoted in Charles E. Silberman, *Crisis in the Classroom* (New York: Random House, 1970), p. 421.
2. *Ibid.*
3. Thomas Sowell, *Ethnic America* (New York: Basic Books, 1981), Chapters 4 and 5.
4. Abraham Lass, "What a School Was," *New York Times*, April 16, 1983, Op-Ed page.
5. See David R. Olson, "From utterance to text: the bias in language in speech and writing," *Harvard Educational Review*, Vol. 47 No. 3, August 1977.
6. *Ibid.*
7. Gene I. Maeroff, *Don't Blame The Kids: The Trouble with America's Public Schools* (New York: McGraw-Hill, 1982), p. 83.
8. *Time*, June 16, 1980, pp. 54–63.

Chapter 4: Attacking Literacy with Pseudoliteracies
1. Roger B. Fransecky and John L. Debes, *Visual Literacy—A Way to Learn—A Way to Reach* (Washington, D.C.: Association for Edu-

cational Communications and Technology, 1972), inside front cover.

2. Harry Foster, "On My Mind—The Media Religion," *American Libraries*, October 1974.

3. John L. Debes, "Some Foundations for Visual Literacy," *Audio-visual Instruction*, November 1968, pp. 961–964.

4. John L. Debes, *Some Semantics of Visual Communication* (Rochester, N.Y.: Eastman Kodak, 1968).

5. Fransecky and Debes, p. 7.

6. "A Selected Bibliography on Visual Literacy," *Audiovisual Instruction*, February 1971, pp. 49–51.

7. Paul A. Kolers, *Aspects of Motion Perception* (New York: Pergamon Press, 1972), p. 187.

8. *The New York Times Magazine*, March 7, 1976, p. 11.

9. Steven Rose, *The Conscious Brain* (New York: Vintage, 1976), p. 335.

10. Douglas O'Connor, "Dwight Allen in Africa," *Change*, Winter/1975–76, p. 33

11. Nancy Cromer, "Why Should We Teach Multi-Media?", *English Journal*, December 1976, pp. 68–71.

12. M. Jean Greenlaw, "Visual Literacy and Reading Instruction: From Books to Media and Back to Books," *Language Arts*, October 1976, p. 789.

Chapter 5: Undermining Literacy with Television

1. William Exton, Jr., *Audiovisual Aids to Instruction* (New York: McGraw-Hill, 1947), foreword.

2. Source: Hope Reports, *Education and Media, 1973–1974–1975* (Rochester, N.Y.: Hope Reports, Inc., 1976), p. 264.

3. James D. Finn, "A Study of Military Audio-Visual Programs," unpublished dissertation, Ohio State University, 1949, pp. 218–219.

4. Richard Schickel, *The Disney Version* (New York: Avon, 1968), pp. 121–123.

5. Donald Spoto, *The Art of Alfred Hitchcock* (New York: Hopkinson and Blake, 1976), pp. 463–499.

6. Examples taken from Robert F. Newby, "Visualanguage Series #1" (The Pennsylvania School for the Deaf: 1969).

7. Rudolf Flesch, *Why Johnny Still Can't Read* (New York: Harper, 1981), p. 18.

8. Robert Newby, "Language and Reading: A Visual Structure," presented at "Update '74: A Decade of Progress" (Lincoln, Nebraska, 1974).

9. Arthur Koestler, *The Act of Creation* (New York: Dell, 1964), p. 158.

10. R. L. Gregory, *Eye and Brain*, Second Edition (New York: McGraw-Hill, 1973), p. 48.

11. Marshall McLuhan, "The Debates," *New York Times*, September 23, 1976, Op. Ed. page.

12. Rose, *The Conscious Brain*, p. 171.

13. *Ibid.*, p. 176.

14. Harry McGurk and John McDonald, "Hearing lips and seeing voices," *Nature*, Vol. 264, December 23/30, 1976, p. 746.

15. *Ibid.*, p. 747.

16. Rosser Reeves, *Reality in Advertising* (New York: Knopf, 1961), pp. 87–89.

17. Rudolph Arnheim, "A Forecast of Television," in *Film as Art* (Berkeley: University of California Press, 1971), p. 195.

Chapter 6: "Illiterates with Doctorates"

1. Peter H. Wagschal, "Illiterates with Doctorates: The Future of Education in an Electronic Age," *The Futurist*, August 1978, pp. 243, 244. Reprinted in the University of Massachusetts, School of Education *Alumni Newsletter*, February 1980, Vol. 5, No. 1, p. 4.

2. John Simon, "Compact with Computers," *Esquire*, February 27, 1979, p. 19. Reprinted in John Simon, *Paradigms Lost* (New York: Penguin, 1981), pp. 154–159.

3. A. H. Lauchner, "How Can the Junior High School Curriculum Be Improved?" *Bulletin* of the National Association of Secondary-School Principals, March 1951, pp. 299–300, quoted in Mortimer Smith, *The Diminished Mind* (New York: Greenwood Press, 1969), pp. 36, 37.

4. *Ibid.*

5. *Ibid.*, p. 24.

6. Wagschal, "Illiterates with Doctorates."

7. *Ibid.*

8. Simon, *Paradigms Lost*, p. 155.

9. Wagschal, "Illiterates with Doctorates."

10. Simon, *Paradigms Lost*, p. 156.

11. Wagschal, "Illiterates with Doctorates."

12. *Ibid.*

13. *Official Report*, The American Association of School Administrators, 1952. Quoted in Mortimer Smith, *The Diminished Mind*, p. 105.

14. "Get the Facts: Both Ours and the Other Fellow's!" *Progressive Education*, January 1952. Quoted in Mortimer Smith, *The Diminished Mind*, p. 105.

15. Cheryl M. Fields, "Study Stirs New Criticism of Exams," *The Chronicle of Higher Education*, September 6, 1977, p. 12.

16. *Ibid.*

Chapter 7: The Damage to Reading Instruction

1. Frank Smith, *Understanding Reading*, First Edition (New York: Holt, Rinehart, Winston, 1971), p. 48.
2. Jeremy Campbell, *Grammatical Man* (New York: Simon and Schuster, 1982), p. 172.
3. *Ibid.*, p. 142.
4. Frank Smith, *Understanding Reading*, Third Edition (New York: Holt, Rinehart, Winston, 1982), p. 178.
5. *Ibid.*, p. 231.
6. Bruno Bettelheim and Karen Zelan, *On Learning to Read: The Child's Fascination With Meaning* (New York: Vintage, 1982), pp. 9, 10.
7. *Ibid.*, pp. 64–67.
8. *Ibid.*, p. 163.
9. *Ibid.*, pp. 89–91.
10. *Ibid.*, p. 239.
11. *Ibid.*, p. 17.
12. Frank Smith, *Understanding Reading*, Third Edition, p. 179.
13. *Ibid.*
14. Albert J. Harris and Edward R. Sipay, *Effective Teaching of Reading* (New York: David McKay, 1971), cited in Bettelheim and Zelan, p. 23.
15. Jeanne S. Chall, *Learning to Read: The Great Debate* (New York: McGraw-Hill, 1967), cited in Bettelheim and Zelan, pp. 23, 24.
16. George Orwell, *1984* (New York: New American Library, 1983) pp. 45, 46.
17. Charles E. Silberman, *Crisis in the Classroom* (New York: Random House, 1970), p. 443.
18. Frank Smith, *Understanding Reading*, Third Edition, p. 144.
19. Eleanor J. Gibson and Harry Levin, *The Psychology of Reading* (Cambridge: MIT Press, 1975), p. 4.
20. Bettelheim and Zelan, *On Learning to Read*, p. 20.
21. George A. Miller quoted in Tom Ferrell, "Pioneering Cognitive Psychologist Has Everyone's Mind On His," *New York Times*, October 12, 1982, p. C1.
22. *Ibid.*
23. Frank Smith, *Comprehension and Learning* (New York: Holt, Rinehart and Winston, 1975), p. 7.
24. Frank Smith, *Understanding Reading*, Third Edition, p. XII.

Chapter 8: "The Right to Fail"

1. Joseph Lelyveld, "Chancellor Harvey Scribner: The Most Powerful Man in the School System—On Paper," *New York Times Magazine*, March 21, 1971, p. 31.
2. *Ibid.*
3. *Ibid.*, p. 90.

4. Reginald G. Damerell, *Triumph in a White Suburb* (New York: William Morrow, 1968), p. 177.
5. Lelyveld, *Times Magazine*, p. 90.
6. *Ibid.*, pp. 31, 90.
7. Damerell, *Triumph in a White Suburb*, p. 176.
8. *Ibid.*, pp. 149–151.
9. *Ibid.*, p. 178.
10. *Ibid.*, 205.
11. Lelyveld, *New York Times Magazine*, p. 90.
12. James D. Koerner, *The Miseducation of American Teachers* (Boston: Houghton Mifflin, 1963), p. 12.
13. Diane Divoky, "Young Ideas in an Old State," *Saturday Review*, April 18, 1970.
14. Lelyveld, *New York Times Magazine*, p. 88.
15. Francis X. Clines, "Assembly Votes High School Curb," *New York Times*, May 20, 1971, p. 1.
16. Leonard Buder, "Board Asks Defeat of a Bill Retaining 4 Specialized Schools' Entrance Tests," *New York Times*, May 17, 1971, p. 26.
17. Andrew H. Malcolm, "Scribner to Name Unit to Study Special-School Entrance Tests," *New York Times* February 24, 1971, p. 50.
18. Lelyveld, *New York Times Magazine*, p. 88.
19. *Ibid.*, p. 90.
20. *Ibid.*
21. Charles E. Silberman, *Crisis in the Classroom* (New York: Random House, 1970), p. xi.
22. Lelyveld, *New York Times Magazine*, p. 89.
23. Abraham H. Lass, "1 + 1 = Terror," *New York Times*, November 20, 1971, Op-Ed page.
24. Alan H. Levine, Letter-to-the-Editor, *New York Times*, December 11, 1971.
25. Maeroff, *Don't Blame The Kids*, p. 51.
26. Samuel Weiss and Edward B. Fiske, "Rigorous High School Courses Attract Fewer in New York City," *New York Times*, March 23, 1978, pp. A1, B12.
27. *Ibid.*
28. Samuel Weiss, "Precollege Courses Rebound in City's Schools," *New York Times*, July 10, 1983, p. 6E.
29. *Ibid.*
30. *Ibid.*
31. Edward B. Fiske, "Community-Run Schools Leave Hopes Unfulfilled," *New York Times*, June 24, 1980, p. B4.
32. Sheila Rule, "Locally Run Schools Disappoint Minority Educators and Parents," *New York Times*, June 27, 1980, p. B3.
33. Edward B. Fiske, *New York Times*, June 24, 1980, p. B4.

34. Marcia Chambers, "Politics and Patronage Dominate Community-Run School Districts," *New York Times*, June 26, 1980, pp. 1, B6.
35. Sheila Rule, *New York Times*, June 27, 1980, pp. 1, B3.
36. Gene I. Maeroff, "Achievement Lagging in Community-Run Schools," *New York Times*, June 25, 1980, p. B4.
37. Sheila Rule, *New York Times*, June 27, 1980, p. B3.
38. Gene I. Maeroff, "Drive to Urge Parents To Use Public Schools," *New York Times*, April 9, 1983, p. 25.
39. *Status of Black New York Report* (New York Urban League: 1984), p. 4.
40. See Edward B. Fiske, "New York School Reading Level Still Low," *New York Times*, January 11, 1978, p. B6, col. 2.
41. Gilbert T. Sewall, *Necessary Lessons* (New York: Free Press, 1983), p. 8 footnote.
42. *Status of Black New York Report*, p. 4.
43. Koerner, *The Miseducation of American Teachers*, p. 17.

Chapter 9: To Make Up Your Mind Anew

1. Hannah Arendt, Reflections, Thinking III, *The New Yorker*, December 5, 1977, p. 183.
2. Harold R. Jacobs, *Geometry* (San Francisco: W. H. Freeman, 1974), p. 128.
3. *Ibid.*, p. 131.
4. R. L. Gregory, *Eye and Brain*, Third Edition, p. 9.

Chapter 10: Third World Within

1. Jonathan Neumann, "Fund use angers COP program participants," *Daily Hampshire Gazette*, January 28, 1975, pp. 1 and 5.
2. Jonathan Neumann, "Quick doctorates earned by many at School of Ed," *Daily Hampshire Gazette*, February 11, 1975, pp. 1 and 5.
3. Neumann, *Gazette*, January 28, 1975, p. 5.
4. Neumann, *Gazette*, February 11, 1975, p. 1.
5. *Ibid.*
6. *Ibid.*, p. 5.
7. *Ibid.*
8. Neumann, *Gazette*, January 28, 1975, pp. 1, 5.
9. *Ibid*, p. 5.
10. *Ibid.*
11. Frederick Cusik, "UMass trustees voice support for Bromery," *Daily Hampshire Gazette*, February 6, 1975, p. 5.
12. Jonathan Neumann and Martha Oravecz, "Possible Ed. School fund misuse is set at $2.4 million, Wood says," *Daily Hampshire Gazette*, February 14, 1975, pp. 1, 5.
13. Neumann, *Gazette*, February 11, 1975, p. 5.
14. *Ibid.*

15. Sowell, *Black Education*, pp. 19, 20.
16. *Ibid.*, p. 16.
17. *Ibid.*, p. 124.
18. Leonard Buder, "Board Ask Defeat of a Bill Retaining 4 Specialized Schools' Entrance Tests," *New York Times*, May 17, 1971, p. 26.
19. Ari L. Goldman, "The City's Elite Schools Are Staying That Way," *New York Times*, November 20, 1977, Section IV, p. 5.
20. Marvine Howe, "Have-Nots Fear 'Manhattanization' As Developers Size Up Chinatown," *New York Times*, September 21, 1984, p. B1.
21. Kirk Johnson, "Asians Galvanize Sales Activity In Flushing," *New York Times,* July 29, 1984, Section 8, p. 14.
22. *Ibid.*
23. Sowell, *Ethnic America*, p. 216.
24. Nathan Glazer and Daniel P. Moynihan, *Beyond the Melting Pot*, Second Edition (Cambridge: M.I.T. Press, 1970), p. 319.
25. *Ibid.*, p. 34.

Chapter 11: Inside the Heads of the Ten-Times Disadvantaged

1. Glazer & Moynihan, *Beyond the Melting Pot*, p. 45.
2. Edward B. Fiske, "U.S. Pupils Lag From Grade 1, Study Finds," *New York Times*, June 17, 1984, p. 30.
3. *Ibid.*
4. Clyde Haberman, "Japan Acts to Revise School System," *New York Times*, August 12, 1984, p. 3.
5. Mortimer Smith, *The Diminished Mind* (Chicago: Regnery, 1954).
6. Neumann, *Gazette*, February 11, 1975, p. 5.
7. Jonathan Neumann, "Volume of doctorates given out by Ed. School raises questions of school's academic procedure," *Daily Hampshire Gazette*, February 10, 1975, p. 5.
8. Diane Ravitch, *The Troubled Crusade: American Education 1945–1980* (New York: Basic Books, 1983), pp. 268, 269.
9. Janice E. Hale, *Black Children: Their Roots, Culture, and Learning Styles* (Provo, Utah: Brigham Young University Press, 1982).
10. *Ibid.*, p. 152.
11. Dena Kleiman, "Children of Immigrants Feel a Real Pride in Their Origins," *New York Times*, October 28, 1982, p. B1.
12. Mary Dean Pentcheff, "A 'Limey' Laments the Loss of Her Immigrant Ticket," *New York Times*, July 1, 1984, p. 20 WC.
13. Hale, *Black Children*, pp. 152, 153.
14. *Ibid.*, p. 154.
15. Glazer & Moynihan, *Beyond the Melting Pot*, pp. 34, 35.
16. Sowell, *Ethnic America*, pp. 216–220.

17. "For West Indians, Cricket Field Is Bit of Home," *New York Times*, July 11, 1983, p. B1.
18. Philip Revzin, "Not Cricket: The West Indians Bowl Over the British," *Wall Street Journal*, August 14, 1984, p. 28.
19. John Duka, "In Paris, a Young Black Society," *New York Times*, April 20, 1984, p. A16.
20. Hale, *Black Children*, Chapter 2.
21. *Ibid.*, p. 158.
22. Nathan Glazer, *Ethnic Dilemmas 1964–1982* (Cambridge: Harvard University Press, 1983), p. 46.
23. Hale, *Black Children*, p. 75.
24. Daniel Bell, *The Reforming of General Education* (New York: Columbia University Press, 1966), p. 111.
25. For one example, see Edward Menaker, "Casualty of a Failed System," *New York Times*, October 3, 1982, p. S1.
26. Douglas L. Edwards, "Rejected by College?", *New York Times*, April 9, 1983, Op-Ed page.
27. Sowell, *Black Education*, p. 25.
28. *Ibid.*, p. 26.
29. *Ibid.*, p. 28.
30. Edward B. Fiske, "U.S. Pupils Lag From Grade 1, Study Finds," *New York Times*, June 17, 1984, p. 30.
31. *Ibid.*
32. Ellen Hume, "Jackson Backers Look To Him to Help Blacks Get 'Our Fair Share'," *Wall Street Journal*, June 1, 1984, p. 1.
33. Carol Hymowitz, "Many Blacks Jump Off Corporate Ladders to Be Entrepreneurs," *Wall Street Journal*, August 2, 1984, p. 1.
34. Charles Murray, *Losing Ground: American Social Policy 1950–1980* (New York: Basic Books, 1984) pp. 96, 97.
35. "Philadelphia Raises Security At School in Attack on Asians," *New York Times*, November 13, 1983, p. 72.
36. Peter Applebome, "Racial Tension Said to Underlie Cambodian's Death in Dallas," *New York Times*, August 2, 1983, p. A10.
37. Glazer, *Ethnic Dilemmas*, p. 332.
38. Sowell, *Ethnic America*, p. 203.
39. *Ibid.*, p. 196.
40. William Henry Cosby, Jr., "An Integration of the Visual Media Via Fat Albert and the Cosby Kids in the Elementary School Curriculum as a Teaching Aid and Vehicle to Achieve Increased Learning," Ed.D. dissertation, School of Education, University of Massachusetts, 1976. Chairperson, Norma Jean Anderson.
41. *Ibid.*, p. 22.
42. Harold G. Shane, "An Interview with W. Willard Witz," *Phi Delta Kappan*, October 1977.

Chapter 12: Education's Big Guns Asmoking

1. Chester E. Finn, Jr., Diane Ravitch, Robert T. Fancher, Eds., *Against Mediocrity: The Humanities in America's Schools* (New York: Holmes & Meier, 1984), p. 254.
2. Gene I. Maeroff, "Report Calls for Limiting High School Enrollments," *New York Times*, February 8, 1984, p. A16.
3. Theodore R. Sizer, *Horace's Compromise: The Dilemma of the American High School* (Boston: Houghton Mifflin, 1984), p. 132.
4. *Ibid.*, p. 7.
5. *Ibid.*, p. 8.
6. *Ibid.*, p. 7.
7. *Ibid.*, pp. 9–21.
8. *Ibid.*, p. 178.
9. Gene I. Maeroff, "Georgia Hires West Germans for Science and Math," *New York Times*, September 24, 1984, p. A14.
10. Sizer, *Horace's Compromise*, p. 109.
11. *Ibid.*, p. 184.
12. *Ibid.*, pp. 104, 105.
13. *Ibid.*, p. 21.
14. *Ibid.*, p. 191.
15. *Ibid.*, p. 194.
16. *Ibid.*, p. 211.
17. *Ibid.*, p. 101, see second complete paragraph.
18. *Ibid.*, p. 8.
19. Cristina Hoff Sommers, "Ethics Without Virtue: Moral Education in America," *American Scholar*, Summer 1984, p. 381.
20. *Ibid.*, p. 383.
21. *Ibid.*, p. 382.
22. *Ibid.*, p. 385.
23. *Ibid.*, p. 387.
24. *Ibid.*, p. 381.
25. Sizer, *Horace's Compromise*, p. 66.
26. Sara Lawrence Lightfoot, *The Good High School: Portrait of Character and Culture* (New York: Basic Books, 1983), p. 23.
27. *Ibid.*, p. 6.
28. *Ibid.*, p. 377.
29. *Ibid.*, p. 63.
30. *Ibid.*, p. 21.
31. *Ibid.*, p. 272.
32. *Ibid.*, p. 273.
33. *Ibid.*, p. 271.
34. *Ibid.*, p. 30.
35. *Ibid.*, p. 122.
36. *Ibid.*, p. 131.

37. *Ibid.*, p. 135.
38. *Ibid.*, p. 160.
39. *Ibid.*, p. 175.
40. *Ibid.*, p. 363.
41. *Ibid.*, p. 358.
42. *Ibid.*, p. 83.
43. *Ibid.*, pp. 319, 320.
44. *Ibid.*, p. 32.
45. *Ibid.*, p. 299.
46. *Ibid.*, p. 360.
47. *Ibid.*, pp. 243, 244.
48. Robert Pear, "Immigration and the Randomness of Ethnic Mix," *New York Times*, October 2, 1984, p. A28.
49. Lightfoot, *The Good High School*, p. 314.
50. Samuel Eliot Morison and Henry Steele Commager, *The Growth of the American Republic* (New York: Oxford, 1942), Vol. 11, p. 367.
51. Lightfoot, *The Good High School*, p. 316.
52. Claude Brown, "Manchild in Harlem," *New York Times Magazine*, September 16, 1984, p. 44.
53. *Ibid.*, p. 78.
54. Edward B. Fiske, "Eight-Year Study of Public Schools Finds Chronic Problems in System," *New York Times*, July 19, 1983, p. 1.
55. John I. Goodlad, *A Place Called School: Prospects for the Future* (New York: McGraw-Hill, 1983), p. 1.
56. Edward B. Fiske, "An Expert Urges Multiple Reforms," *New York Times*, July 26, 1983, p. C7.
57. Thomas Sowell, "The intellect of the intellectuals," *The Chronicle of Higher Education*, December 8, 1975, p. 20.
58. Goodlad, *A Place Called School*, p. 267.
59. *Ibid.*, p. 197.
60. *Ibid.*, p. 209.
61. *Ibid.*, p. 206.
62. David Burnham, "The Suave, Sophisticated and Illiterate Capital," *New York Times*, October 9, 1984, p. A26.
63. Goodlad, *A Place Called School*, pp. 160, 161.
64. Sowell, "The Intellect of the Intellectuals."
65. Edward B. Fiske, "Study Asks Tighter Curriculums," *New York Times*, September 16, 1983, p. A13.
66. Ernest L. Boyer, *High School: A Report on Secondary Education in America* (New York: Harper & Row, 1983), p. XI.
67. *Ibid.*, p. 175.
68. *Ibid.*

69. *Ibid.*, p. 176.
70. Quoted in Daniel Bell, *The Reforming of General Education*, p. 287.
71. Boyer, *High School*, p. 193.
72. *Ibid.*, p. 190.
73. *Ibid.*, p. 198.
74. *Ibid.*
75. *Ibid.*, pp. 199, 200.
76. Virginia Inman, "Educational Testing Service Adopts Tactics From Business World as Old Markets Shrink," *Wall Street Journal*, November 30, 1982, p. 33.
77. Edward B. Fiske, "Test Misuse Is Charged by Its Maker," *New York Times*, November 29, 1983, p. C11.
78. *Ibid.*
79. Willard Wirtz *et al*, *On Further Examination: Report of the Advisory Board on the Scholastic Aptitude Test Score Decline* (New York: College Entrance Examination Board, 1977), p. 9.
80. Fred M. Hechinger, "Standing Guard Over Aptitude Tests," *New York Times*, August 30, 1983, p. C9.
81. Sewall, *Necessary Lessons*. pp. ix, x.
82. *Ibid.*
83. Boyer, *High School*, p. 6.
84. Edward B. Fiske, "Noted Educator Foresees Resurgence in Teaching," *New York Times*, June 5, 1984, p. C11.
85. Jacques Barzun, *The House of Intellect* (New York: Harper, 1959), p. 99.
86. Colin Campbell, "Experts on Thinking Fear a Decline of Reasoning," *New York Times*, August 27, 1984, p. A8.
87. *Ibid.*
88. *Ibid.*
89. Eugene H. Methvin, "Guess Who Spells DISASTER For Education?" *Reader's Digest*, May 1984, pp. 89–94.
90. Gene I. Maeroff, "Teachers' Gathering Has the Trappings of a Party Convention," *New York Times*, July 5, 1984, p. A10.
91. Gilbert T. Sewall, "Teachers' Unions and the Issue of Academic Standards," *Wall Street Journal*, January 6, 1983, p. 16.
92. Chester E. Finn, Jr., quoted in Methvin, *Reader's Digest*, p. 92.
93. A 1973 NEA manual designed for classroom use, *Education and Racism*, quoted in Sewall, *Necessary Lessons*, p. 70.
94. Mary Futrell, *The American Spectator*, September 1984, p. 19.
95. Gene I. Maeroff, "Federation Calls For Better Teacher Training," *New York Times*, August 24, 1984, p. A26.
96. Kathleen Teltsch, "Foundations Warned Against Complacency," *New York Times*, April 29, 1984, p. 30.
97. *Ibid.*

98. Edward B. Fiske, " 'Tide of Mediocrity' May Not Be Rising as Fast as It Seems," *New York Times*, September 18, 1983, p. 20E.

99. Fred M. Hechinger, "Rush of Contradictory Ideas on School Reform," *New York Times*, August 2, 1983, p. C7.

100. Fred M. Hechinger, "But Will Anything Come of All Those Reports?" *New York Times*, October 4, 1983, p. C8.

101. Chester E. Finn, Jr. and Diane Ravitch, "Conclusions and Recommendations," in *Against Mediocrity: The Humanities in America's High Schools* (New York: Holmes & Meier, 1984), p. 254.

102. Chester E. Finn, Jr., "The Future of Education's Liberal Concensus," *Change*, September 1980, p. 25.

103. Christopher Lehmann-Haupt, "Books of The Times," *New York Times*, September 7, 1983, p. C21.

104. Chester E. Finn, Jr., Diane Ravitch, and Robert T. Fancher, *Against Mediocrity*, pp. 9, 10.

105. Quoted by Daniel Machalaza in "An English Professor Grades Colleagues," *Wall Street Journal*, January 13, 1978, p. 1.

106. James Sloan Allen, "The Humanities Are Guilty of Betraying Humanism," *Wall Street Journal*, February 2, 1982, p. 30.

107. Simon, *Paradigms Lost*, pp. 169–171.

108. Thomas Sowell, "The intellect of the intellectuals."

109. Stewart Dill McBride, "The literary Galbraith on the art of writing," *Christian Science Monitor*, December 9, 1975, p. 17.

Chapter 13: "The Near Nihilism of the Present"

1. Daniel Patrick Moynihan address, "On the Present Discontent," delivered at the convocation for the 140th Anniversity of the School of Education, State University of New York at Albany, September 22, 1984.

2. James D. Koerner, "The Second Coming of Educational Technology," *Change*, September 1977, p. 50.

3. C. Emily Feistritzer, *The Making of A Teacher: A Report on Teacher Education and Certification* (Washington, D.C.: National Center for Education Information, 1984), p. 30.

4. *Ibid.*, p. 34.

5. *Ibid.*, p. 31.

6. *Ibid.*, p. 34.

7. Richard Darwick, "Spare Us Your Saviors," *New York Times*, July 14, 1984, Op-Ed page.

Chapter 14: To Make Teaching Professional

1. Koerner, *The Miseducation of American Teachers*, p. 39.

2. *Ibid.*, pp. 39, 40.

3. Neumann, *Daily Hampshire Gazette*, February 13, 1975, p. 1.

4. Albert Shanker, "Where We Stand," *New York Times*, July 1, 1984, p. E9.
5. *Radical Teacher*, Issue #23 (Cambridge: Boston Women's Teachers' Group, Inc.), p. 37.
6. *Ibid.*, p. 34.
7. *Ibid.*, p. 37.
8. From J. S. Bruner et al, *Studies in cognitive growth* (New York: Wiley, 1966), as shown in David R. Olson, *Cognitive Development* (New York: Academic Press, 1970), p. 6.
9. Edward B. Fiske, "Learning Disabled: A New Awareness," *New York Times Fall Education Survey*, Section 12, November 11, 1984, p. 44.
10. *Ibid.*
11. Olson, *Cognitive Development*, p. 73.
12. *Ibid.*, p. 74.
13. Marva Collins and Civia Tamarkin, *Marva Collins' Way*, (Tarcher: Los Angeles, 1982).
14. Smith, *The Diminished Mind*, p. 130.
15. U.S. Department of Education Study, "What Ed Knows About Private School Participation Under ECIA Chapter 2," prepared by Judith Anderson-Ng and Carol Chelmer.
16. Source: *The Metropolitan Life Survey of the American Teacher*, by Louis Harris and Associates, Inc., Table 24, p. 40.
17. Ellie McGrath, *Time*, January 30, 1984, p. 80.
18. Silberman, *Crisis in the Classroom*, p. 341.
19. David D. Dill, "New Strategies for Schools of Education Ought to Include Schools of Teaching," *Chronicle of Higher Education*, January 18, 1984, p. 80.
20. Jean Bethke Elshtain, "Time to Politize the Schools," *The Nation*, September 25, 1982, p. 271.
21. Kenneth Seib, "How the Laws of Acadynamics Work to Prevent Change," *Chronicle of Higher Education*, January 25, 1984, p. 72.
22. Glazer, *Ethnic Dilemmas*, pp. 55, 56.

Index